Speech Planning and Dynamics

Speech Production and Perception

Edited by
Susanne Fuchs and Pascal Perrier

Volume 1

PETER LANG
Frankfurt am Main · Berlin · Bern · Bruxelles · New York · Oxford · Wien

Speech Planning and Dynamics

Edited by
Susanne Fuchs
Melanie Weirich
Daniel Pape
Pascal Perrier

PETER LANG
Internationaler Verlag der Wissenschaften

Bibliographic Information published by the Deutsche Nationalbibliothek
The Deutsche Nationalbibliothek lists this publication in the Deutsche Nationalbibliografie; detailed bibliographic data is available in the internet at http://dnb.d-nb.de.

ISSN 2191-8651
ISBN 978-3-631-61479-2

www.peterlang.de

Contents

Preface

Prior to uttering a sentence, the speaker needs to plan it. The planning process is highly complex and consists of at least two tasks, a cognitive-linguistic task and a motor task. The cognitive-linguistic task involves the conceptualization of meaning (What to say?), the framing of meaning within the rules of a given language (Which syntax? Which words? Which prosody?), and the selection of phonological units (phonemes, syllables...). The motor task involves planning the spatial and temporal coordination of the speech articulators. Controlling these articulators is complex and is like controlling an orchestra of muscle activations over time, because the resulting movements have to be accurate in space and time to convey linguistic meaning.

One of the most influential psycholinguistic models of language production was proposed by Levelt and colleagues (Levelt, 1989; Levelt et al., 1999). This model describes the cognitive-linguistic components of speech planning in hierarchical layers going from intention to articulation. One weakness of Levelt's model is that it fails to address the impact of the requirements of the motor control system on cognitive-linguistic planning. Smith and Goffman (2004) and Smith (2006) have provided evidence that there are bottom-up influences from the dynamics of the motor control system to the cognitive-linguistic system. This debate is not the primary focus of the book, but it is relevant to certain chapters.

The aim of this book is to provide the reader with the latest research in speech planning, from both a cognitive-linguistic and a motor control perspective. In most models of speech planning, a speech sequence is organized and produced not as a whole, but as a sequence of connected chunks. These chunks are called units, which give the sequence a specific structure. Units take on different characteristics and properties in the various chapters here. In general, studies from the cognitive-linguistic perspective emphasize units, which are meaningful words or prosodic constituents, whereas studies from the motor control perspective focus on the motor goals (auditory and articulatory) and the dynamics of the motor system (accounting for forces at the origin of the movement). The planned units are also dynamic (as the title of the book proposes), in the sense that they change in time. Changes in time are

discussed in various ways, for instance in terms of speech acquisition or in diachronic sound changes.
The book consists of the following eight chapters:

Pierre Hallé and **Alejandrina Cristia** provide a comprehensive literature review of the prelexical and lexical mental representations during speech acquisition. Lexical representations for speech production develop from whole-word into phoneme-like units. For speech perception vowels and consonants play different roles within the developmental path. Children show a high sensitivity to phonetic details in consonant perception from an early age, but this does not apply to vowels.

Jonathan Harrington, Felicitas Kleber and **Ulrich Reubold** present two examples of diachronic sound changes in Southern British English and in East Franconian German. They demonstrate how diachronic changes can be driven by synchronic coarticulatory variation and the processing of these variations by the perceptual system.

Marianne Pouplier presents an overview of the gestural model of syllable structure originally proposed by Browman and Goldstein (1988). She discusses data on German consonant clusters and shows, how the internal structure of the consonant clusters influences articulatory coordinations. Her results confirm the predominance of the in-phase coordination for syllable onsets.

Linda Wheeldon studies the scope of advanced planning in spoken language production. She focuses on the relationship between conceptual and grammatical processes. Her results provide evidence that the minimal unit speakers plan is a phrasal chunk corresponding to a thematic unit. Several experiments have been carried out on English and Japanese.

Sam Tilsen gives an introduction to the stress-clash phenomenon and its phonological interpretations. Furthermore, he provides evidence that stress-clash depends on the extent to which an utterance was prepaired before or not. The results of his study have further implications on the interaction between prosody and time-constraints in speech planning.

Jelena Krivokapić presents results clarifying how speakers plan the prosodic structure of an utterance. More specifically she investigates the effect of phrase length and prosodic structure on speech planning. She shows that both local and distant prosodic phrases have an effect on the speech planning process, and suggests that prosodic structure could determine the nature of the planned units in this process.

Pascal Perrier provides a literature review on the existence of dynamic internal models in the Central Nervous System. These models are crucial in the planning process. After a description of the basic principles underlying the use of dynamic internal models in motor planning, empirical findings from the motor control and speech motor control literature are discussed, putting the strengths and weaknesses of these models in perspective.

Leonardo Lancia and **Mark Tiede** present a selection of methods for the description and comparison of movement data, which enable to describe time series in a holistic way. Functional data analysis, the cross wavelet transform and cross recurrence analysis are introduced and their applications are discussed.

This book has its origins in the third summer school on "Speech Production, Perception and the Production-Perception Interaction" that was held in Berlin in September 2010. The summer school was organized in the context of the PILIOS project between the Centre for General Linguistics in Berlin and the Gipsa-lab (UMR CNRS 5216) in Grenoble. It could take place thanks to the financial support by the French-German University (Saarbrücken), the Ministry of Education and Research (BMBF), the French Embassy in Berlin, and the Stendhal University in Grenoble.

References

Browman, C. P. and Goldstein, L. (1988). Some notes on syllable structure in Articulatory Phonology. *Phonetica*, 45(2-4):140–155.

Levelt, W. J. M. (1989). *Speaking: From Intention to Articulation.* MIT Press, Cambridge MA.

Levelt, W. J. M., Roelofs, A., and Meyer, A. S. (1999). A theory of lexical access in speech production. *Brain and Behavioral Sciences*, 22:1–38.

Smith, A. (2006). Speech motor development: Integrating muscles, movements, and linguistic units. *Journal of Communication Disorders*, 39:331–349.

Smith, A. and Goffman, L. (2004). Interaction of language and motor factors in speech production. In Maasen, B., Kent, R. D., Peters, H. F. M., Peters, H., van Lieshout, P., and Hulstijn, W., editors, *Speech motor control in normal and disordered speech*, pages 225–252. Oxford University Press.

Global and detailed speech representations in early language acquisition

PIERRE HALLÉ
ALEJANDRINA CRISTIA

Abstract: We review data and hypotheses dealing with the mental representations for perceived and produced speech that infants build and use over the course of learning a language. In the early stages of speech perception and vocal production, before the emergence of a receptive or a productive lexicon, the dominant picture emerging from the literature suggests rather non-analytic representations based on units of the size of the syllable: Young children seem to parse speech into syllable-sized units in spite of their ability to detect sound equivalence based on shared phonetic features. Once a productive lexicon has emerged, word form representations are initially rather underspecified phonetically but gradually become more specified with lexical growth, up to the phoneme level. The situation is different for the receptive lexicon, in which phonetic specification for consonants and vowels seem to follow different developmental paths. Consonants in stressed syllables are somewhat well specified already at the first signs of a receptive lexicon, and become even better specified with lexical growth. Vowels seem to follow a different developmental path, with increasing flexibility throughout lexical development. Thus, children come to exhibit a consonant-vowel asymmetry in lexical representations, which is clear in adult representations.

1 Introduction

To begin with, what do we mean by speech representations? We simply refer to the mental representations that speakers/listeners of a given language have built during acquisition and use to produce and understand spoken utterances of their language. We adopt the generativist view according to which production and perception of speech is accomplished via the manipulation -in production or perception- of basic speech units that combine into higher order units through the application of grammatical rules. Words are combined units with respect to, for example, phonemes but are basic units with respect to multi-word sentences. In that sense, words play a pivotal role at the interface between basic sound units and sentences. Importantly, the units we are talking about are not just useful to describe languages and how languages work but are meant to have a psychological reality in language users' minds, following the goals of modern linguistics, as summarized in the following passage:

"There has always been a tension between two ways of understanding linguistics: On one view [...] (which was dominant in the first part of this century), [language] has a structure that can be explored independently of any efforts to figure out what particular speakers may do or think [...]. On the other view of linguistics (a view that has come to be relatively dominant in the past several decades), *the goal of linguistics is to model what it is that goes inside a speaker's head.*" Goldsmith (1999, p.5, our stress).

The discussion in this chapter will therefore revolve around the mental representations speakers/listeners use in processing speech. We restrict ourselves to prelexical and lexical units and will not cover the issue of how the rules that combine units are themselves represented. Although many other questions could be posed, this chapter mainly focuses on the following questions:
How detailed, in terms of phonetic specification, are the speech representations used by children acquiring their mother tongue?
Do representations change throughout development?
The literature on language acquisition, from Ferguson and Farwell (1975) onwards, converges to suggest that, overall, children follow a holistic-to-analytic progression in the way they code words (from whole-word units to decomposed representations), at least in production. The motivation of such a progression is clear: The need to adopt systematic strategies to code words increases with vocabulary size, eventually leading to analytic representations into unit combinations. Work in the last 20 years has led to a refinement of this proposal by exploring lexical specification in both production and perception. In addition, some of this work suggests that there is an asymmetry in terms of the level of specification of consonants and vowels. In this chapter, we present a global view of both classical and recent results bearing on this proposal. This chapter is or-

ganized as follows: Sections 2 and 3 deal with prelexical infants' speech representations in production, beginning with the babbling; and in perception, beginning with newborns' speech perception. The following two sections address the lexical representations that emerge around 10-11 months and often grow dramatically around 18-20 months. Section 4 briefly surveys the "child phonology" literature on early word representations in production; section 5 summarizes recent findings on early lexical representations in the receptive lexicon and on how these representations develop as a function of language acquisition. The final section (section 6) surveys adult perception and linguistic data indicating that consonants and vowels serve somewhat different linguistic functions and reviews recent child data bearing on a consonant-vowel asymmetry in lexical representations.

2 Speech representations for production in prelexical children

Before they produce (or are discovered to produce) their first words, young children normally go through different stages of vocal productions (see, among others, Oller, 1980, 2000; Stark, 1980; Kent and Murray, 1982). Among these, vocalizations and babbling undoubtedly are intentional, voluntary productions. The early vocalizations of young children usually are long, sustained vowels modulated in pitch and intensity, with the occasional occurrence of consonant-like onsets, thereby forming "proto-syllables" (Oller, 1980). Vocalizations thus are certainly not rich in terms of phonetic detail. The picture changes notably with babbling. Babbling is followed by the child's first words and is characterized by the production of syllables roughly conforming with the syllables of adult speech in terms of timing. These syllables are often reduplicated a few times (canonical babbling) but possibly also differ from one another with respect to vowel or consonant (variegated babbling). Although the dominant opinion is that variegated and canonical babbling appear more or less simultaneously (MacNeilage and Davis, 2002), this issue is still debated (Vihman et al., 1985). The disagreement may be due to the difficulty of defining phonetic variation vs. phonetic constancy when it comes to describing the phonetic content of babbling productions. In other words, the phonetic substance of babbling productions might not be well defined in terms of phonetic categories. This suggests phonetically underspecified rather than detailed mental representations in production, although it could be the case that phonetic variation in babbling is in part explained by an incomplete maturation of the vocal production system. At any rate, babbling productions are more readily described in terms of syllables than of consonants and vowels, as the defining characteristic of babbling itself suggests: Babbling consists of adult-like syllables.

In the frame-then-content (henceforth, F-then-C) view of children's babbling and first word productions promoted by MacNeilage and Davis (Davis and MacNeilage, 1990, 1995; MacNeilage, 1997), the syllable indeed explicitly appears as the basic unit of production: One syllable corresponds to precisely one cycle of mandibular oscillation, that is, to one "frame". The F-then-C account proposes that frames are initially underspecified segmentally. Early frames are "pure frames", only specified by a cyclic closing-opening movement of the jaw superimposed on laryngeal voice excitation. The result is heard as CVs whose Cs and Vs mechanically reflect unintentional, targetless positioning of tongue (and lips) riding passively on the jaw oscillatory cycle (typically a labial obstruent and a central vowel): Thus, these frames have no "content" (see Hodge (1989) for a similar idea). Content appears when voluntary maneuvers of the articulators are superimposed on the closing-opening cycle. At this stage, three more elaborate frames emerge, namely "front frames", "back frames", and "nasal frames", in which just one single articulatory parameter is set: Tongue position for front vs. back frames and velum opening for nasal frames (Matyear et al., 1998). Such minimal specifications are thought to prevail until rather late in language development, that is, until around 16-18 months (MacNeilage, 1996, 1997). In particular, the three basic frames "pure", "front", and "back" seem to explain most of the consonant-vowel cooccurrence data, although the dominant patterns of cooccurrence are somewhat debated (for a review, see Chen and Kent, 2005). The F-then-C account contends that the CV cooccurrence patterns observed for children during speech acquisition reflect a universal trend (MacNeilage and Davis, 2000). Whether or not such a universal trend exists (see Whalen et al. in press, for a discussion), babbling and early word productions are largely underspecified according to the F-then-C account: Only four types of frames, hence four classes of syllables make up the building bricks of intended utterances and each class is defined by a single parameter. The articulatory phonology approach (Browman and Goldstein, 1989, 1992) similarly holds that the syllable is the time frame wherein oscillatory systems are synched to produce consonant and vowel gestures. However, instead of positing syllabic gestures specified by a single parameter for both consonants and vowels, this approach considers that consonant and vowel gestures, although initially achieved with great imprecision, are *intended* separately. That certain CV cooccurrences are favored over others (e.g., front vowels follow alveolar rather than velar consonants) and are more noticeable in child than adult speech is attributable to gestural overlap. Young children still do not control well phasing relationships and durations - which are at the heart of articulatory phonology - thereby producing variable and unwanted gestural overlap. Articulatory phonology thus proposes a similar account for early speech CV cooccurrences and for assimilation processes: gestural overlap. Browman and Goldstein (1992) suggest that children's early speech productions reduce to a few "dynamically stable patterns", wherein C and V gestures remain undifferentiated and are not accurately phased together. Children then progressively learn to differentiate these patterns into separate C and V gestures, eventually acquiring CV combinations specific to the language they learn (de Boysson-Bardies, 1993). The gestural approach thus also describes early speech production as initially underspecified for consonants and vowels and implicitly suggests that later emerging CV specification is still constrained by the syllabic time frame.

To sum up, children's early speech productions seem to be underspecified in terms of consonants and vowels and, rather, to be specified in terms of syllables as whole units. The F-then-C account holds that syllable-based speech productions - mostly specified by place only - are still the rule at the stage of early words and that children gradually escape this pattern through C and V variegation. Articulatory phonology assumes a less constrained development, which tends toward children's learning of phasing relationships within CV syllables.

3 Speech representations for perception in pre-lexical children

In the preceding section, the nature of speech representations in production was inferred from the extent to which vowels and consonants are independently controlled in children's productions. Speech representations in perception can be inferred from several other sources of evidence. However, the relevant data seem to converge toward a similar conclusion: Young children code speech in terms of syllables. One source of evidence is provided by the capacity of newborns to "count" syllables rather than phonemes within simple utterances. This finding was first reported by Bijeljac-Babic et al. (1993). These authors used a habituation-dishabituation paradigm based on the classic High Amplitude Sucking (henceforth, HAS) procedure (Eimas et al., 1971). In one experiment, four-day-old infants habituated to a set of disyllabic CVCV speech stimuli, such as {*rifu, kepa...*}, dishabituated when presented with a set of trisyllabic CVCVCV stimuli, e.g. {*mazopu, rekiva...*}, and vice-versa. Discrimination was not based on overall stimulus duration but on stimulus syllabic structure, as shown by another experiment in which the distributions of stimulus durations for the two sets were made to overlap by expanding and compressing the stimuli. This manipulation preserved the discrimination between the two- and three-syllable sets. An alternative explanation for these results simply is that infants discriminate between four- and six-phoneme utterances (CVCVs and CVCVCVs).

Bijeljac-Babic et al. tested this possibility in comparing stimuli with four vs. six phonemes but all with two syllables (e.g., {*rifu, iblo*} vs. {*treklu, suldri*}). Infants did not discriminate 4-phoneme from 6-phoneme disyllabic items. Altogether, these data therefore strongly suggest that infants are more sensitive to syllabic rather than to phonemic units in the input speech. Another study by the same group further suggested that French infants count syllables rather than moras (Bertoncini et al., 1995): Amongst disyllabic items, infants did not discriminate 2-mora items (e.g., {*kago, mika, seki, buke*}) from 3-mora ones (e.g., {*kaNgo, mikaN, seQki, buuke*}).

Another source of evidence, in line with the idea that infants perceive speech as a string of syllables, is provided by Bertoncini and Mehler (1981). The same acoustic contrast may be discriminated or not by two-month-olds (French-learning) according to whether the stimuli sound like speech, with a salient syllabic structure, or not. French two-month-olds do not discriminate [tʃp]-[pʃt] but do discriminate [utʃpu]-[upʃtu]. Indeed, syllabic structure is presumably much more salient in the latter than the former contrast, at least for French-learning infants. A more salient syllabic structure would allow infants to process the stimuli as speech and parse them into syllables they can discriminate.
A third line of evidence is provided by experiments that addressed the level of detail infants code within the syllable using the standard HAS procedure. For example, in Jusczyk (1987), American two-month-olds were habituated to a set of CVs sharing C ([bi, bo, bɚ, ba]). After habituation (post-shift phase), a new CV stimulus with a new C ([di]), a new V ([bu]), or both a new C and V ([du]) was added to the initial set of stimuli. The assumption was that infants would dishabituate with the [d] but not the [b] new stimuli, had they been able to extract and code [b] as a "sound" common to all the habituation CVs. But infants dishabituated for [d] and [b] equally. There was thus no evidence that two-month-olds can identify a syllable-initial consonant as a property shared by several syllables with different vowels. In other words, infants at that age do not seem to extract and code a consonant within a syllable. Bertoncini et al. (1988) replicated Jusczyk and Derrah's (1987) results, using the same stimuli and procedure, with French two-month-olds. They also tested newborns who differed from two-month-olds in that they dishabituated only when the new stimulus introduced a new vowel (i.e., for [bu] and [du], not [da]). In a second experiment, infants were tested with an habituation set of CVs sharing V ([bi, si, li, mi]), and post-shift new CV stimuli with a new V ([ba]), a new C ([di]), or both a new V and C ([da]). The very same pattern of results obtained: Two-month-olds dishabituated for any new CV stimulus, whereas newborns dishabituated only when the new stimulus introduced a new vowel (i.e., for [ba] and [da], not [di]). These data were taken to suggest that very young infants code CV syllables as whole units, and that newborns are insensitive to consonant variation. The newborns' reduced sensitivity to consonants compared to vowels may reflect their experience in utero,

which filters much of the high-frequency energy relevant for consonantal contrasts while relatively preserving vowels. Do older prelexical infants come to represent consonants and vowels separately? The answer to this question may come from a more recent line of research, where young infants' encoding of sound sequences has been investigated. In this work, infants hear a large number of word forms (50-100), all of which bear the same abstract sequence; for example, nasal vowels are always followed by fricative consonants, and oral vowels by stops. At test, infants are presented with new word forms, some of which follow the abstract pattern (i.e., a new nasal vowel is followed by a fricative) while others do not (a new nasal vowel is followed by a stop). Prelexical infants, some tested as young as 4 months, exhibit stable preferences, typically for the more novel-sounding illegal patterns (see a summary in Cristia et al., 2011). This appears to indicate that prelexical infants come to represent consonants and vowels specifically. However, a recent study (Cristia and Peperkamp, 2011) suggests that such results may be best accommodated through acoustic, whole-word representations. In this study, six-month-olds were first familiarized with word forms sharing onset voicing. They were then tested on new word forms in which onset voicing and novelty (from the familiarization set or not) were manipulated. They preferred the new voicing and this was not due to novelty only since they showed no preference for novel over familiarization word forms when voicing was kept constant. At first sight, the infants' behavior could be explained by their reliance on the [voice] feature value in onsets. Yet, the results better fitted acoustic distances between word forms computed on entire items than on item onsets only. This suggested that the infants' behavior actually reflected acoustic- or auditory-based comparison between whole-word forms rather than feature-based analytic representations.

To summarize, prelexical infants appear to rely on syllabic representations, or perhaps on whole-word forms, in which consonants and vowels are bound together. Now what about the lexical stage? Do young children who are starting a productive or a receptive lexicon represent words (be they production targets or recognized spoken items) as composed of syllables or, for example, of consonants and vowels?

4 Lexical representations in production: Children's early words

Most evidence suggests that children first go through a whole-word stage during which the word is the basic unit (the "prosodic word" Macken, 1978, 1979; Vihman, 1996). Following that stage, children gradually develop more adult-like phonological representations, that is, rule-based representations gradually leading to principled segmental and featural units. Some children, usually during the second year, develop a few templates (i.e., word patterns) consisting of a stable skeleton of consonants - or of consonants and vowels - that constrains all their attempted words. This is well illustrated in Macken's classic longitudinal study (Macken, 1978) from 1;6 to 2;5 years of the words produced by "Si", a child raised in a Mexican Spanish environment. From 1;7 to 1;9, virtually all the words attempted by this child followed a "labial-dental" disyllabic word pattern, whether this pattern reflected the adult model or not. For example, she produced *zapato* ('shoe') as [pwatːo], closely following the adult model, but also *sopa* ('soup') as [pwæta], reversing the dental-labial order of the adult model, or even *reloj* ('clock') as [budːo], although the adult model had no labial consonant. These single word patterns have been interpreted as reflecting non-analytic representations of produced speech into "whole-word" units. The rigid single pattern followed in virtually all produced words indeed suggests nondecomposed representations in terms of consonants or in terms of syllables. Neither the consonant skeleton nor the vowel pattern of the adult model are usually preserved in the productions of the children who follow the path of a single template whole-word stage, suggesting these children do not analyze words into segments. However, children are quite variable with respect to the observable path they follow in acquiring words. This is illustrated in Table 1, drawn from de Boysson-Bardies (1996): At comparable chronological age and/or estimated productive vocabulary size, early words are close to their adult model in some children (suggesting analytic coding), but rather underspecified in other children. Despite such individual variation, children's first words often are rather holistic approximations of the adult word forms. De Boysson-Bardies' data (e.g., Table 1) suggest that this holistic stage is difficult to notice in some children. Whole- word rather than analytic representations may underlie holistic approximations, as was proposed in the classic paper by Ferguson and Farwell (1975).

Table 1: First words produced by two 14-month-old French children (with a productive vocabulary estimated at 30-40 words), from de Boysson-Bardies (1996); adult glosses in italics. Marie's productions may be described as "analytic" and those of Émilie as "holistic".

Émilie		Marie	
[ba]	balle	[ættæ]	attend
[bø]	bouton	[hatø]	bateau
[bebe]	bébé	[bebe]	bébé
[poe]	pomme	[dodo]	dodo q
[pɔ]	chapeau	[təbɔ]	c'est beau
[popo]	petit pot	[ebotsa]	c'est beau ça
[ka]	canard	[taːtinn]	tartine
[ke]	clef	[papɨdzɐ̧]	papillon
[kkɪ]	cuillère	[voaɧy]	voiture
[kχ]	Mickey	[hemjetsɐ]	mimichat
[qa]	sac	[popi]	poupée

Throughout development, however, word form representations become more and more clearly organized in terms of segments in that their consonants and vowels do not depart from those of adult forms in an erratic way but, rather, in a progressively more systematic way (see, for example, Vihman and Greenlee, 1987). This increasing systematicity is quite appealing for phonologists and a huge "Child Phonology" literature has been devoted to describing in terms of phonological processes how child forms differ from adult forms. We will not expand on that aspect and simply note that most of the processes described in this literature involve consonants rather than vowels (Vihman and Greenlee (1987), but see Pollock and Berni (2003) on both normal and disordered acquisition of English vowels). This might be an indication that consonants are more important than vowels in children's early lexical representations or, possibly, that vocalic variations in children's early words are less easily noticed by adult hearers and therefore get underreported (see section 6 on adults' greater sensitivity to consonant than vowel variation). To sum up, a gross analogy is observed between prelexical and lexical representations for production in that both become increasingly detailed throughout development.

5 Children's receptive lexical representations in word-learning and word-recognition

Children recognize word forms earlier than they can produce them intentionally. A further, and logically more difficult accomplishment, is to consistently associate word forms with meanings. Many studies have used a variety of "word-learning" tasks, whereby children learn made-up associations between novel words and novel objects, and have directly addressed the issue of how much phonetic detail children are able to code for newly learned words. A somewhat different line of research has focused on how children code the words they have learned either during experimental training or from natural exposure to the language spoken in their linguistic environment, and has addressed that issue with "word recognition" tasks. We will see that the two approaches yield somewhat different pictures of children's representations of word forms. Six-eight months is about the youngest age investigated by word recognition studies, such as those conducted by Peter Jusczyk's group. Those studies show that 8-month-old American infants can "segment", or pull out monosyllabic words out of continuous speech and retain them at least for the duration of an experimental session. For example, Jusczyk and Aslin (1995) trained 6- and 7.5-month-olds with two words (*cup* and *dog* for half the infants, *foot* and *bike* for the others) appearing repeatedly in a few sentences during a familiarization phase, then tested them on their preference for trained over untrained words, using the now classical Headturn Preference Procedure (henceforth, HPP). They found that 7.5-month-olds but not 6-month olds preferred listening to the two words they had been trained on over the two other, untrained words. However, this preference, suggesting word recognition, did not resist a change in word-initial consonant: Infants trained with *cup* and *dog* did not prefer *tup* and *bawg* over untrained words. Hence, word form representations at this age seem phonetically detailed, at least with respect to the onset consonant. Older infants (at about 11 months) have been shown to recognize words presumably familiar to them through natural, not experimental exposure (Hallé and de Boysson-Bardies, 1994; Vihman et al., 2004; Swingley, 2005). For example, 11-month-old French infants prefer listening to *ballon* ('balloon') than *félin* ('feline': presumably not a familiar word for children) right away, that is, without experimental training on *ballon* (Hallé and de Boysson-Bardies, 1994). This suggested 11-month-olds have coded some familiar words in long term memory, in an early receptive lexicon. Further studies examined how strictly infants might code word forms: How detailed are word form representations in infants' early receptive lexicon? Hallé and de Boysson-Bardies (1996) used mispronunciations of familiar words to address that issue. They found that 11-month-old French infants still preferred mispronounced familiar over unfamiliar words, when the mispronunciation affected the word-initial consonant (e.g., *poupée* ('doll') > *boupée* or *foupée*). Moreover, they did not prefer unaltered over mispronounced familiar word forms. The preference for mispronounced familiar over unfamiliar words tended to fade away when the mispronunciation affected the word-medial consonant (e.g., *poupée* > *poufée*). Omission of the word-initial consonant resulted in no preference at all for mispronounced familiar words (e.g., *poupée* > *oupée*). As proposed by Hallé and de Boysson-Bardies (1996), these data thus show a relative elasticity of 11-month-olds' word form representations. It might seem surprising that infants tolerate word-initial but not word-medial consonant mispronunciation. More recent work by Vihman et al. (2004) provides a clue to this question. Vihman et al. (2004) tested 11-month-old British infants with familiar vs. unfamiliar disyllabic English words or noun phrases (so as to manipulate stress placement). The results they obtained were similar to those in Hallé and de Boysson-Bardies (1996) but with an important difference. The British infants tolerated mispronunciations of word medial consonant but not of word initial consonant (e.g., *dirty* > *dirny* tolerated; *dirty* > *nirty* not tolerated). This pattern is the opposite of that found for French. Since English and French words have opposite dominant metric patterns (trochaic and iambic, respectively), a sensible interpretation is that 11-month-olds rather strictly code stressed syllables and less strictly so unstressed syllables in their early receptive lexicon (Figure 1). This is compatible with the earlier finding by Jusczyk and Aslin (1995) that 7.5-month-olds fail to recognize *tup* and *bawg* after they have been trained on *cup* and *dog*, since monosyllabic content words are stressed. Similarly, Swingley (2005) replicated the preference for familiar over novel words in Dutch 11-month-olds, using monosyllabic words. In line with our explanation, this preference was abolished if the words were mispronounced (e.g., *mont* ('mouth') > *nont* or *monk*) and infants systematically preferred unaltered over mispronounced familiar words.

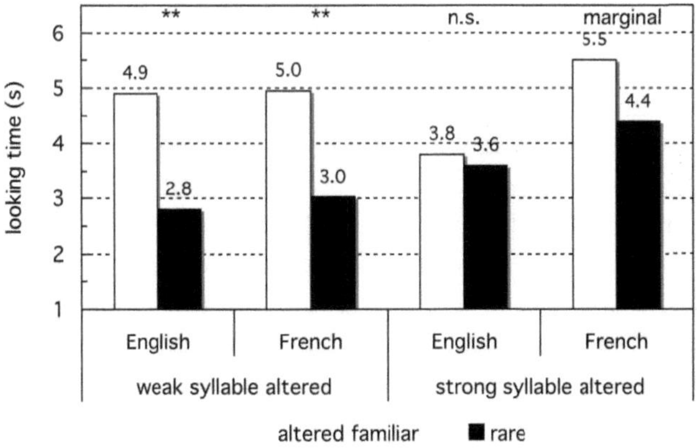

Figure 1: Looking times to disyllabic unfamiliar vs. familiar words, place-altered on the initial consonant of the weak vs. strong syllable. Recognition of familiar words obtains for weak but not strong syllable alteration (from Hallé and de Boysson-Bardies, 1996; Vihman et al., 2004).

Further data with slightly older children confirm the view that infants' word form representations in early receptive lexicon are rather detailed phonetically. These data come from studies using the preferential looking procedure, whereby infants are presented with two pictures on a screen (one target, one distracter), then prompted with a sentence such as "Where is the [target]?". Longer looking times to the target than the distracter are assumed to indicate word recognition (together with knowledge of word-picture association). Swingley and Aslin (2002) found that 14-month-olds recognize both *dog* and *tog* as referring to the picture of a dog rather than that of a shoe, but look longer to that picture when presented with *dog* than *tog*. Bailey and Plunkett (2002) obtained an even more radical advantage for *dog* over *tog*, with 14-month-olds recognizing *dog* but not *tog*. When children learn new, arbitrary word-object associations, they seem to show some difficulty at coding words with full phonetic detail.

At 14 months, American children, when tested on a word-learning paradigm known as the "Switch" procedure (an habituation-dishabituation paradigm on word-object associations, see Werker et al., 1998), do not distinguish *bih* from *dih* (Stager and Werker, 1997; Werker et al., 2002). Children do not succeed in this task before 17 months (Werker et al., 2002). However, when the contrasted words are familiar minimal pairs, such as *ball* vs. *doll* (presumably well known by young children), even 14- month-olds succeed in the Switch task (Fennell and Werker, 2003). But this is not the whole story, as recent data bearing on the "bih-dih issue" suggest: Children's success at associating *bih* and *dih* (or similar minimal pairs) to different referent objects depends on a variety of non-phonetic factors, such as the testing procedure - new minimal pairs can be learned at 14 months with the preferential looking procedure - (Ballem and Plunkett, 2005; Fennell and Waxman, 2010), the distracter items used (Thiessen, 2007), or the simple fact that referent objects move in synchrony with target speech items or not (see Lakshmi Gogate's research on 8-month-olds: e.g., Gogate, 2010). In other words, the picture of phonetic detail in word-learning is quite heterogeneous. If we limit our purpose to drawing a meaningful developmental trajectory, the data obtained with the Switch procedure might be the most telling, since they clearly reveal infants' improving ability to code phonetic detail in newly learned words. We therefore rely on these data so as to draw a coherent picture of children's sensitivity to phonetic detail in newly learned words.

Altogether, then, current research on lexical development, especially that using the Switch procedure, suggests that when children "learn" words, they code word forms in a less phonetically specified way than for the long term representations they have built in their early receptive lexicon over the course of normal language acquisition. Yet, this difference is probably quantitative rather than qualitative: Coding word forms during a word-learning task, after a limited exposure to arbitrary word-object pairs (typically presented only 3-9 times), is logically more demanding than detecting and memorizing recurring word forms from natural exposure to speech over the course of weeks or months. We therefore propose that children use similar word form representations in both word-learning and in familiar word-recognition. The observed delay in forming phonetically detailed representations in word-learning tasks therefore suggests a developmental trend from initially somewhat underspecified toward fully specified word form representations.

The literature reviewed so far examined the issue of phonetic detail in children's word form representations for consonants (e.g., *ball* vs. *doll*) but not for vowels, or non-systematically so, as in Swingley and Aslin (2000) whose materials include *apple* vs. *opple*. In the next section, we review the recent data obtained for vowel compared to consonant variation.

6 Vowels versus consonants in children's lexical representations

During the first decade or so of its existence, the research on children's word form representations in reception focused exclusively on consonants, from Jusczyck and Aslin's onwards (Jusczyk and Aslin, 1995). This is in itself revealing of an implicit assumption made by researchers that consonants matter more than vowels for lexical forms. There are indeed reasons to believe so. Recently, the logical arguments for a consonant-vowel dissociation in terms of their functional roles were neatly laid out in an often cited paper by Nespor et al. (2003). In this work, the argument is made that lexical forms are mainly specified by consonants; in contrast, vowels carry prosodic, syntactic, and morphosyntactic information, and are less important for lexical identity.

To test these claims, Mehler's group at SISSA ("Scuola Internazionale Superiore di Studi Avanzati" in Trieste) has conducted numerous artificial grammar studies which suggest that adults segment out word forms from a continuous stream of syllables more readily when "words" are defined by consonant rather than vowel patterns (Bonatti et al., 2005). In contrast, other artificial grammar studies suggest that abstract regularities (e.g., structural sequencing such as reduplication, or simple patterns such as AAB, ABA, etc.) can be extracted by listeners when they are defined on vowels but not when they are defined on consonants (adults: Peña et al., 2002; Toro et al., 2008) (infants: Pons and Toro, 2010), in line with the idea that consonants specify words and vowels specify rules (Nespor et al., 2003). Evidence that is more immediately relevant to our question of whether consonants and vowels are coded equally in word representations comes from an older line of work. Word-reconstruction studies provide more convincing evidence for the lexical motivation of consonants because they bear on natural word form representations in long-term lexicon. In these experiments, listeners are asked to produce a word form closest to a pseudoword derived from a word by either vowel or consonant change. For example, *keebra* is derived from *cobra* by a vowel change or from *zebra* by a consonant change. Listeners more often and more easily "reconstruct" *cobra* than *zebra* from *keebra*, thereby preserving consonant rather than vowel information (van Ooijen, 1996; Sharp et al., 2005, the latter for recent behavioral and brain imagery data). Note that this result obtains regardless of phonological inventory. That is, one might imagine that the observed consonant-vowel asymmetry only holds for languages such as English, in which there are many vowels and vowels vary with regional accent. In fact, the asymmetry also obtains in Spanish or Japanese (which have only a handful of vowels) as clearly as in English (Cutler et al., 2000; Cutler and Otake, 2002). Listeners tend to provide words that match the consonantal frame more frequently than those that match the vocalic frame, suggesting that word form representations are universally based on consonants more than vowels. Now, is there evidence for the lexical coding C-V asymmetry in child data? Nazzi's study (Nazzi, 2005) marks a turning point in the children's lexical representation research in that it showed, for the first time, that consonants weigh more than vowels in 20-months-olds' word form representations. Nazzi (2005) used the "name-based categorization" paradigm (henceforth, NBC): In this paradigm, children are first taught three name-object pairings, in which two different objects share the same label (e.g., /pize/) and the third object has a different label (e.g., /tize/). In the test phase after each such triplet, the child's task is to put together the objects that share the same label; their success in the task indicates, among other things, their ability to learn two different labels (Nazzi and Gopnik, 2001). Of interest here is how the two labels differ. Nazzi (2005) manipulated this difference in various ways. In particular, he compared differences in consonant with differences in vowel (e.g., /pize/-/tize/ vs. /pize/-/pyze/); he found that 20-months-old French children performed better for consonant than vowel differences, showing a "consonantal bias" in word-learning. Further follow-up experiments using the NBC procedure demonstrated that this bias was not confounded with a positional bias, that is, a possible advantage for syllable-initial phonemes (Nazzi and Bertoncini, 2009). The consonantal bias was also found for younger children, at 16 months, using a simplified version of the NBC task (Havy and Nazzi, 2009). Using variants of the NBC paradigm, Nazzi and colleagues (Nazzi et al., 2009) found that both French- and English-learning 30-months-olds are able to learn a single feature vowel change (/pize/-/pyze/) but still rely more on consonants when asked to match a mispronounced form with a learned label (e.g., they match /pide/ with /pyde/ rather than /tide/[1]). Altogether, this line of research suggests a developmental trend toward more attention paid to vowel variation (at 30 months), but still with an advantage for consonants over vowels. We return to this developmental issue in the general discussion.

A recent study by the SISSA's group suggests this consonant-vowel functional distinction also holds for 12-months-olds. Using a variant of the preferential looking paradigm, whereby an auditory word predicts the apparition of an associated picture at one side of the screen (Kovács and Mehler, 2009), Hochmann showed that, when encoding words, 12-months-olds give more weight to consonants than vowels (Hochmann, 2010; Hochmann et al., 2011): After they learn to associate *keke* with side A and *dudu* with side B, they orient in anticipation to side A rather than B when presented with *kuku*, and vice versa with *dede*.[2] That is, the consonant code prevails over the vowel code for word recognition.

In an other experiment, Hochmann et al. (2011) showed that, when extracting a second order regularity, 12-months-olds give more weight to vowels than consonants: They do learn to associate vowel but not consonant reduplication with one side of the screen. Altogether, then, these

---

1 This experimental design is thus strongly reminiscent of the word-reconstruction paradigm used with adults. Note that it allows for directly comparing tolerance to consonant vs. vowel variation.

2 This experimental design is a constant target design, in contrast to most other studies, thus avoiding possible confounding factors in the consonant-vowel comparison.

children behaved just like adults: They rely on consonants to code lexical forms and on vowels to extract rules.

Another line of research, conducted by Plunkett's group (using the preferential looking procedure), investigated the consonantal bias in word--recognition for well-known words. Mani and Plunkett (2007) found that English-learning children, aged 15, 18, and 24 months, were sensitive to both consonant and vowel mispronunciations. They did not look at the image of a *bib* (a well known word for children this age) when hearing either *bab* or *dib* (vowel or consonant mispronunciation, respectively), although 15-month-olds non-significantly tended to look at the *bib* upon hearing *bab*. Mani and Plunkett (2010) also found that British 12-month-olds were as sensitive to vowel as to consonant changes in familiar words (e.g., *cups* mispronounced *keps* or *tups*). Do these results contradict those obtained in Nazzi's group? A possible reason for the observed discrepancies might be the difference in word form representation for word-learning and word-recognition, as we discussed earlier. However, Mani and Plunkett (2008) obtained vowel-mispronunciation effects using novel words learned by 14-month-olds (e.g., learned *padge* mispronounced *poudge*). Likewise, Curtin et al. (2009) (see also Dietrich et al., 2007), using the Switch procedure, found that English-learning 14-month-olds successfully learned a *deet-dit* pair (although not a *deet-doot* pair or a *dit-doot* pair). Note that these negative results with respect to the consonantal bias run contrary to the current findings with adult listeners from various languages mentioned above.

To sum up, the consonantal bias in children's word form representations is still a matter of debate. The discrepancies found across the various studies just reviewed may be due to a variety of factors: Children's target language, children'age, type of lexical representation (for word-learning vs. word-recognition), type of word form (e.g., mono- vs. disyllabic), or experimental procedure. Yet, on theoretical grounds and on the basis of data consistency, the dominant picture is an advantage of consonants over vowels for lexical coding. Interestingly, we note that the consonant bias in adults, which is rather well established, may have consequences in their report of children's early produced word forms: Child phonology studies have mainly focused on the regular or quasi-regular consonant variation in children's early words.

Alternatively, it might be the case that vowel variation in these productions is random rather than regular. This point certainly deserves systematic research.

7 General discussion

In this review of prelexical and lexical representations in children, we came across rather different issues, addressed by various research studies. Yet, one aspect seems to characterize the entire spectrum of data: Children start with somewhat vague, global, holistic, underspecified representations of sound sequences and later of words, in both perception and production; they then orient toward more precise, analytic, phonetically specified representations.

Representations certainly cover different realities for perception and production, for prelexical sound sequences and for words. We focus in this discussion on *word form* representations but occasionally refer to prelexical representations. While representations for production definitely develop from whole-word to analytic representations into phoneme-like elements at around 2 years of age (Macken, 1978, 1979), those for perception follow a less clear, and less agreed-on developmental trajectory. The differences between word-learning and word-recognition might help understand this trajectory. As we argued, the kinds of representations that infants use in word-learning tasks and for coding/recognizing words in long term memory (in their receptive lexicon) are conceivably similar and should follow parallel, although somewhat time-delayed developmental trajectories. Whereas little change is observed for word recognition representations in terms of phonetic detail, a change from holistic to analytic is more apparent for word-learning between about 14 and 18 months (section 5). Such a change is also predictable on theoretical grounds: According to Metsala, "...representations of lexical items may become increasingly segmented (phonemic) with development from the pressure of an increasing vocabulary size." Metsala (1997, p.161) (see also, Metsala and Walley, 1998; Walley, 1993; Walley and Metsala, 1990). We therefore surmise that word form representations in children's early receptive lexicons gradually shift from holistic to analytic formats during the second year of life.

Now, this holistic-to-analytic shift is not the whole story. Indeed, as the recent research highlights, consonants and vowels play different roles and it seems that consonants are eventually more strictly coded than vowels in the receptive lexicon. Thus, the holistic-to analytic picture needs some qualification. The current literature on consonant-vowel asymmetries suggests that consonants are strictly coded very early on: Even 7.5 month-olds recognize *cup* but not *tup* after they are familiarized with *cup* (Jusczyk and Aslin, 1995). But some confusion exists in the currently available data with respect to vowels. Prelexical data suggest that vowels initially have more weight that consonants (Bertoncini et al., 1988), which is also in line with the classical findings that vowels are perceived in a language specific way earlier than consonants (vowels: around 5-6 months (Kuhl et al., 1992); consonants: around 8-10 months (Werker and Tees, 1984)). For lexical coding, Mani and Plunkett's data (Mani and Plunkett, 2007) suggest a more elastic coding of vowels at 15 than 18 or 24 months. Nazzi et al.'s data (Nazzi et al., 2009) suggest that sensitivity to vowel variation increases between 20 and 30 months. Yet it seems that these data also depend on which consonant or vowel contrast is tested (consonants: Pomiechowska (2011); vowels: Curtin et al. (2009)). It is therefore clear that more research is needed in this domain. A study by Best and colleagues (Best et al., 2009) might serendipitously shed light on that issue. Although it was primarily aimed at detecting the emergence of "phonological constancy", this study suggests that 15-month-old American children are sensitive to vowel quality for the familiar words in their receptive lexicon. Indeed, 15-month-olds did not recognize familiar words[3] when spoken in Jamaican English, although they did recognize them when spoken in their natice Connecticut American English. Importantly, vowel quality is the main difference between these two English dialects.[4] At 19 months, children recognized familiar words, whether spoken in American or Jamaican English. That is,

3 Best et al. (2009) used a conditioned-fixation version of Hallé and de Boysson-Bardies's (1994) familiar-word preference task.

4 Jamaican and American English mainly differ on vowels: different locations in vowel space (Wassink, 2006), different diphthongs, and different tense-lax distinctions. Jamaican English also tends to avoid vowel reduction, hence to be more syllable-timed than American English. The two dialects differ on some consonants (e.g., Jamaican English merges /f/ and /θ/, and sometimes drops /h/ or /r/, etc.); they also may differ on lexical stress patterns (Patrick, 1999).

somewhere between 15 and 19 months, children develop the ability to ignore irrelevant vowel variation in lexical items. In our perspective, vowel information in known words becomes coded in a more and more flexible way with linguistic experience. Such a developmental trajectory seems more cogent with a general developmental trend from infancy to adulthood. In the adult state, vowels indeed have a lesser weight than consonants for coding lexical information. As we mentioned earlier, the consonant-vowel asymmetry in adults is demonstrated in word-reconstruction studies (Cutler et al., 2000; Sharp et al., 2005; van Ooijen, 1996), as well as in artificial grammar studies (Bonatti et al., 2005). Note that the perception data reviewed in section 3 for newborns vs. 2-month-olds (Bertoncini et al., 1988) may suggest a precursor of the change toward the C-V asymmetry observed in adults: Newborns appear more sensitive to vowel than consonant variation, whereas 2-month-olds are equally sensitive to both and seem to only attend to CV whole syllables. To conclude, whereas we agree with the general notion that lexical coding becomes more and more specified overall throughout the development of both productive and receptive lexicons - logically under the pressure of lexical growth -, we believe this notion needs an important qualification in the case of the receptive lexicon. With respect to consonants, high sensitivity to phonetic detail in word form representations can be observed very early on, at least in stressed syllables, and may only slightly increase in older children. Children's sensitivity to vowels seems to follow an opposite trajectory. We propose that, contrary to the general holistic-analytic developmental trend, children's lexical representations become more and more flexible for vowels with increased experience with the language they learn. Only this developmental path is compatible with the adult state of affairs, whereby the consonant-vowel asymmetry is clearly established.

References

Bailey, T. M. and Plunkett, K. (2002). Phonological specificity in early words. *Cognitive Development*, 17:1265–1282.

Ballem, K. and Plunkett, K. (2005). Phonological specificity in children at 1;2. *Journal of Child Language*, 32:159–173.

Bertoncini, J., Bijeljac-Babic, R., Jusczyk, P., Kennedy, L., and Mehler, J. (1988). An investigation of young infants' perceptual representations of speech sounds. *Journal of Experimental Psychology: General*, 117:21–33.

Bertoncini, J., Floccia, C., Nazzi, T., and Mehler, J. (1995). Morae and syllables: Rhythmical basis of speech representations in neonates. *Language and Speech*, 38:311–329.

Bertoncini, J. and Mehler, J. (1981). Syllables as units in infant speech perception. *Infant Behavior and Development*, 4:247–260.

Best, C., Tyler, M., Gooding, T., Orlando, C., and Quann, C. (2009). Development of phonological constancy: Toddlers' perception of native- and Jamaican-accented words. *Psychological Science*, 20:539–542.

Bijeljac-Babic, R., Bertoncini, J., and Mehler, J. (1993). How do four-day-old infants categorize multisyllabic utterances. *Developmental Psychology*, 29:711–721.

Bonatti, L., Peña, M., Nespor, M., and Mehler, J. (2005). Linguistic constraints on statistical computations: The role of consonants and vowels in continuous speech processing. *Psychological Science*, 16:451–459.

Browman, C. P. and Goldstein, L. (1989). Articulatory gestures as phonological units. *Phonology*, 6:201–251.

Browman, C. P. and Goldstein, L. (1992). Articulatory phonology: An overview. *Phonetica*, 49:155–180.

Chen, L.-M. and Kent, R. (2005). Consonant-vowel co-occurrence patterns in Mandarin-learning infants. *Journal of Child Language*, 32:507–534.

Cristia, A. and Peperkamp, S. (2011). Generalizing without encoding specifics: Infants infer phonotactic patterns on sound classes. In *Communication at the 36th annual Boston University Conference on Language Development*.

Cristia, A., Seidl, A., and Francis, A. (2011). Phonological features in infancy. In Clements, G. and Ridouane, R., editors, *Where do Phonological Contrasts Come from? Cognitive, Physical and Developmental Bases of Phonological Features*, pages 303–326. Benjamins, Amsterdam.

Curtin, S., Fennell, C., and Escudero, P. (2009). Weighting of vowel cues explains patterns of word-object associative learning. *Developmental Science*, 12:725–731.

Cutler, A. and Otake, T. (2002). Rhythmic categories in spoken-word recognition. *Journal of Memory and Language*, 46:296–322.

Cutler, A., Sebastian-Galles, N., Soler-Vilageliu, O., and van Ooijen, B. (2000). Constraints of vowels and consonants on lexical selection: Cross-linguistic comparisons. *Memory & Cognition*, 28:746–755.

Davis, B. and MacNeilage, P. (1990). Acquisition of correct vowel production: A quantitative case study. *Journal of Speech and Hearing Research*, 33:16–27.

Davis, B. and MacNeilage, P. (1995). The articulatory basis of babbling. *Journal of Speech and Hearing Research*, 38:1199–1211.

de Boysson-Bardies, B. (1993). Ontogeny of language-specific syllabic productions. In de Boysson-Bardies, B., de Schonen, S., Jusczyk, P., MacNeilage, P., and Morton, J., editors, *Developmental Neurocognition: Speech and Face Processing in the First Year of Life*. Kluwer, Dordrecht.

de Boysson-Bardies, B. (1996). *Comment la Parole Vient aux Enfants*. Odile Jacob, Paris.

Dietrich, C., Swingley, D., and Werker, J. F. (2007). One-year- olds' language-specific phonological categorization in word learning: A cross-linguistic study. *PNAS*, 104(41):16027–16031.

Eimas, P., Siqueland, E.and Jusczyk, P., and Vigorito, J. (1971). Speech perception in infants. *Science*, 171:303–306.

Fennell, C. and Waxman, S. (2010). What paradox? Referential cues allow for infant use of phonetic detail in word learning. *Child Development*, 81:1376–1383.

Fennell, C. and Werker, J. (2003). Early word learners' ability to access phonetic detail in well-known words. *Language and Speech*, 46:245–264.

Ferguson, C. and Farwell, C. (1975). Words and sounds in early language acquisition. *Language*, 51:419–439.

Gogate, L. (2010). Learning of syllable-object relations by preverbal infants: The role of temporal synchrony and syllable distinctiveness. *Journal of Experimental Child Psychology*, 105:178–197.

Goldsmith, J. A. (1999). Introduction. In Goldsmith, J., editor, *Phonological Theory: The Essential Readings*, pages 1–16. Blackwell, Malden MA.

Hallé, P. and de Boysson-Bardies, B. (1994). Emergence of an early lexicon: Infants' recognition of words. *Infant Behavior and Development*, 17:119–129.

Hallé, P. and de Boysson-Bardies, B. (1996). The format of representation of recognized words in infants' early receptive lexicon. *Infant Behavior and Development*, 19:465–483.

Havy, M. and Nazzi, T. (2009). Better processing of consonantal over vocalic information in word learning at 16 months of age. *Infancy*, 14:439–456.

Hochmann, J. R. (2010). *Categories, words and rules in language acquisition*. PhD thesis, SISSA, Trieste, Italy.

Hochmann, J. R., Benavides-Varela, S., Nespor, M., and Mehler, J. (2011). Consonants and vowels: Different roles in early language acquisition. *Developmental Science*, 14:1445–1458.

Hodge, M. (1989). *A comparison of spectral-temporal measures across speaker age: Implications for an acoustic characterization of speech maturation.* PhD thesis, University of Wisconsin-Madison.

Jusczyk, P. W. and.Derrah, C. (1987). A study of phonetic categorization in 2-month-olds. *Developmental Psychology*, 23:648–654.

Jusczyk, P. and Aslin, R. (1995). Infants' detection of the sound patterns of words in fluent speech. *Cognitive Psychology*, 29:1–23.

Kent, R. D. and Murray, A. D. (1982). Acoustic features of infant vocalic utterances at 3, 6 and 9 months. *Journal of the Acoustic Society of America*, 72:353–365.

Kovács, A. and Mehler, J. (2009). Flexible learning of multiple speech structures in bilingual infants. *Science*, 325:611–612.

Kuhl, P., Williams, K., Lacerda, F., Stevens, K., and Lindblom, B. (1992). Linguistic experience alters phonetic perception in infants by 6 months of age. *Science*, 255:606–608.

Macken, M. A. (1978). Permitted complexity in phonological development: One child's acquisition of spanish consonants. *Lingua*, 44:219–253.

Macken, M. A. (1979). Developmental reorganization of phonology: A hierarchy of basic units of acquisition. *Lingua*, 49:11–49.

MacNeilage, P. (1996). Formal versus functional approaches to the acquisition of speech production. In *Paper presented at the Symposium on Research in Child Language Disorders.*

MacNeilage, P. (1997). Acquisition of speech. In Hardcastle, W. and Laver, J., editors, *The Handbook of Phonetic Sciences*, pages 301–332. Blackwell, Cambridge MA.

MacNeilage, P. and Davis, B. (2000). On the origin of internal structure of word forms. *Science*, 288:527–531.

MacNeilage, P. and Davis, B. (2002). On the origins of intersyllabic complexity. In Malle, B., editor, *The Rise of Language out of Pre-language*, pages 118–136. John Benjamins, Amsterdam.

Mani, N. and Plunkett, K. (2007). Phonological specificity of vowels and consonants in early lexical representations. *Journal of Memory and Language*, 57:252–272.

Mani, N. and Plunkett, K. (2008). Fourteen-month-olds pay attention to vowels in novel words. *Developmental Science*, 11:53–59.

Mani, N. and Plunkett, K. (2010). Twelve-month-olds know their 'cups' from their 'keps' and 'tups'. *Infancy*, 15:445–470.

Matyear, C., MacNeilage, P., and Davis, B. (1998). Nasalization of vowels in nasal environments in babbling: Evidence for frame dominance. *Phonetica*, 55:1–17.

Metsala, J. (1997). Spoken word recognition in reading disabled children. *Journal of Education Psychology*, 89:159 –169.

Metsala, J. and Walley, A. (1998). Spoken vocabulary growth and the segmental restructuring of lexical representations: Precursors to phonemic awareness and early reading ability. In Metsala, J. and Ehri, L., editors, *Word Recognition in Beginning Literacy*, pages 89–120. Erlbaum, Mahwah NJ.

Nazzi, T. (2005). Use of phonetic specificity during the acquisition of new words: Differences between consonants and vowels. *Cognition*, 98:13–30.

Nazzi, T. and Bertoncini, J. (2009). Consonant specificity in onset and coda positions in early lexical acquisition. *Language & Speech*, 52:463–480.

Nazzi, T., Floccia, C., Moquet, B., and Butler, J. (2009). Bias for consonantal information over vocalic information in 30-month-olds: Cross-linguistic evidence from French. *Journal of Experimental Child Psychology*, 102:522–537.

Nazzi, T. and Gopnik, A. (2001). Linguistic and cognitive abilities in infancy: When does language become a tool for categorization? *Cognition*, 80:B11–B20.

Nespor, M., Peña, M., and Mehler, J. (2003). On the different roles of vowels and consonants in speech processing and language acquisition. *Lingue e Linguaggio*, 2:221–247.

Oller, D. K. (1980). The emergence of the sounds of speech in infancy. In Yeni-Komshian, G., Kavanagh, C., and Ferguson, C., editors, *Child Phonology 1: Production*, pages 93–112. Academic Press, New York.

Oller, D. K. (2000). *The Emergence of the Speech Capacity*. Lawrence Erlbaum Associates, Mahwah N.J.

Patrick, P. (1999). *Urban Jamaican Creole: Variation in the Mesolect*. Benjamins, Amsterdam.

Peña, M., Bonatti, L. L., Nespor, M., and Mehler, J. (2002). Signal-driven computations in speech processing. *Science*, 298:604–607.

Pollock, K. and Berni, M. (2003). Incidence of non-rhotic vowel errors in children: Data from the Memphis Vowel Project. *Clinical Linguistics and Phonetics*, 17(3-4):393–401.

Pomiechowska, B. (2011). Consonantal bias in word learning at 3 years of age: A crosslinguistic study. Master's thesis, LPP Paris.

Pons, F. and Toro, J. (2010). Structural generalizations over consonants and vowels in 11-month-old infants. *Cognition*, 116:361–367.

Sharp, D., Scott, S., Cutler, A., and Wise, R. (2005). Lexical retrieval constrained by sound structure: The role of the left inferior frontal gyrus. *Brain and Language*, 92:309–319.

Stager, C. and Werker, J. (1997). Infants listen for more phonetic detail in speech perception than in word learning tasks. *Nature*, 388:381–382.

Stark, R. E. (1980). Stages of speech development in the first year of life. In Yeni-Komshian, G., Kavanagh, J., and Ferguson, C., editors, *Child Phonology 1: Production*, pages 73–90. Academic Press, New York.

Swingley, D. (2005). 11-month-olds' knowledge of how familiar words sound. *Developmental Science*, 8:432–443.

Swingley, D. and Aslin, R. N. (2000). Spoken word recognition and lexical representation in very young children. *Cognition*, 76:147–166.

Swingley, D. and Aslin, R. N. (2002). Lexical neighborhoods and the word-form representations of 14-month-olds. *Psychological Science*, 13:480–484.

Thiessen, E. (2007). The effect of distributional information on children's use of phonemic contrasts. *Journal of Memory and Language*, 56:16–34.

Toro, J., Bonatti, L., Nespor, M., and Mehler, J. (2008). Finding words and rules in a speech stream: Functional differences between vowels and consonants. *Psychological Science*, 19:137–144.

van Ooijen, B. (1996). Vowel mutability and lexical selection in English: Evidence from a word reconstruction task. *Memory & Cognition*, 24:573–583.

Vihman, M. (1996). *Phonological Development: The Origins of Language in the Child.* Blackwell, Oxford.

Vihman, M., dePaolis, R., Nakai, S., and Hallé, P. (2004). The role of accentual pattern in early lexical representation. *Journal of Memory and Language*, 50:336–353.

Vihman, M. and Greenlee, M. (1987). Individual differences in phonological development: Ages one and three years. *Journal of Speech and Hearing Research*, 30:503–521.

Vihman, M., Macken, M., Miller, R., Simmons, H., and Miller, J. (1985). From babbling to speech: A re-assessment of the continuity issue. *Language*, 51:397–445.

Walley, A. (1993). The role of vocabulary development in children's spoken word recognition and segmentation ability. *Developmental Review*, 13:286–350.

Walley, A. and Metsala, J. (1990). The growth of lexical constraints on spoken word recognition. *Perception and Psychophysics*, 47:267–280.

Wassink, A. (2006). A geometric representation of spectral and temporal vowel features: Quantification of vowel overlap in three linguistic varieties. *Journal of the Acoustical Society of America*, 119:2334–2350.

Werker, J., Cohen, L., Lloyd, V., Casasola, M., and Stager, C. (1998). Acquisition of word-object associations by 14-month-old infants. *Developmental Psychology*, 34:1289–1309.

Werker, J. and Tees, R. (1984). Cross-language speech perception: Evidence for perceptual reorganization during the first year of life. *Infant Behavior and Development*, 7:49–63.

Werker, J. F., Fennell, C. T., Corcoran, K., and Stager, C. L. (2002). Infants' ability to learn phonetically similar words: Effects of age and vocabulary size. *Infancy*, 3:1–30.

Whalen, D., Giulivi, S., Nam, H., Levitt, A., Hallé, P., and Goldstein, L. (in press). Biomechanically preferred consonant-vowel combinations fail to appear in adult spoken corpora. *Language and Speech*.

The production and perception of coarticulation in two types of sound changes in progress

JONATHAN HARRINGTON
FELICITAS KLEBER
ULRICH REUBOLD

Abstract: This paper presents two studies that are concerned with the mechanisms by which historical sound change develops from synchronic coarticulatory variation with reference to the diachronic fronting of high back vowels in Standard Southern British and the development of a post-vocalic voicing contrast in the East Franconian variety under the influence of Standard German. The direction and extent of the sound changes in progress were inferred through comparisons between older and younger speakers on production and perception tasks. Both studies suggest that diachronic change has developed out of synchronic coarticulatory variation. We then differentiate this from other aspects of the sound change, including its spread to other contexts unrelated to the direction of the diachronic change and, for the East Franconian data, the development of a trading relationship between coarticulatory source and effect. Taken together, the results show that the complex of sound change is composed of many different parts that are activated in either production or perception at different stages in its development.

1 Introduction

Synchronic variation is both ubiquitous in languages and infinite: as much empirical research has shown, post-lexical variation including the apparent deletion of the final /t/ in phrases such as 'perfect memory' (Browman and Goldstein, 1990, 1995) or the vocalisation of /l/ in English varieties in certain prosodic positions (Scobbie and Pouplier, 2010) arises out of continuous processes of spatial reduction and temporal overlap. Synchronic processes such as the effects of consonant voicing on intrinsic pitch in the vowel (Löfqvist et al., 1989) or anticipatory vowel nasalisation due to a following nasal consonant have been shown to be closely related to historical sound change such as tonogenesis (Hombert et al., 1979) or the development of phonological oral-nasal vowel contrasts (Beddor, 2007). But how exactly does continuous synchronic variation turn into categorical diachronic change? This issue is central both to developing a phonetic 'path' to sound change (Beddor, 2009) and more generally to investigations in laboratory phonology of how phonetic variability and phonological categories are inter-related.

Phonetic models of sound change are often based on the idea that listeners occasionally de-contextualise synchronic variation in speech production. According to Ohala (1993), sound change can originate when a listener fails to factor out or compensate for the effects of context: in this model, a fronted realisation of the vowel due to consonant-on-vowel coarticulatory influences in contexts such as /tut/ can be perceived as /y/ and not as /u/, should the listener fail to attribute the fronting to the coarticulatory source from which it originates, the alveolar consonants. In Lindblom et al. (1995), the listener's occasional decontextualisation of hypoarticulated variants that tend to occur at semantically redundant points in the speech signal can cause novel phonetic forms of words to be remembered: usually, the listener engages extensive top-down processing in reconstructing hypoarticulated speech production, and it is exceptionally when this top-down processing is disengaged that the hypoarticulated production of the word can be added to the listener's lexicon. One of the reasons why listeners might sometimes not interpret the speech signal in relation to the context in which it was produced is if they are inexperienced users of the language. As Ohala (1993) emphasises, only a small fraction of synchronic variation is converted to sound change, precisely because adult listeners are so adept at normalising for context, as studies of the perceptual compensation for coarticulation (Mann and Repp, 1980) suggest. Perhaps then inexperienced listeners like children might be frequent initiators of sound change because they have not fully acquired the knowledge for interpreting the speech signal in its context (Ohala, 1981), just as in vision they may take until the age of ten years to reach adult-like competency in the visual normalisation for size (Doherty et al., 2010).

Another reason why a listener's and speaker's interpretation of context may be divergent is because adults may have learned context-effects slightly differently. This possibility is suggested both by numerous production studies showing that there is a great deal of variability even amongst speakers of the same variety in the magnitude and extent of coarticulation (van den Heuvel et al., 1996; Magen, 1997; Grosvald, 2009) and also by various perception studies showing that listeners can differ in the extent to which they normalise or compensate for coarticulation (Beddor, 2009). This variability in contextual normalisation is likely to be exacerbated when two varieties of a language or two different languages come into contact with each other, given the additional influences of variety (Scobbie and Pouplier, 2010) and language (Mok, 2010) on coarticulation and phonetic detail in both production (Öhman, 1966) and in perception (Beddor and Krakow, 1999; Beddor et al., 2002).

Some further mechanisms may be needed in order to explain how speaker- and listener-dependent variations in coarticulation actually develop into sound change. One of these may be that tracking (and by extension mis-tracking) fine phonetic detail and coarticulatory relationships is an integral part of perceiving speech (Alfonso and Baer, 1982; Fowler and Smith, 1986; Martin and Bunnel, 1982). Another is imitation of speech production that may derive from mimicry in human neonates (Meltzoff and Moore, 1997) and which may also be implicated in language acquisition and the development of the lexicon (Studdert-Kennedy, 2005). Adult imitation has been demonstrated in shadowing tasks (Goldinger, 1997; Shockley et al., 2004), in the production of isolated words (Babel, 2012; Delvaux and Soquet, 2007; Nielsen, 2007, 2011) and in conversational exchanges (Pardo, 2006; Pardo et al., 2012). Imitation in speech may be part of a more general tendency of entrainment in which postural sway is matched during a conversation even in the absence of any intention to entrain (Fowler et al., 2008; Shockley et al., 2009). Imitation may also be responsible for the shift in adults' pronunciation in the direction of diachronic changes over a long time-scale (Harrington et al., 2000). Perhaps diachronic change is propagated as adults imitate each others' slightly different coarticulatory relationships.

The general aim in this study is to explore whether two types of sound changes in progress can be modelled in terms of some of the mechanisms outlined above such as the decontextualisation of speech and imitation. The analysis for doing so is based on apparent time studies (Weinreich et al., 1968) in which the magnitude and direction of diachronic change are inferred through phonetic comparisons of two age groups that share the same linguistic background. The first study in the following analysis was concerned with a sound change in progress in the standard accent of English in which high back vowels have fronted diachronically: the main aim here was to determine whether the diachronic change took place in equal measure in contexts to which it was, and was not, synchronically related and whether these changes have occurred in both speech production and perception. The focus of the second study is the development of a phonological voicing contrast in a variety of German under the influence of Standard German. Here the concern was to explore whether the changes take place in both perception and production and how such changes are related to synchronic processes of coarticulation in two age groups of the same variety.

2 Fronting of high back vowels in Standard Southern British

The starting point for comparing the shift in the production and perception of speech due to a sound-change in progress is the diachronic fronting of tense /u/(*who'd*) and lax /ʊ/ (*hood*) in the standard accent of English, Standard Southern British (SSB) which, some 40-50 years ago were mid-back vowels with phonetically fronted variants in the context of alveolar (e.g. *noon, soot*) and following initial palatal (e.g. *cue, few*) consonants (Gimson, 1966; Wells, 1982). Various acoustic and auditory analyses have shown that these vowels have fronted diachronically (Bauer, 1985; Hawkins and Midgley, 2005; Henton, 1983; de Jong et al., 2007; McDougall and Nolan, 2007) in the last 40-50 years. A recent physiological analysis has also shown that the movement of the tongue dorsum in present-day SSB /u, ʊ/ patterns much more closely with the front vowels /i, ɪ/ than with the back vowels /ɔ/ (*saw*) and /ɒ/ (*pod*) and that the extent of lip-rounding in /ɔ, ɒ, u, ʊ/ is quite similar (Harrington et al., 2011): taken together, these studies suggest that, whereas 40-50 years ago both a retracted tongue-dorsum position and greater lip-rounding distinguished /i, ɪ/ from /u, ʊ/ respectively, the main basis for the distinction between these pairs of vowels in present-day SSB is lip-rounding and not tongue-fronting. Apparent time studies are typically based on acoustic analyses of speech production of the kind shown in Figure 1: these data, which are taken from Harrington et al. (2008) and Kleber et al. (2012) show the mean positions of the second formant frequency (F2) at the vowel target of tense /u/ and lax /ʊ/ in older and younger speakers of the same variety.

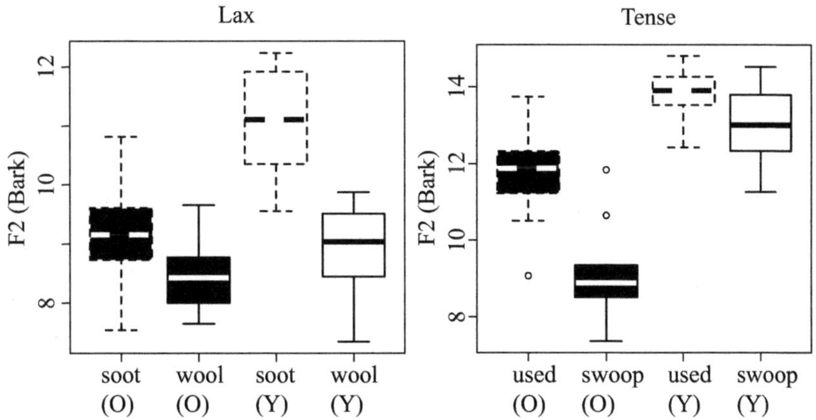

Figure 1: Boxplots (interquartile ranges) showing the distributions of the second formant frequency for younger and older speakers of a Standard Southern British variety. The data for lax vowels (left), which were taken from Kleber et al. (2012) include 18 younger subjects (9 females, 9 males) aged between 19 and 21 years and with an average age of 20.2 years and 15 older subjects (8 females, 7 males) aged between 54 and 89 years and with an average age of 75.4 years. The data for tense vowels (right), which were taken from Harrington et al. (2008), included 14 younger (Y) subjects (3 male, 11 female) aged between 18 and 20 years and with an average age of 18.9 years and 17 older (O) subjects (10 male, 7 female) aged over 50 years and with an average age of 69.2 years. Seven younger and nine older subjects who produced the lax vowels (left) had also participated in the study of tense vowels (right). The boxplots include one data point per subject that is a subject-mean at the point in the voiced vowel corresponding most closely to the voiced vowel target. The words whose distributions are shown in this figure were produced in isolation. The F2 values were extracted at the point in the vowel corresponding most closely to the acoustic vowel target.

These data are shown for two contexts: one of these is a fronting context and includes the tense vowel in *used* (past tense, /just/) and the lax vowel in *soot* (/sʊt/). In both cases, /u, ʊ/ are expected to front (synchronically) due to the coarticulatory influences of the flanking alveolar or palatal consonants. The other is a non-fronting context that includes the tense vowel in *swoop* and the lax vowel in *wool*. Coarticulatory influences of the consonants on these words' vowels induce F2 lowering, either because of the effects of lip-rounding in the labial consonants and/or because of the tongue-dorsum retraction in /w/ and in the velarised /l/ that occurs syllable-finally in this variety.

Two trends are apparent in the data in Figure 1. The first is that, as expected, the variants in *used* and *soot* were evidently fronted relative to those in *swoop* and *wool*, as judged from the higher F2 values in the fronting context. The second is that F2 was lower for the older than for the younger speakers which suggests diachronic fronting in the tense and lax vowels. There was, however, also an interaction between the age groups, vowel tensity, and context. For the lax vowel data, the extent of diachronic fronting as inferred from comparisons across the age groups was greater in the fronting context than in the non-fronting context: the evidence for this is that older and younger speakers differed on F2 to a much greater extent in the variant of *soot* compared with that of *wool*. However, for the tense vowels, there is the opposite pattern: the older and younger speakers differed on F2 much more in the non-fronting variant *swoop* than they did in the fronting variant of *used*.

Figure 2 shows a model of the diachronic fronting in a hypothetical language that has /u/ in /tut/ (synchronically fronting) and /pup/ (non-fronting) contexts that will be used to account for the diachronic changes in these SSB vowels. In this model, the relationship between /tut/ and /pup/ is the same both before and after the sound change has taken place: thus, the only difference between the two contexts both before and after the diachronic change is due to synchronic coarticulation so that the vowel in /tut/ is synchronically phonetically fronted relative to that of /pup/. As the sound change takes hold, it affects /tut/ before it does /pup/ and, as a result, these variants come to be widely separated (middle panel). The completion of the sound change (between the middle and right panels) comes about when /u/ in non-fronting /pup/ 'catches up' diachronically with /tut/ so that the relationship between the two contexts is once again the same before (left panel) and after (right panel) the sound change. Figure 2 also shows how the sound change is presumed to be manifested across three generations relative to a hypothetical time-line between *t*=0 years when the sound change begins and *t*=30 years when it is nearing completion. The sound change is initially manifested through contextual differences between the two generations *A* (aged 50 years) and *B* (aged 20 years) at *t*=0 years: the difference between /u/ in /tut/ and /pup/ is due only to synchronic coarticulation for generation *A* which is unaffected by the sound change; but for generation *B*, the difference between /u/ across the two contexts is greater because /u/ in /tut/ has additionally fronted diachronically. Thus according to this model, the variants between the fronting and non-fronting contexts are predicted to be widely spaced for the younger generation *B*, in comparison with those of the older generation *A* in the initial stages of a sound change.

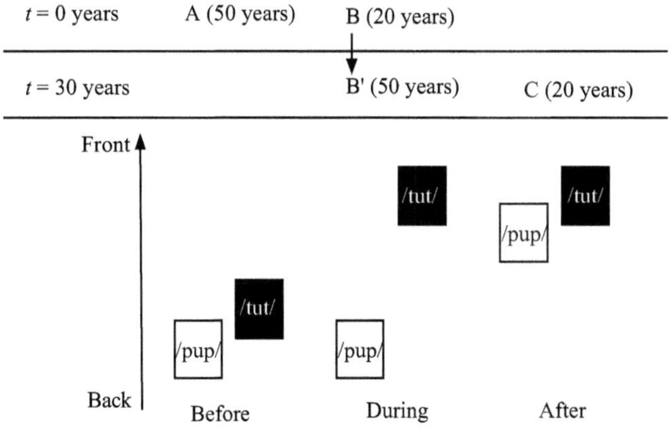

Figure 2: A model of the changes to /u/ in /tut/ (synchronically fronting) and /pup/ (synchronically non-fronting) contexts in a hypothetical language in which /u/ fronts diachronically from phonetically back to front. The stages shown are before the sound changes take place (left), during the sound change (middle), and close to the completion of the sound change (right). The top part of the figure shows how the sound change is expected to be manifested across three generations, *A*, *B*, *C* during its early stages when the sound change begins at *t*=0 years and close to its completion at *t*=30 years. The hypothetical ages of these three generations at these two timelines are shown (*B* and *B′* refer to the same speakers aged 20 years and 50 years respectively).

Just this relationship is presumed to characterise the difference across the generations in SSB /ʊ/ (left panel, Figure 1) in which the divergence between *soot* and *wool* was found to be much greater for the younger (analogous to generation *B* in Figure 2) than it was for the older speakers (analogous to generation *A* in Figure 2). As the sound change nears completion (which is modelled to take place over a 30 year period), generation *B* now aged 50 years (shown as *B′* in Figure 2) is assumed to show similarly widely spaced /u/-variants in /tut/ and /pup/. But for the next generation C, the sound change /u/ in non-fronting /pup/ has shifted diachronically towards /u/ in /tut/: thus these two generations differ primarily in the relative position of /u/ in non-fronting /pup/ which is further back for the older generation *B′* relative to that of the younger generation C at time *t*=30 years. Such differences are characteristic of the data in the right panel of Figure 1 for the tense vowel /u/ which is a sound change in SSB that, according to Hawkins and Midgley (2005), took hold well before diachronic /ʊ/-fronting began (and is therefore closer to completion than for its lax counterpart): thus the variants in fronting *used* and non-fronting *swoop* in Figure 1 were found to be widely spaced for the older generation (analogous to generation *B′* of Figure 2) but narrowly spaced for the younger generation (analogous to generation C of Figure 2). The same speakers whose production data are shown in Figure 1 also participated in forced-choice perception experiments in which they labelled synthetic continua that differed only in the second formant frequency in minimal-pair fronting and non-fronting contexts (see Harrington et al., 2008; Kleber et al., 2012, for further details). For the tense vowel, the two synthetic contexts that were presented in the forced-choice perception experiment were *yeast-used* (fronting) and *sweep-swoop* (non-fronting); and for the lax vowel they were *sit-soot* (fronting) and *will-wool* (non-fronting). The results for psychometric curves and 50% cross-over boundaries averaged by age group show the well-known effect of perceptual compensation for coarticulation (Mann and Repp, 1980): evidently, the curves and boundaries were shifted to the left, towards the /i, ɪ/ end of the continua in the fronting context in both age groups, compatibly with their speech production data in which F2 was also raised in the fronting relative to that of the non-fronting context.

There is also a parity between the perception and production data for the tense vowel because both the interval separating the 50% cross-over boundaries in the two contexts (*yeast-used* and *sweep-swoop*) as well as the F2-distances between the corresponding variants in production (i.e., between those in *used* and *swoop*) were less for younger than they were for the older subjects. But there is no analogous parity between the modalities for lax vowels because, whereas the F2-distance between fronting (*soot*) and non-fronting (*wool*) contexts in production was evidently much greater for younger than for older speakers (Figure 1), younger listeners' psychometric curves and cross-over boundaries were marginally *closer* together than they were for older listeners (Figure 3).

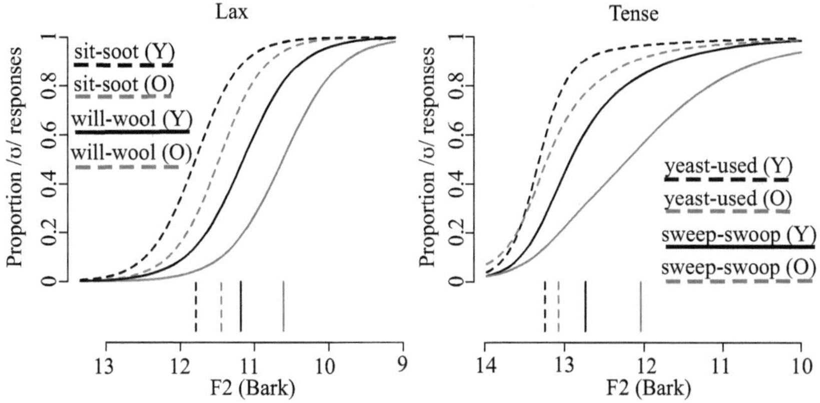

Figure 3: Averaged psychometric curves showing the proportion of /ʊ/ responses for the lax vowels (left) and the proportion of /u/ responses for the tense vowels (right) with the 50% decision boundaries marked as vertical lines for the same speaker groups whose production data are shown in Figure 1. The forced-choice responses were to stimuli created in the fronting and non-fronting contexts shown in the panels of the figures by reducing F2 in equal Bark steps over the range of values shown on the x-axis.

We argued earlier that diachronic fronting in production has applied scarcely at all to younger speakers' *wool*. But on the other hand, diachronic fronting must have applied perceptually in this non-fronting context because the 50% cross-over boundary in younger listeners' *will-wool* is positioned nearer to the /ɪ/-end of the continuum relative to that of older listeners and significantly so (t_{31}=4.6, p<0.001). From this it would follow that younger subjects' diachronic /ʊ/-fronting in contexts like *wool* is at a more advanced stage in perception than it is in production (see Kleber et al., 2012, for further details).

The present results, showing a production-perception asymmetry for the lax vowel data, are potentially inconsistent with two types of findings: firstly with compensation experiments in which speakers adjust their acoustic output due to artificially induced perturbations to auditory feedback (Munhall et al., 2009; Reubold, 2012); and secondly, with various studies suggesting that there is necessarily parity between the production and perception of coarticulation (Fowler, 2005). As far as the first of these is concerned, the results from compensation in speech production to altered auditory feedback and to the effects induced by bite-blocks (Lindblom et al., 1979) may be only marginally relevant to the present results given that they are concerned with short-term perturbations to on-line feedback whereas the data for the presented investigation are based instead on considerations of longer-term diachronic changes to the way in which coarticulatory relationships are perceived in relation to production. Of potentially greater relevance to the present results is the issue of whether parity between produced and perceived coarticulation can ever be violated. Our results, which suggest that it can be, are commensurate with other studies showing that listeners do not always compensate sufficiently in perception for coarticulation that occurs in production (Beddor, 2009; Fowler and Brown, 2000). Moreover, it is just this type of mismatch that can create an unstable relationship between the production and perception of speech that could lead to sound change (Kleber et al., 2012).

Finally, there is a third set of studies on near-mergers that are both similar to those found for the present SSB lax vowel study but also different. They are similar in that near mergers represent a stage in the development of sound change in which a measurable difference in speech production is not perceptible (Di Paolo and Faber, 1990; Faber and Di Paolo, 1995; Labov et al., 1972). Thus as Labov et al. (1991, p.46) note: "The existence of near-mergers puts into question the symmetry of production and perception. From the productive viewpoint, there are two categories; from a perceptual one, only one". At the same time, there are structural differences between the allophonic variation found in the present investigation on the one hand, and the variation between two phonemic categories in near-mergers on the other.

Whether the same mechanism can account for these perception-production asymmetries in coarticulatory phonetic (the present study) and phonemic (near-mergers) relationships will require further investigation.

3 Post-vocalic stop voicing in Franconian

The study in this section is concerned with a very different type of sound-change in the East Franconian variety of German which is spoken in a region of Northern Bavaria encompassing the cities of Nürnberg and Würzburg and extending northwards into Thuringia. In the standard variety of German, the ratio of the duration of the vowel to that of the following closure (henceforth the voicing ratio) is critical for the post-vocalic voicing distinction in minimal pairs such as *leiten* ('to lead') and *leiden* ('to suffer'): thus in the standard variety (and indeed in many other languages including English), post-vocalic voiceless stops are associated with a shorter vowel duration and longer closure duration (i.e., a lower voicing ratio) compared with those found in voiced stops; perceptually, the voicing ratio has been shown to be one of the most effective cues for the post-vocalic voicing distinction (Kohler, 1979). Some auditory studies have suggested that the voicing contrast is neutralized towards lenis, i.e. towards the voiced stop, in East Franconian so that words like *leiten/leiden* that are distinct in Standard German may be homophones in this variety (Barbour and Stevenson, 1990; Rowley, 1990). The issue to be explored in the present paper is whether a post-vocalic voicing contrast may be developing diachronically as a result of an increasing influence of the Standard on the East Franconian variety. The analysis was based on an extension of a production and perception study by Müller et al. (2011) of 16 younger (3 male, 13 female; age range 15-25 years) and 16 older (4 male, 12 female; age range 51-74 years) subjects of an East Franconian variety of German. In addition, data were obtained from five speakers (4 male, 1 female; age range 25-52 years) and 21 (different) listeners of a standard variety (10 male, 11 female, 20-32 years) in order to assess whether any age-related changes in East Franconian were in the direction of the standard variety in either production or perception.

For the production data, the younger and older East Franconians as well as the five Standard speakers produced a number of isolated disyllabic words with a trochaic stress pattern and a tense vowel in the first syllable: these included both distracters and three sets of target word minimal pairs differing only in post-vocalic /t, d/ that occurs in the standard variety: these included *mieten/mieden* ('to rent'/'to avoid'), *baten/baden* ('asked for'/'to bathe') and *leiten/leiden* ('to lead'/'to suffer') which, in the standard variety, are often produced with nasal plosion as /miːtn, miːdn, laɪtn, laɪdn, baːtn, baːdn/. The same older and younger East Franconian subjects and the different set of 21 Standard subjects referred to above participated as listeners in two-alternative forced-choice labelling experiments in which they identified one of *leiten/leiden* or *mieten/mieden* from two continua that had been resynthesised by manipulating the voicing ratio in 11 equal steps between voiceless *leiten/mieten* (voicing ratios: *leiten*=0.665, *mieten*=0.478) and voiced *leiden/mieden* (voicing ratios: *leiden*=0.749, *mieden*=0.740) ends of the continuum. Only the voicing ratio was changed (through shortening and lengthening of the relative duration of the voiced vowel and consonant closure, respectively) between the stimuli: this ensured that the listeners depended on a single cue for the voicing distinction. The test words contained no schwa and all phonetic voicing (i.e. vocal fold vibration) during the closure was set to zero. The duration of the vowel+closure dyad was identical in all stimuli.

These data were used to address the following two issues: firstly, whether there was a trend for a greater differentiation between voiced and voiceless stops on the voicing ratio from older East Franconian to younger East Franconian to Standard speakers; and secondly, whether this trend was evident in equal measure in both the production and perception of speech. (In the presentation of the results below, we will henceforth refer to these three subject groups as *younger*, *older*, and *Standard* respectively). The results showed a significant trend in production (X^2_2=33.2, p<0.001) such that there was a progressively greater difference in voicing ratios between voiced and voiceless stops from older to younger to Standard speakers (Figure 4, left panel). The results from the forced-choice classification experiments (Figure 4, right panel) were to a certain extent compatible with those from production: there were progressively more pronounced S-shapes in the psychometric curves from older to younger to Standard listeners (X_2^2=25.8, p<0.001). Thus whereas the Standard listeners exhibited the most categorical-like response with an almost 100% identification of voiced and voiceless at either end of the continuum, the older listeners showed continuous responses and labelled most stimuli with /d/ which indicates that this group perceptually neutralized the contrast towards lenis (Barbour and Stevenson, 1990).

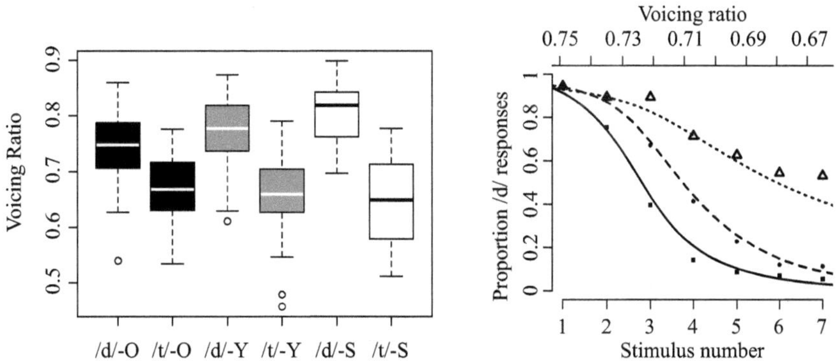

Figure 4: Boxplots (interquartile ranges) showing the voicing ratio calculated from V/(V+C) where V and C are the durations of the voiced vowel and consonant closure respectively for /t/ in isolated word productions of *baten, leiten,* and *mieten,* and for /d/ in *baden, leiden,* and *mieden* in older East Franconian (n = 16), younger East Franconian (n = 16), and Standard German (n = 5) speakers. The boxplots include three aggregated values (one per word type) per speaker. Right: Averaged psychometric curves showing the proportion of /d/ responses for the same speaker groups (dotted/triangles: older East Franconian; dashed/circles: younger East Franconian; solid/squares: Standard) whose production data are shown in Figure 1. The forced-choice responses were to stimuli created by changing the voicing-ratio in *leiten/leiden* and *mieten/mieden* in seven equal steps.

As far as the responses from the younger listeners were concerned, these were intermediate between those of the other two groups: that is, although their responses were categorical (as shown by the clear S-shape in the right panel of Figure 4), the categorical change was not as marked as it was for Standard listeners. The results from these production and perception experiments are compatible with a sound change in progress by which there has been a progressively greater differentiation in East Franconian between post-vocalic voiced and voiceless stops on the voicing ratio under the influence of the standard variety in which the distinction on this parameter is categorical.

The data also show that there was a clear difference between the older subjects on the one hand and the other two groups on the other in the extent to which the production and perception data were matched: whereas for the younger and Standard subjects the psychometric curves' 50% cross-over boundaries occurred close to voicing ratio values that separate their /t, d/ distributions in production (Figure 4, left panel), there was evidently no such correspondence between production and perception for the older subjects. Thus, on the one hand the older subjects' /t, d/ were separated at a voicing ratio value (of just over 0.7) that was quite similar to those of the other two groups in production; but on the other hand, older listeners had no 50% cross-over boundary within the voicing ratios presented in the perception experiment because, even at the 'voiceless' end of the continuum (stimulus number 7 in Figure 4, right panel) the older listeners' preferred response was /d/ and not /t/. Older subjects' difference between /t, d/ on the voicing ratio in production as opposed to their performance in perception in which they labelled almost the entire continuum as /d/ might suggest that the categorical development of the /t, d/ contrast in East Franconian has taken place in production before it has done so in perception. However, when voicing ratios were obtained from read speech in which the same words were embedded in longer passages that were constructed in such a way that the research objective (to measure the voicing distinction in minimal word pairs) would not be obvious to the reader, then, as Figure 5 shows, the distinction of post-vocalic /t, d/ on the voicing ratio collapsed (and was not significant) for the older speakers, but it was maintained for the other two groups. Thus, the apparent /t, d/ distinction in older speakers' isolated word productions is unlikely to have a phonological origin, given that the distinction collapsed in continuous speech and that they showed no categorical /t, d/ response in perception.

A possible explanation for older speakers' /t, d/ distinction on the voicing ratio in isolated word productions is that it was brought about as an indirect consequence of a strong oral release of /t/. It was evident to us that post-vocalic /t/ for many of the older East Franconian speakers was often produced with a strongly audible oral release (and they also exploited this cue in perception as subsequent tests that are not reported in this paper have indicated), whereas for the other two groups, the post-vocalic /t/ was often both weakly and nasally released. Perhaps then a strongly and orally released /t/ was responsible for reducing its voicing ratio because of truncation by /t/ of the preceding vowel (which would produce a shorter vowel, thereby also decreasing the voicing ratio).

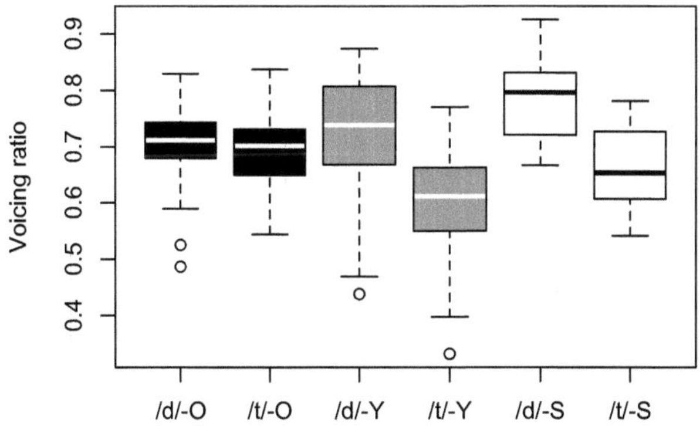

Figure 5: Boxplots (interquartile ranges) showing the voicing ratio for /t/ and /d/ produced in read speech for the same speaker groups and word types as shown in Figure 4.

There is independently of these considerations evidence from both physiological studies (Hoole and Mooshammer, 2002) and from studies of intonation (Grabe, 1998) that vowels in German are often truncated by following voiceless consonants and there is also some electromyographic evidence (cited in Lisker, 1974) to show that voiceless stops begin earlier in the vowel than do voiced stops. If the strength of the release of /t/ produced a shortening of the voicing ratio for older Franconian speakers, then these two variables should be negatively correlated: that is, stronger releases should be associated with shorter voicing ratios. Some evidence in support of this is shown in the left panel of Figure 6 in which voice onset time, measured from the release of the stop to the onset of periodicity in the second weak syllable of *baten, leiten*, and *mieten* was plotted as a function of the voicing ratio: for the older speakers, there was a general trend for longer /t/ releases to be associated with shorter voicing ratios. The relationship between these parameters was quite different for younger East Franconian (middle panel, Figure 6) and Standard (right panel, Figure 6) speakers who produced the postvocalic /t/ either with short voicing ratios or with longer releases of the stop: these two cues co-varied so that if the stop was unreleased (i.e. VOT is zero), then /t/ was distinguished from /d/ in production by correspondingly shorter voicing ratios.

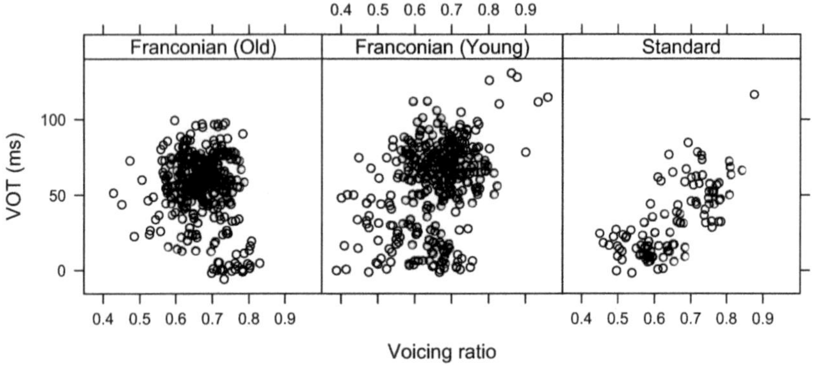

Figure 6: The voicing ratio as a function of voice onset time calculated from the stop release to the onset of periodicity in the following weak vowel for the same word types and speakers shown in Figures 3 and 4. Each point is an individual token (seven tokens per word type per speaker).

One of the reasons for the positive relationship between these parameters for younger and Standard speakers is that the voicing ratio and VOT may have entered into a trading relationship for these groups: of relevance here are findings by Jessen (1998) showing a perceptual trading relationship between stop closure duration and voice onset time in forced choice judgements by 20 listeners of Standard German to a postvocalic /t-d/ continuum. It also seems clear from Figure 6 that there was a stronger positive relationship between VOT and voicing ratio (and thus closure duration) for the Standard than for the younger East Franconian speakers (although this may be an artefact of the greater number of speakers in the latter group) suggesting once again a developmental diachronic change from older to younger to Standard speakers.

The general conclusion from these data is that a phonetic distinction that is manifested in hyperarticulated isolated word productions in East Franconian has been phonologized under the influence of the standard variety and that as part of this phonologization, the voicing ratio and the phonetic source that can give rise to voicing ratio differences in older East Franconians' isolated word productions have, as in the standard variety, entered into a trading relationship for younger East Franconian speakers.

4 General discussion

The two types of sound change, while very different, share the following characteristic: in both cases, existing synchronic variation due to coarticulation seems to have become magnified during a sound change in progress. In Standard Southern British, /u, ʊ/ are synchronically fronted due to coarticulation in certain contexts such as when they follow alveolar or palatal consonants. There is some evidence that the diachronic change has taken place in these fronting contexts ahead of that in non-fronting contexts: this was the explanation given both for the large acoustic separation in production between fronting and non-fronting /ʊ/ variants in younger speakers' variants and for the acoustic proximity between the age groups in the /ʊ/-variant of *wool* (whereas older and younger speakers' /ʊ/-variants in *soot* were far apart). As far as East Franconian is concerned, the existing synchronic, coarticulatory variation that has come to be magnified is the phonetic influence of the postvocalic /t, d/ contrast on the voicing ratio, that is on the ratio of the vowel duration to that of the vowel and following stop closure. This phonetic variation is likely to have existed in East Franconian because older speakers showed a voicing ratio distinction in (possibly hyper-articulated) isolated word productions, even though they were not as listeners able to make use of the voicing ratio perceptually for distinguishing post-vocalic voiced from voiceless stops. It is the exaggeration of this coarticulatory variation in production that leads diachronically to a categorical, phonological distinction between post-vocalic stops both in perception and in production.
Phonetic imitation of similar but not identical coarticulatory patterns may have propagated these sound changes in East Franconian. For ex-

ample, both East Franconian and speakers of Standard German showed similar patterns of coarticulation because for both groups /t/ encroached upon the vowel to a greater extent than it did on /d/. But they also differed: the extent to which /t, d/ affected the preceding vowel duration was greater for Standard German speakers than for older East Franconians. We would propose that it is the broad similarity between the groups in coarticulatory patterns that might provide the basis for the East Franconians to entrain to the Standard speakers: the outcome of this entrainment has been a shift in the direction of the Standard variety, as shown by the intermediate extent of voicing ratio distinctions in production and perception for younger East Franconians.

The spread to other contexts that are synchronically unrelated to the direction of the diachronic change may be another separate stage in the development of the sound change. Our evidence for this is that diachronic /u, ʊ/ fronting in labialized and velarized contexts (which is a change unrelated to the synchronic coarticulatory influences of these consonants on the vowel) in SSB may take place after it does in those contexts (alveolar, palatal) that influence the vowel synchronically in the same direction as the diachronic change. Our data also suggest that this extension to other contexts may come about in perception before it does in production: the evidence for this is that the perceptual boundaries between the fronting and non-fronting context for lax /ʊ/ were closer together for younger subjects than the coarticulatory differences between their fronting and non-fronting variants in production would suggest. Diachronic change may be slowed in production relative to perception in contexts such as these if it is opposed to coarticulatory influences of context for physiological reasons. In the present case, the requirements for the tongue dorsum to be back in the contexts of /w/ and syllable-final /l/ may extinguish the diachronic tongue-dorsum fronting in the vowel. This is especially likely in *wool* given firstly that the velarised /l/ that is typical in syllable-final position in this variety is resistant to coarticulation (Recasens and Espinosa, 2005) and given other evidence showing that segments that resist coarticulation also tend to exert strong coarticulatory influences in others (Fowler and Saltzman, 1993).

A further and quite separate component of sound change is the development of trading relationships between the coarticulatory source and effect as the diachronic change takes hold. Based on a number of perception experiments, Beddor (2009) has shown how trading relationships between anticipatory coarticulatory nasalization in the vowel and the duration of the following nasal consonant (that is the source for these coarticulatory effects) may be one of the main mechanisms leading to the diachronic development of phonological vowel nasalization combined with the subsequent loss of the nasal consonant. Compatibly, our apparent-time study has suggested that diachronic change is accompanied by the development of a trading relationship between the effect (the voicing ratio) and the source that gives rise to it (the strength of the voiceless stop release). The reason why the development of such a trading-relationship is likely to lead to the waning and possible extinction of the source that produced the coarticulatory effect is because, whereas in older speakers the cues of the source and effect were additive in the sense that strongly released voiceless stops were accompanied by short voicing ratios that both cued /t/, they had instead a complementary association for younger East Franconian and Standard speakers such that short voicing ratios that provide cues for /t/ were matched with weak releases that do not. Consequently, the diachronic development of the voicing ratio as the main basis for the /t, d/ distinction necessarily results in the waning and possibly destruction of the source cue (the strong oral release of the /t/) that originally gave rise to voicing ratio differences, if the coarticulatory source and effect enter a trading relationship as the latter is phonologised during the sound change in progress.

The general conclusion from this analysis is that the complex of what is called sound change is made up of several different components. These include the phonetic conditions that give rise to the sound change, the development of the change through the entrainment of different speaker groups in contexts to which the diachronic change is related synchronically, its spread to other contexts possibly in perception ahead of changes in production, and the development in certain cases of trading relationships. Many more analyses of the production and perception of coarticulatory relationships for various types of sound changes in progress in different languages are needed to determine how these and other components that contribute to the complex of diachronic change are interconnected.

5 Acknowledgements

We are very grateful for the constructive criticisms of an earlier draft of this paper by two anonymous reviewers. This research was supported by German Research Council Grant No. HA 3512/3-2, "Sound change, lexical frequency, and variability: an experimental study of Southern British English, Received Pronunciation."

References

Alfonso, P. J. and Baer, T. (1982). Dynamics of vowel articulation. *Language and Speech*, 25:151–173.

Babel, M. (2012). Evidence for phonetic and social selectivity in spontaneous phonetic imitation. *Journal of Phonetics*, 40:177–189.

Barbour, S. and Stevenson, P. (1990). *Variation in German: A Critical Approach to German Sociolinguistics*. Cambridge University Press, Cambridge.

Bauer, L. (1985). Tracing phonetic change in the received pronunciation of British English. *Journal of Phonetics*, 13:61–81.

Beddor, P., Harnsberger, J., and Lindemann, S. (2002). Language-specific patterns of vowel-to-vowel coarticulation: Acoustic structures and their perceptual correlates. *Journal of Phonetics*, 30(4):591–627.

Beddor, P. S. (2007). Nasals and nasalization: The relation between segmental and coarticulatory timing. In Trouvain, J. and Barry, W., editors, *Proceedings of the 16th International Congress of Phonetic Sciences*, pages 249–254.

Beddor, P. S. (2009). A coarticulatory path to sound change. *Language*, 85(4):785–821.

Beddor, P. S. and Krakow, R. A. (1999). Perception of coarticulatory nasalization by speakers of English and Thai: Evidence for partial compensation. *Journal of the Acoustical Society of America*, 106(5):2868–2887.

Browman, C. and Goldstein, L. M. (1995). Gestural syllable position effects in American English. In Bell-Berti, F. and Raphael, L. J., editors, *Producing Speech: Contemporary Issues*, pages 19–33. AIP Press, Woodbury NY.

Browman, C. P. and Goldstein, L. M. (1990). Gestural specification using dynamically defined articulatory structures. *Journal of Phonetics*, 18:299–320.

de Jong, G., McDougall, K., Hudson, T., and Nolan, F. (2007). The speaker discriminating power of sounds undergoing historical change: A formant-based study. In

Trouvain, J. and Barry, W., editors, *Proceedings of the 16th International Congress of Phonetic Sciences*, pages 1813–1816.

Delvaux, V. and Soquet, A. (2007). The influence of ambient speech on adult speech productions through unintentional imitation. *Phonetica*, 64:145–173.

Di Paolo, M. and Faber, A. (1990). Phonation differences and the phonetic content of the tense-lax contrast in Utah English. *Language Variation and Change*, 2:155–204.

Doherty, M. J., Campbell, N. M., Tsuji, H., and Phillips, W. (2010). The Ebbinghaus illusion deceives adults but not young children. *Developmental Science*, 13(5):714–721.

Faber, A. and Di Paolo, M. (1995). The discriminability of nearly merged sounds. *Language Variation and Change*, 7:35–78.

Fowler, C. and Brown, J. (2000). Perceptual parsing of acoustic consequences of velum lowering from information for vowels. *Perception & Psychophysics*, 62:21–32.

Fowler, C., Richardson, M., Marsh, K., and Shockley, K. (2008). Language use, coordination, and the emergence of cooperative action. In Fuchs, A. and Jirsa, V., editors, *Understanding Complex Systems*, pages 261–279. Springer, Berlin.

Fowler, C. and Smith, M. (1986). Speech perception as 'vector analysis': An approach to the problems of invariance and segmentation. In Perkell, J. S. and Klatt, D., editors, *Invariance and Variability in Speech Processes*, pages 123–139. Lawrence Erlbaum Associates Inc., Hillsdale NJ.

Fowler, C. A. (2005). Parsing coarticulated speech in perception: Effects of coarticulation resistance. *Journal of Phonetics*, 33:199–213.

Fowler, C. A. and Saltzman, E. (1993). Coordination and coarticulation in speech production. *Language and Speech*, 36:171–195.

Gimson, A. C. (1966). *An Introduction to the Pronunciation of English.* E. Arnold, London.

Goldinger, S. (1997). Speech perception and production in an episodic lexicon. In Johnson, K. and Mullennix, J. W., editors, *Talker Variability in Speech Processing*, pages 33–66. Academic Press, New York.

Grabe, E. (1998). Pitch accent realization in English and German. *Journal of Phonetics*, 26(2):129–143.

Grosvald, M. (2009). Interspeaker variation in the extent and perception of long-distance vowel-to-vowel coarticulation. *Journal of Phonetics*, 37(2):173–188.

Harrington, J., Kleber, F., and Reubold, U. (2008). Compensation for coarticulation, /u/-fronting, and sound change in Standard Southern British: An acoustic and perceptual study. *Journal of the Acoustical Society of America*, 123:2825–2835.

Harrington, J., Kleber, F., and Reubold, U. (2011). The contributions of the lips and the tongue to the diachronic fronting of high back vowels in Standard Southern British English. *Journal of the International Phonetic Association*, 41(2):137–156.

Harrington, J., Palethorpe, S., and Watson, C. (2000). Monophthongal vowel changes in Received Pronunciation: An acoustic analysis of the Queen's christmas broadcasts. *Journal of the International Phonetic Association*, 30:63–78.

Hawkins, S. and Midgley, J. (2005). Formant frequencies of RP monophthongs in four age groups of speakers. *Journal of the International Phonetics Association*, 35:183–199.

Henton, C. G. (1983). Changes in the vowels of Received Pronunciation. *Journal of Phonetics*, 11:353–371.

Hombert, J.-M., Ohala, J. J., and Ewan, W. (1979). Phonetic explanations for the development of tones. *Language*, 55(1):37–58.

Hoole, P. and Mooshammer, C. (2002). Articulatory analysis of the German vowel system. In Auer, P., Gilles, P., and Spiekermann, H., editors, *Silbenschnitt und Tonakzente*, pages 129–152. Niemeyer, Tübingen.

Jessen, M. (1998). *Phonetics and Phonology of Tense and Lax Obstruents in German*. John Benjamins, Amsterdam and Philadelphia.

Kleber, F., Harrington, J., and Reubold, U. (2012). The relationship between the perception and production of coarticulation during a sound change in progress. *Language and Speech*.

Kohler, K. J. (1979). Dimensions in the perception of fortis and lenis plosives. *Phonetica*, 36:332–343.

Labov, W., Karen, M., and Miller, C. (1991). Near-mergers and the suspension of phonemic contrast. *Language Variation and Change*, 3:33–74.

Labov, W., Yaeger, M., and Steiner, R. (1972). *A Quantitative Study of Sound Change in Progress*. Philadelphia, U.S. Regional Survey.

Lindblom, B., Guion, S., Hura, S., Moon, S.-J., and Willerman, R. (1995). Is sound change adaptive? *Rivista Di Linguistica*, 7:5–37.

Lindblom, B., Lubker, J., and Gay, T. (1979). Formant frequencies of some fixed-mandible vowels and a model of speech motor programmming by predictive simulation. *Journal of Phonetics*, 7:147–161.

Lisker, L. (1974). On time and timing in speech. In Sebeok, T. A., editor, *Current Trends in Linguistics*, volume 12, pages 2387–2418. Mouton, The Hague.

Löfqvist, A., Baer, T., McGarr, N., and Story, R. (1989). The cricothyroid muscle in voicing control. *Journal of the Acoustical Society of America*, 85:1314–1321.

Magen, H. S. (1997). The extent of vowel-to-vowel coarticulation in English. *Journal of Phonetics*, 25(2):187–205.

Mann, V. A. and Repp, B. H. (1980). Influence of vocalic context on the perception of [ʃ-s] distinction: I. Temporal factors. *Perception & Psychophysics*, 28:213–228.

Martin, J. G. and Bunnel, H. T. (1982). Perception of anticipatory coarticulation effects in vowel-stop-vowel sequences. *Journal of Experimental Psychology: Human Perception and Performance*, 8:473–488.

McDougall, K. and Nolan, F. (2007). Discrimination of speakers using the formant dynamics of /u:/ in British English. In *Proceedings of the 16th International Congress of Phonetic Sciences, Saarbrücken, Germany*, pages 1825–1828.

Meltzoff, A. N. and Moore, M. K. (1997). Explaining facial imitation: A theoretical model. *Early Development and Parenting*, 6:179–192.

Mok, P. K. P. (2010). Language-specific realizations of syllable structure and vowel-to-vowel coarticulation. *Journal of the Acoustical Society of America*, 128(3):1346–1356.

Müller, V., Harrington, J., Kleber, F., and Reubold, U. (2011). Age-dependent differences in the neutralization of the intervocalic voicing contrast: Evidence from an apparent-time study on East Franconian. In *Proceedings of Interspeech, Florence.*

Munhall, K. G., MacDonald, E. N., Byrne, S. K., and Johnsrude, I. (2009). Talkers alter vowel production in response to real-time formant perturbation even when instructed not to compensate. *Journal of the Acoustical Society of America*, 125:384–390.

Nielsen, K. (2007). Implicit phonetic imitation is constrained by phonemic contrast. In Trouvain, J. and Barry, W., editors, *Proceedings of the 16th International Congress of Phonetic Sciences, Saarbruecken*, pages 1961–1964.

Nielsen, K. (2011). Specificity and abstractness of VOT imitation. *Journal of Phonetics*, 39:132–142.

Ohala, J. J. (1981). The listener as a source of sound change. In Masek, C. S., Hendrick, R. A., and Miller, M. F., editors, *Papers from the Parasession on Language and Behavior*, pages 178–203. Chicago: Chicago Ling. Soc.

Ohala, J. J. (1993). Sound change as nature's speech perception experiment. *Speech Communication*, 13:155–161.

Öhman, S. E. G. (1966). Coarticulation in VCV utterances: Spectrographic measurements. *Journal of the Acoustical Society of America*, 39:151–168.

Pardo, J. (2006). On phonetic convergence during conversational interaction. *Journal of the Acoustical Society of America*, 119:2382–2393.

Pardo, J., Gibbons, R., Suppes, A., and Krauss, J. (2012). Phonetic convergence in college roommates. *Journal of Phonetics*, 40:190–197.

Recasens, D. and Espinosa, A. (2005). Articulatory, positional and coarticulatory characteristics for clear /l/ and dark /l/: Evidence from two Catalan dialects. *Journal of the International Phonetic Association*, 35(1):1–25.

Reubold, U. . (2012). *Über die Zusammenhänge zwischen Grundfrequenz und Vokalhöhe: Evidenzen aus longitudinalen Altersstimmenstudien, Perturbations- und Vokalerkennungsexperimenten.* PhD thesis, Ludwig-Maximilians-University of Munich.

Rowley, A. (1990). East Franconian. In Russ, C., editor, *The Dialects of Modern German*, pages 394–416. Routledge, London.

Scobbie, J. M. and Pouplier, M. (2010). Conditioning factors in external sandhi: An EPG study of vocalisation and retraction of word-final English /l/. *Journal of Phonetics*, 38(2):240–259.

Shockley, K., Richardson, D., and Dale, R. (2009). Conversation and coordinative structures. *Topics in Cognitive Science*, 1:305–319.

Shockley, K., Sabadini, L., and Fowler, C. A. (2004). Imitation in shadowing words. *Perception and Psychophysics*, 66:422–429.

Studdert-Kennedy, M. (2005). How did language go discrete. In Tallerman, M., editor, *Language Origins: Perspectives on Language*, pages 48–67. Oxford University Press, Oxford.

van den Heuvel, H., Cranen, B., and Rietveld, T. (1996). Speaker variability in the coarticulation of /a, i, u/. *Speech Communication*, 18(2):113–130.

Weinreich, U., Labov, W., and Herzog, M. (1968). Empirical foundations for a theory of language change. In Lehmann, W. and Malkiel, Y., editors, *Directions for Historical Linguistics*, pages 97–195. University of Texas Press, Austin.

Wells, J. (1982). *Accents of English: An Introduction.* Cambridge, Cambridge University Press.

The gestural approach to syllable structure: Universal, language- and cluster-specific aspects

MARIANNE POUPLIER

Abstract: This paper presents a discussion of the gestural model of syllable structure (Browman and Goldstein, 1988). This model assumes that the linguistic structure of spoken language can be captured on the basis of dynamical primitive units (gestures) which cohere into larger structures on the basis of intergestural coupling relations. Besides providing an overview of the empirical support the gestural model of syllable structure has received so far, this paper also presents some data on German clusters investigating how differences in timing within clusters interacts with syllable-position specific timing (onset-vowel coordination). Results show that the internal structure of clusters has a greater effect on onset-vowel timing than on coda-vowel timing. This supports the assumption of the gestural model that onsets, but not codas constitute a higher-level constituent of syllabic organization. The data also add to recent work showing that the gestural model of syllable structure has to be extended to account for language- and cluster-specific effects on timing relations within the syllable.

1 Introduction

The syllable continues to be a topic of fascination for both formal and empirical speech researchers: the syllabic organization of spoken language is a primary example of how the physiological boundary conditions of spoken language are intertwined with grammar. In particular, strong universal tendencies in syllabic organization are seen as key candidates for physiological explanations, such as the cross-linguistic preference for onsets over codas, and generally for CV syllables. Since these are, however, universal preferences and not inviolable laws, any physiological explanation must be non-deterministic and allow for language-particular choices and deviations from the general pattern. There is no doubt that many particulars of syllabic organization are, as any aspect of grammar, language-specific. The challenge thus remains to negotiate universal principles of syllabic organization, presumably rooted in speech physiology, with language-particular syllable characteristics. While there is general agreement on the cross-linguistic existence and importance of syllabic organization (for recent discussions of exceptions see Hyman, 2008, 2011), joining up the details of our knowledge about the syllable from a grammatical and a physical perspective has been anything but trivial: the identification of consistent correlates of syllabic organization in speech production is still an open challenge.

The purpose of this paper is to provide a discussion of the gestural theory of syllable structure as first proposed by Browman and Goldstein (1988) as one particular approach that aims to draw a direct link between physiological and grammatical principles of syllabic organization. Thereby the gestural model of syllable structure has clearly emphasized the universal aspects of syllabic organization. First proposals on how to incorporate language- and consonant-specific aspects have been made only recently, as an understanding of the range of phenomena that need to be accounted for is beginning to emerge. Few studies so far have investigated how cluster-internal timing differences and syllable-position timing effects may interact in both onset and coda, and it is the aim of the data presented here to begin to fill that gap. After the presentation of the main theoretical claims of the model, we will provide an overview of published studies that have explicitly tested the model empirically, and add to the existing literature by presenting some new data on German clusters in this paper.

2 The gestural theory of syllable structure

2.1 The c-center hypothesis

Units of phonological analysis, such as features, segments and syllables, are idealized representations of linguistic sound structure; they symbolize abstractions over the physical, infinitely variable details of utterance production. These discrete units only very limitedly specify the physical, spatio-temporal patterns of articulator motion which characterize the production of any given sound. However, since speech sounds are always produced in an overlapping fashion, many phenomena in spoken language require an explicit account of how articulatory gestures relate to each other in physical space and time (Fowler, 1980; Öhmann, 1966). Against this background, Browman and Goldstein and colleagues have challenged the adequacy of positing symbolic phonological units. Instead, they have proposed in their Articulatory Phonology framework that the primitive units of phonological analysis must incorporate the spatio-temporal patterns of articulator motion (Fowler, 1980; Goldstein et al., 2006; Saltzman and Munhall, 1989). In the gestural model, utterance planning as much as the gestures themselves are modeled as complex systems of coupled oscillators. By coupling gestures to each other, higher level functional units such as segments, onsets etc. emerge. Linguistic units therefore are manifest in the relative temporal coordination of gestures.

Syllabic structure has occupied a central position within the gestural model, since, as argued above, the syllable is one of the primary interface points between cognitive and physical aspects of spoken language. Particularly the work of Rena Krakow (1993) has been foundational for the gestural theory of syllable structure. Her studies on nasal and lateral onset and coda consonants in English have shown how inter-gestural timing varies systematically as a function of syllable position. Krakow recorded velum movement data for sequences differing in syllable structure such as *see$me* versus *seem$E*, and confirmed that for a coda nasal, the velum lowers early during the vowel, with the velum movement being asynchronous with the corresponding lip/oral gesture of the nasal. The latter starts its closing movement only when the velum has already attained its target. In onset position, velum and lingual/lip movement of a nasal are roughly synchronous. Based on these and similar findings, Browman and Goldstein have argued that syllabic structure is epiphenomenal to different relative timing relations that characterize gestural organization pre- and postvocalically (Browman and Goldstein, 1995; Kelso et al., 1986).

In linguistic analysis, the syllable hierarchy describes the fact that multiple pre- and postvocalic consonants form constituents such as onset and rhyme, which are targeted as single units by certain grammatical rules or constraints. Browman and Goldstein (1988, 2000) find that the phonological constituency of onsets is indeed reflected in articulation: the global temporal coordination of an onset cluster with the vowel remains stable irrespectively of the number of consonants the cluster comprises. Building on these findings, they advance the idea that universally, languages employ two basic phase relationships for onset and coda coordination: in-phase (0°) and anti-phase (180° out-of-phase). Onset consonants are, by hypothesis, coupled in-phase to the following vowel and anti-phase with each other. This results in a 'c-center' timing pattern, as shall be detailed below, meaning that the onset as a single unit is in a stable relationship to the vowel, irrespectively of how many or which types of gestures a given onset comprises. This contrasts with coda consonants, which are coupled anti-phase only. Only the first post-vocalic consonant is coupled to the vowel, a second coda consonant is coupled only to the preceding one, but not to the vowel; hence this has been termed 'sequential' or 'left-edge' coordination. This implies that codas are quite different as syllable constituents compared to onsets. Codas are linear sequences of consonants, with only one coda gesture being directly coupled to the vowel. Onsets, however, have a much more complex coupling structure with each gesture of the onset being coupled to the vowel and to the other onset consonant(s). Note that in this point the gestural syllable model differs from the traditional view that vowel-coda (cluster or not) form a constituent to the exclusion of the onset; there is no direct correlate of a rhyme in this model.

2.2 Characterization of surface timing patterns

The underlying phase specifications give rise to characteristic relative timing patterns on the surface. For example, the observation that in a tautosyllabic CV sequence, the vowel may begin its movement before the consonant has achieved closure (Löfqvist and Gracco, 1999) has been taken as evidence in support of underlying in-phase coupling in onsets. Krakow's (1993) work on the timing of liquids and nasals in the different syllable positions has already been mentioned. Computational modeling studies have served to corroborate inferred relationships between timing and phasing (Nam and Saltzman, 2003; Shaw et al., 2009). Further, changes in relative timing between onset/coda consonants and the nucleus under changing cluster complexity have been used as a diagnostic for underlying phase relationships. Since many previous studies have used changing syllable margin complexity in order to test the pre-

dictions of the gestural syllable model, and this strategy will also be taken up for the German data reported here, we will explain the reasoning of this method now.
Throughout this paper, the first member of a cluster will always be denoted to as C1; we will refer to the individual consonants of an onset cluster as C1C2V, and to the consonants in a coda cluster as VC1C2. The consonants immediately adjacent to the vowel will be referred to as *vowel-adjacent consonants* (C2 of onset, C1 of coda clusters), and the non-vowel adjacent consonants will be referred to as *vowel-remote consonants* (C1 of onset, C2 of coda clusters).

2.2.1 Shift analysis

One measurement which has been used to establish underlying coordination relationships concerns the timing of the vowel-adjacent and vowel-remote consonants to the vowel under changes in syllable margin complexity. A fixed reference point in the vowel (or, for measurement convenience, an appropriate consonant) is used as an anchorpoint relative to which consonant-vowel timing is assessed. According to the gestural syllable model, we expect that, as more consonants are added to an onset, the vowel-adjacent consonant shifts temporally more and more towards the anchorpoint. This is so because the onset as a whole (as a global unit) is in a stable relationship to the vowel, not the individual consonants of the onset. In Figure 1a, the RE measurement point in the vowel-adjacent consonant (/k/ in *Konto*) is closer to the anchorpoint in the singleton (top) than in the cluster (bottom) condition (/k/ of *Skonto*). The vowel-remote consonant (LE measurement point in Figure 1a; /s/ in *Skonto*) will shift away from the anchorpoint compared to the singleton (/k/ in *Konto*), whereby both onset consonants are expected to shift to an approximately equal degree relative to the singleton. Now if we regard not the individual consonants, but the onset as a whole, there is no change in relative timing to the anchorpoint across conditions. Observe how for onsets, the c-center measurement point in Figure 1a lines up between singleton and cluster conditions, that is, the c-center maintains its timing to the anchor under changing onset complexity (thereby the c-center is defined as the temporal midpoint of the onset as a whole). Codas, on the other hand, show only sequential or 'left-edge' coordination, meaning increasing coda complexity does not affect the timing of the vowel-adjacent consonant to the anchor; there is no shift. The LE measurement point in Figure 1b has the same relative temporal distance to the anchor across conditions (/k/ in *Muck* has the same distance to the anchor as /k/ in *Mucks*).

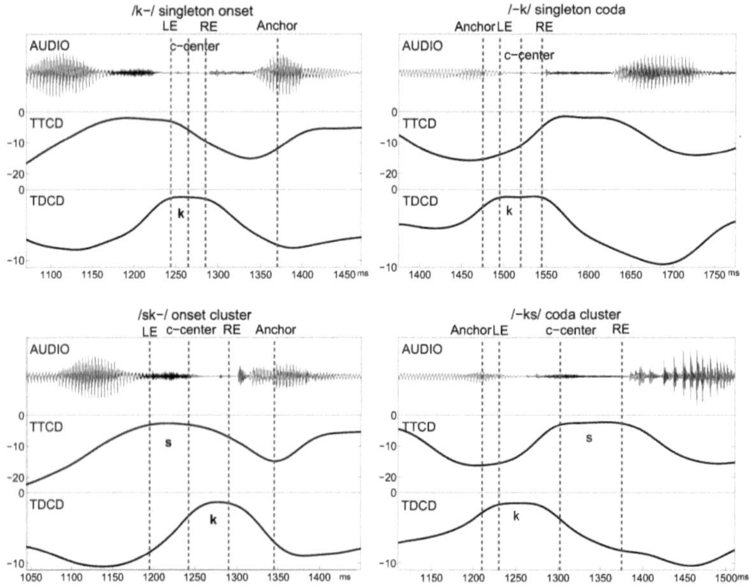

Figure 1a. Onset **Figure 1b. Coda**

Figure 1: Articulatory timing patterns as they are predicted to result from the underlying phase relationships. Subject A, typical rendition of /s#k-/ and /#sk-/ (*Omas Konto, Oma Skonto*) for onset on the left (Figure 1a) and for /-k#s/, /-ks#/ for coda (*Muck sachte, Mucks achte*) on the right (Figure 1b). Singleton conditions are on the top row, cluster conditions on the bottom row. TTCD and TDCD indicate tongue tip constriction degree and tongue dorsum constriction degree, respectively. The fixed anchorpoint (acoustic midpoint of the vowel) is indicated, as well as the landmarks left-edge (LE), c-center and right-edge (RE). The singleton-cluster figures have been aligned at the fixed anchorpoint relative to which c-center calculations are performed (see main text). Observe how for onset (Figure 1a) the c-center aligns between the singleton (top) and cluster (bottom) conditions, but not the left-edge or right-edge. For coda (Figure 1b), however, it is the left-edge that aligns between singleton (top) and cluster (bottom) conditions, not c-center or right-edge.

In contrast, the c-center measurement point and the RE measurement point (vowel remote consonant) do not line up across conditions. This is so because the consonants are just 'added' linearly one after the other. In sum, the gestural syllable model predicts for the vowel-adjacent onset consonant a shift towards the anchorpoint as onset complexity increases, but no such shift for the vowel-adjacent coda consonant.

2.2.2 Stability analysis

A second, related strategy to identify phase relationships has been to regard the variability of various 'landmarks' (measurement points) of an onset or coda by observing to which degree the timing of each measurement point to the anchor varies as cluster size changes. For onsets, the temporal midpoint of the entire cluster, the c-center, does not vary significantly in its timing to the anchorpoint, no matter how many consonants are part of the onset cluster. For codas, only the vowel-adjacent consonant, the 'left-edge' landmark of the coda, is in a stable relationship to the vowel (cf. Figure 1) and is thus expected to show the least variability across conditions (e.g., lowest standard deviation).

2.3 Universal and language-specific aspects

The gestural model has advanced the strong claim that universally, syllable structure is organized on the basis of just these two coupling modes: in-phase and anti-phase. The rationale for assuming a universal status for these two modes draws on knowledge from coordination dynamics in biological systems (Kelso, 1995). In-phase coordination is known more generally to have a privileged status in movement coordination. This pattern requires no learning and is the one that systems revert to if more complex patterns break down; it is fundamentally stable. The idea is that languages will naturally exploit these two coordination modes due to their "intrinsic" character (i.e., naturalness), and indeed in-phase and anti-phase are posited as the only two accessible modes at all for syllabic organization (most recently formulated in Goldstein et al. (2008)). In the gestural theory of syllable structure, this *physiological* universal (the basic stability of in-phase coordination) is linked to the *linguistic* universal of onset preference and generally provides the basis for a gestural concept of markedness. CV is universally the preferred syllable type in that for instance, no language permits codas to the exclusion of onsets, but the reverse is perfectly possible. Onsets show a greater resistance to sound change compared to codas and do, in contrast to codas, generally not contribute to moraic weight. However, some languages may deviate from the near-universal CV preference; this has for instance been claimed for the Australian Aboriginal languages (Butcher, 2006). In this case, Nam et al. (2009) have used computational simulations to argue that if VC is the most dominant pattern in a given ambient language, children will acquire VC patterns relatively more quickly compared to a language in which CV is the dominant structure, but nonetheless for any language the CV pattern would be the one to emerge/stabilize first, given the hypothesis that onsets universally exhibit the more intrinsically accessible in-phase coordination mode.

Two other studies have drawn a connection between phonological or typological markedness and the absence of in-phase onset coupling. Hermes et al. (2008) contrasted Italian onset clusters /pl-/ and /pr-/ with 'impure-s' clusters (/sC(C)-/), which are known to have a different status in Italian grammar compared to other clusters. While generally onset clusters showed a c-center effect, this was not the case for those with impure-s. The /s/ was just 'added' to the left of the onset cluster, as it were, it did not form a single functional unit with the rest of the onset (indicated by a lack of a shift of the vowel-adjacent consonant for /s/-clusters, and a lack of c-center line-up). The different status of these clusters in grammar seems to go hand in hand with a different articulatory coordination pattern, that is, there seems to be a direct correspondence between linguistic and physiological (non-)default patterns. Pouplier and Beňuš (2011) have recently argued that syllabic consonants in Slovak (e.g., *smrk*, with /r/ being the nucleus) do not allow for an in-phase onset-nucleus coordination pattern. Syllabic consonants constitute a case in which the segmental identity of the gestures involved plays a bigger role than envisioned by the gestural syllable model in its simplest form: Onset-nucleus coordination differs depending on whether the nucleus is a vowel or a consonant[1]. Pouplier and Beňuš raise the

1 Note that there were not only differences in onset-nucleus timing depending on the identity of the nucleus (which may be conditioned by the different articulators used

possibility that there may be a causal link between the absence of in-phase coordination for syllabic consonants and the fact that syllabic consonants with complex onsets are typologically rare. At the same time, the stability analysis for Slovak does not support the predictions of the gestural syllable model, neither for canonical syllables with a vocalic nucleus, nor for those with a syllabic consonant. This work opens up the possibility that the range of timing patterns observed in languages may be greater than anticipated.

In the light of the hypothesis that universally, languages employ in-phase coordination for onset and anti-phase coordination for codas, and that any deviations from those patterns imply some form of markedness of a given structure, the question arises which role known timing differences within different types of onset and coda clusters play in this model. While it is well known that articulatory timing within a cluster may differ cross-linguistically as well as within a language as a function of the segmental composition of the cluster, it is poorly understood how these timing difference interact with syllable-position effects on timing. That the identity of the segments involved may play a role for timing relations in coda clusters was revealed in a recent articulatory (EMA) study by Marin and Pouplier (2010). We systematically tested the gestural model of syllable structure for American English looking at /sp-, sk-, sm-, pl-, kl-/ for onsets and /-ps, -sp, -ks, -sk, -ms, -lp, -lk/ for codas (see also Byrd (1995); Honorof and Browman (1995)). While for onsets, results were as predicted in terms of the shift and stability analyses laid out above, for coda consonants, the results were more complex. The /s/-clusters showed, as expected, stable left-edge coordination irrespective of coda complexity. For the two /-lp/ and /-lk/ clusters, however, the tongue tip gesture for /l/ occurred temporally closer to the anchor-point in *gulp* compared to *gull*; the same held for the /l/ in *bulk* and *ball*. Concomitantly, the stability analysis did not support left-edge coordination for these clusters. These results mean that the identity of the segments involved plays a bigger role than originally envisioned. En-

---

for consonants and vowels), but there were also differences in consonant-consonant coordination for the same consonant sequence depending on whether the same two consonants were an onset/coda cluster or whether one of the consonants was in the nucleus. For more details the reader is referred to the Pouplier and Beňuš (2011) publication.

glish /l/ is known to be composed of two gestures, a tongue-tip raising and a dorsal retraction gesture (Giles and Moll, 1975). We speculated in the Marin and Pouplier paper that the dorsal gesture of the liquid can overlap with the vowel without endangering its perceptibility, hence /l/ clusters may be less constrained in their timing compared to obstruent clusters. Moreover, coda gestures participate in less coupling relations compared to onsets and thus have more degrees of freedom, possibly allowing for a greater variety of coordination patterns (onset /l/-clusters /pl-, kl-/ did not behave differently from the other clusters we investigated).

A further study rendered unexpected patterns for three-consonantal /s/-clusters in English: Waltl and Marin (2010) failed to find a c-center effect for /spl-, skl-/ onset clusters, even though they confirmed the effect for the two-consonantal counterparts (/sp-, sk-, pl-, kl-/): in their data no shift of the vowel-adjacent consonant towards the anchorpoint occurred in going from *played* to *splayed*, nor was the c-center a stable relative timing point across conditions (subjects and experimental details were the same as in the Marin and Pouplier study). They conjectured that the low lexical frequency of these clusters in English may play a role given known effects of lexical frequency on consonant overlap. How lexical frequency may affect onset-vowel timing has not been investigated so far.

In a study of Romanian onsets, Marin (2011) investigated obstruent (/sp-, sk-, ps-, ks-, kt-/), liquid (/pl-, kl-/), and nasal onset clusters (/sm-,kn-/). Her results showed among others, that the order of the consonants in clusters significantly affects timing: While /sp-, sk-/ patterned as predicted by c-center theory, this was not the case for the reverse order of the same consonants (/ps-, ks-/): for these clusters, the vowel-adjacent consonant (/s/) shifted away from the anchorpoint as cluster complexity increased, opposite to the predicted pattern. The stability analysis supported a c-center organization pattern only for the /s/-initial clusters /sp-, sk-, sm-/, but not for the other clusters included in the study. For the other clusters, no particular landmark emerged as more stable than the other ones, although there was a trend for c-center stability for /pl-, kl-/. Sibilants are known to show a high degree of resistance to vowel coarticulation (Recasens et al., 1997), and the order effect in Marin's data might be interpreted to the effect that the coarticulation resistance of C2 in a C1C2 onset cluster may interact with a c-center effect. The c-center effect leads to an increasing overlap of the vowel-adjacent consonant with the vowel, which may not be possible for sibilants, given their general low propensity for coarticulation[2]. Order effects of a different kind have previously been observed in several studies: the relative order of place of articulation of the two consonants of a cluster has been found to be a significant factor determining articulatory timing. Chitoran et al. (2002) have shown for Georgian that front-to-back onset clusters such as /bg/ show more overlap than back-to-front clusters such as /gb/, and there is also some evidence that global onset coordination for these two clusters is not the same (Goldstein et al., 2008), although a comprehensive study is missing. Segmental composition may significantly affect cluster-vowel timing in onsets also beyond a place order effect, as shown by Bombien et al. for German (Bombien, 2011; Bombien et al., 2010). The authors find that in addition to a place-order effect parallel to Georgian, overlap differed even within the same place order. For instance /kn-/ was systematically less overlapped than /kl-/, both are back-to-front clusters. Onset-vowel timing was unfortunately not investigated in that study; it is unknown whether both clusters would show shift and stability measures consistent with the c-center hypothesis. Kühnert et al. (2006) present a case in which timing differences within the cluster do not seem to affect the c-center onset pattern. The authors report for data from two speakers that the consonant timing in French C/n/ and C/l/ clusters differed significantly depending on whether C is a stop or a fricative (with /f/ exhibiting more overlap than /p, k/) and on whether the place of articulation order was front-to-back or back-to-front (e.g., /fl/ being more overlapped than /kl/). Despite these significant cluster-internal timing differences, global onset-vowel timing was the same across five of their six cluster types (measured as the temporal distance cluster midpoint - vowel). This contrasts with

2 Note that Marin's /sk-/ data do not fully support this interpretation. In Recasens' model, in which degree of active tongue dorsum control is the main determinant of coarticulation resistance, /k/ is among the consonants most resistant to coarticulation, but in Marin's data the /sk-/ onset cluster shows the expected c-center pattern. On the other hand, generally coarticulation resistance in sibilants takes a very different form from velar coarticulation resistance, since the place of articulation in velars shifts considerably as a function of vowel context, but less so for sibilants (Iskarous et al., 2011; Öhmann, 1967).

Georgian, in which back-to-front onset clusters differed in global timing to the vowel compared to front-to-back clusters (note some contradictory data in Goldstein et al. (2007) though, in which a back-to-front cluster shows a c-center effect, although place order effects are not tested in that study). However, a direct comparison of the results of all of these experiments is difficult, since very different measures were employed and the studies had different questions as their main focus. It is thus unclear whether this is a methodological effect or a true difference between the languages.

2.4 Summary

While the c-center has thus emerged as an overall stable phenomenon across languages for onsets, there is also some evidence that the segmental composition of the cluster may play a bigger role than expected. Yet most studies have had either syllable-position timing effects or the internal structure of clusters at their focus, but not both, making it difficult to compare the results. Such a comprehensive investigation is, however, necessary in order to advance our understanding of how the internal composition of clusters may interact with syllable-position specific timing. The data presented in the remainder of the paper systematically compare onset and coda clusters for German, aiming to shed light on the question whether and how differences in overlap within clusters can be understood within the gestural model of syllable structure.

3 Experiment: Onset and coda coordination in German

3.1 Method

Data were collected using a Carstens Medizinelektronik 5-D articulography system. Standard calibration and postprocessing procedures were performed for each experiment. The kinematic data were sampled at 200Hz and filtered during postprocessing with 20Hz (5Hz for the reference coils). Acoustic data, sampled at 16kHz, were recorded at the same time and synchronized with the kinematic signals during postprocess-

ing. Four receiver coils were attached to the tongue, roughly equally spaced: ranging from about 1cm behind the actual tongue tip for the most anterior coil to the dorsal region of the tongue body for the most posterior coil. Additional sensors were placed on the lower incisors and on the upper and lower lips. Reference sensors allowing for the correction of head movement were attached to the nose ridge, maxilla and on the mastoid process on each side. The data were rotated to each subject's occlusal plane. A palate trace was obtained for each speaker by sliding a sensor coil attached to the experimenter's finger midline down the hard palate.
This paper reports data from four native speakers of German. All subjects spoke Standard High German without any pronounced dialectal features and were naïve as to the purposes of the experiment.

3.1.1 Stimuli

The utterances were designed to allow for a comparison of the consonant-vowel timing between simple onsets/codas and complex onsets/codas; therefore the stimuli consisted of target words containing onset and coda consonant clusters as well as corresponding singletons (Table 1).
For each V#C1C2V onset and VC1C2#V coda cluster, singleton conditions were collected in the form of a corresponding cross-word cluster (VC#CV). For example, the /bl-/ cluster in *prima [**bl**]aues* ('excellent blue') was compared to the /l-/ in *ga[**p**] [**l**]aues* ('there was blue'). Correspondingly for a coda cluster, the timing of the /-lm/ cluster in *Ha[**lm**] acht* ('blade eight') was compared to the timing of /-l/ in *Ha[**l**] [**m**]acht* ('echo makes'). The target words were embedded in carrier phrases, which varied slightly across cluster types to avoid monotony (e.g. "*Es **gab laues/prima blaues** Wasser zu trinken*" ('There was lukewarm/excellent blue water for drinking'); "*Ich habe **Hall macht/ Halm acht** aufgeschrieben*" ('I wrote down echo makes/blade eight')).
Eight repetitions were collected in randomized blocks with a different randomization for each subject, rendering 640 tokens (4 speakers x 20 target phrases x 8 repetitions). Due to technical problems, for some speakers some repetitions could not be analyzed; overall 601 tokens entered into the analysis across conditions and subjects.

Table 1: Target stimulus phrases for onset and coda. The top row shows the orthographic representation, the middle row an IPA transcription, the bottom row gives an approximate English gloss. Consonants of interest are in bold face. Note that voiced word-final stops are devoiced in German (underlying voicing is represented in the orthography).

Set	**ONSET** Cluster	Singleton	Set	**CODA** Cluster	Singleton
/bl-/	prima **bl**aues ˈpʁiːmɐˈblaʊəs *excellent blue*	gab **l**aues gap ˈlaʊəs *there was blue*	/-lm/	Ha**lm** acht halm ʔaxt *blade eight*	Ha**ll** macht hal maxt *echo makes*
/pl-/	prima **Pl**atten ˈpʁiːmɐˈplatən *excellent tiles*	gab **L**atten gap ˈlatən *there were bars*	/-lp/	A**lp** hasst ʔalp hast *alp hates*	A**ll** passt ʔal p^{h}ast *universe fits*
/gm-/	prima **Gm**ünder ˈpʁiːmɐˈgmyndɐ *excellent people from Gmünd*	mag **M**ünder mak ˈmyndɐ *likes mouths*			
/km-/	prima **Khm**er ˈpʁiːmɐˈkmeːɐ *excellent Khmer (name)*	mag **M**eer mak meːɐ *likes the sea*			
/sk-/	Oma **Sk**onto ˈʔoːmɐˈskɔnto *grandmother discount*	Omas **K**onto ˈʔoːmɐs ˈkɔnto *grandmother's bank account*	/-ks/	Muc**ks** achte mʊks ˈʔaxtə *to the small noise pay attention*	Muc**k** sachte mʊk ˈzaxtə *Muck (name) carefully*
			/-kt/	Pa**kt** eilt p^{h}akt aɪlt *pact is urgent*	Pac**k** teilt p^{h}ak taɪlt *pack shares*
			/-bt/	A**bt** hakt(nach) ʔapt haːkt *abbot asks further*	A**b** tagt ʔap taːkt *Ab (name) meets*

3.1.2 Measurements

For the tongue sensors, constriction degree was calculated as the Euclidean distance of each sample of the relevant transducer coil to all sample points on the palate. The minimal distance was taken as the constriction degree for that sample. Lip aperture was computed as the Euclidean distance between the upper lip and lower lip transducer coil. A semi-automatic labeling algorithm provided by Mark Tiede from Haskins Laboratories was used to identify constrictions. For a given time series, kinematic events (in the derived constriction degree signal) were detected semi-automatically using a 20% threshold of the peak velocity: movement onset, peak velocity, target achievement, and release. The temporal midpoint of the target plateau (henceforth referred to as target-midpoint) was calculated as the timepoint half-way between target achievement and release. The acoustic midpoint of the tautosyllabic vowel was defined as anchorpoint relative to which the shift and stability analyses were performed.

3.1.3 Shift analysis: Lag ratios

For each token, the relative timing of the consonant gestures to the anchorpoint was calculated as the temporal lag between the target-midpoint of the relevant consonant and the acoustic vowel midpoint. The relative shift for each Set between the singleton and cluster condition was calculated by taking the ratio of the anchorlag in the cluster condition over the anchorlag in the singleton condition. For example, for the /bl-/ Set, we computed the ratio of the /l/-anchorlag in *blaues* over the /l/-anchorlag in *laues* for the vowel-adjacent consonant and the ratio of the /b/-anchorlag in *blaues* over the /l/-anchorlag in *laues* for the vowel-remote consonant. A value < 1 indicates a shift towards the vowel, while a value > 1 indicates a shift away from the vowel. A value of 1 means the relative timing between consonant and anchor has not changed between conditions.

3.1.4 Stability analysis

As laid out in the Introduction, the stability of various landmarks or measurement points in onset/coda position has been taken as an index of underlying phase relationships. In onset, the c-center landmark is predicted to be most stable, while in coda, it is left-edge that is expected to show least variability. For this analysis, the onset (coda) is treated as a single unit, and it is investigated which relative timing point of the onset (coda) with respect to the anchor is most stable under changes in onset (coda) complexity. That is, for each onset (coda), the timing of the left-edge, c-center and right-edge of the onset (coda) to the acoustic anchorpoint was calculated (following Browman and Goldstein, 1988; Byrd, 1995; Honorof and Browman, 1995). The left-edge is defined as the target achievement of C1, the right-edge is defined as the release of C2, and the c-center is defined as the arithmetic temporal midpoint between left-edge and right-edge (see Figure 1). For singletons, the timepoints of target achievement, target-midpoint and release constitute the left-edge, c-center and right-edge alignment points. Statistical tests are used to assess the stability of each of these landmarks under increasing onset (coda) complexity.

3.1.5 Overlap analysis

We compute degree of overlap by subtracting the timepoint of the release of C1 from the timepoint of target achievement of C2. Therefore larger numbers mean less overlap; negative values mean that C2 has already achieved its target when C1 is released. Overlap values are reported both as absolute and as normalized values. Normalization was achieved by dividing each overlap value by the total duration of the cluster. Cluster duration was defined as the time interval between target achievement of C1 and release of C2 in a C1C2 sequence.

3.2 Results

Recall that c-center theory predicts for onsets that the vowel-adjacent consonant temporally shifts towards the anchor as more consonants are added, we thus expect ratios <1. If there is left-edge coordination for codas, the relative timing of the vowel-adjacent consonant to the anchor should not change between the singleton and cluster conditions, therefore the ratio should be around 1. For the vowel-remote consonants, we should see less of a change in onsets compared to codas. Figure 2 displays the mean ratios for the vowel-adjacent and vowel-remote consonants of each cluster averaged across the four subjects (by-subject data are shown in the Appendix).

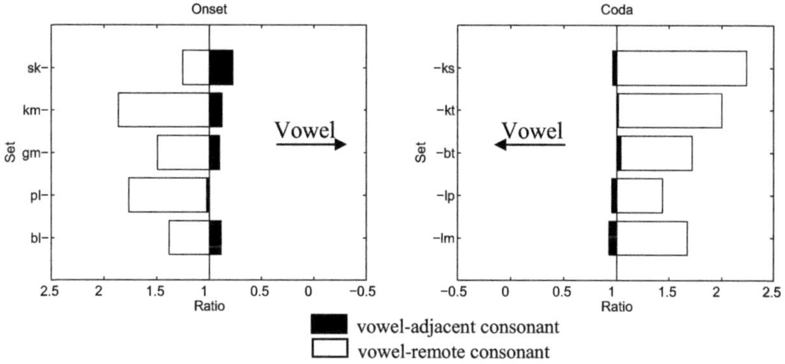

Figure 2: Lag ratios for onset and coda clusters. Ratios < 1 mean that the consonant has shifted closer to the anchorpoint between the singleton and cluster conditions, ratios > 1 mean the consonant has shifted away from the anchorpoint between conditions.

3.2.1 Vowel-adjacent consonant timing

We first present results for vowel-adjacent consonant timing (filled bars in Figure 2). For onsets, we generally observe values < 1 as expected; only the /pl-/ Set shows a different pattern with a ratio close to 1. For codas, we see mostly values just under 1; the clusters /-kt/ and /-bt/ have ratios slightly greater than 1. Overall, the degree of change in timing between conditions is larger for onsets compared to codas. Statistically, we compared whether the difference in anchorlag (i.e. the shift) between singleton and coda condition is significant. A univariate ANOVA was conducted by Subject and by Set separately for onset and coda. Fixed factor was Complexity (singleton vs. cluster), the dependent variable was anchorlag. For onset, the factor Complexity was significant by Set ($F(1,4)=8.22$; $p=.046$) and by Subject ($F(1,3)=136.52$; $p=.001$) showing that there is a significant difference in anchorlag for the vowel-adjacent consonant in the singleton and cluster conditions. For codas, Complexity was significant neither by Set ($F(1,4)=1.37$, $p=.306$), nor by Subject

($F(1,3)=1.52$, $p=.305$). A univariate ANOVA with the fixed factor Cluster (onset, coda) was significant ($F(1,38)=7.74$, $p=.008$), confirming the overall timing difference between onset and coda. Figure 2 suggests that the size of the complexity effect (i.e. the timing difference between singleton and cluster conditions) is not the same for the different cluster types, at least for onsets. To evaluate whether the Sets differed significantly in the degree of timing change between the complexity conditions, we ran, separately for onset and coda, a univariate ANOVA on the ratios with fixed factor Set and random factor Subject. Set was significant for onsets ($F(4,12)=9.87$; $p=.001$), but not for codas ($F(4,12)=1.07$, $p=.413$). This means that there is a significant difference in onset-vowel timing depending on the cluster type, but coda-vowel timing remains the same independently of cluster composition. For onsets, a Bonferroni posthoc test reveals that /pl-/ differs (near-) significantly from all other Sets (/pl-/ vs. /bl-/ $p=.079$; /pl-/ vs. /gm-/ n.s., /pl-/ vs. /km-/ $p=.057$; /pl-/ vs. /sk-/ $p<.001$). None of the other Sets differed significantly from each other.

3.2.2 Vowel-remote consonant timing

We now regard the timing of the vowel-remote consonant (empty bars in Figure 2). To recapitulate, c-center theory predicts that in onsets, there should be an approximately equal shift for the vowel-adjacent and the vowel-remote consonant, and overall the vowel-remote consonant should show a lesser shift in onsets compared to codas. For onsets, the /sk-/ Set is as predicted in terms of a symmetric displacement of both C1 and C2 relative to the singleton timing. The other Sets show a different picture: /pl-/ essentially patterns like a coda cluster in that the timing of the /l/ is stable across conditions, and /p/ is just 'added' to the left; there is no evidence for global onset timing for this cluster. For onsets, vowel-remote consonants have on average a ratio closer to 1 compared to codas (mean onset=1.55, mean coda=1.81). A two-sided Wilcoxon test showed that this difference between onsets and codas was at trend level ($Z(4)=-1.83$; $p=.068$). Set effects in remote-vowel consonant timing were significant for both onset and coda (univariate ANOVA with random factor Subject and fixed factor Set; coda: $F(4,2)=5.4$, $p<.01$; onset: ($F(4,2)=34$, $p<.001$). For coda, a Bonferroni posthoc test shows that

/-lp/ and /-ks/ differ marginally from each other (p=.083). For onsets, /km-/ differs significantly from /bl-, gm-, sk-/ and /pl-/ differs from /bl-, sk-/ at the .01 level.

Overall, the results corroborate that onsets and codas can be distinguished both on the basis of vowel-adjacent and on the basis of vowel-remote consonant timing. For coda, cluster composition did not affect the timing of the vowel-adjacent consonant, and only marginally affected the timing of the vowel-remote consonant. In onset, there was a clearer interaction with cluster-internal composition: there was a stronger Set effect compared to coda for both consonants; the voiceless C1 stop clusters differed significantly from the voiced C1 stop clusters, as well as from the fricative-initial cluster /sk-/. We will now report the results of the stability analysis before proceeding to the analysis of consonant-consonant timing within the clusters.

3.2.3 Stability analysis

This analysis was designed to test whether there is evidence for onset or coda clusters being coordinated to the vowel as a unit (higher-level constituency). Stability of the three different landmarks was assessed as follows: We computed for each speaker, across the multiple repetitions of the same stimulus, the standard deviation for each landmark (left-edge, c-center, right-edge). For the ANOVA, the standard deviations were then averaged across Sets, separately for each speaker and landmark; this averaged lag SD served as dependent variable. In order to be able to conflate the landmarks for the two positions, they were recoded as vowel-adjacent edge (right-edge of onset, left-edge of coda), c-center, and vowel-remote edge (left-edge of onset, right-edge of coda). Table 2 gives the means and standard deviations for the dependent variable lag SD. Independent variables were the factors Position (onset, coda) and Landmark (V-adjacent edge, c-center, V-remote edge), Subject served as random factor. The main factor Position was not significant ($F(1,3)=3.62$, $p=.15$). Landmark reached significance ($F(2,6)=74.02$, $p<.001$), as did the Position*Landmark interaction ($F(2,6)=13.8$, $p=.006$). It is noticeable in Table 2 that there is greater inter-subject variability for onsets (higher SDs of the lag SD) compared to codas, this was also reflected in a significant Position*Subject interaction ($F(3,6)=15.05$, $p=.003$). A Bonferroni

posthoc test showed that the significant Landmark effect is due to the V-remote edge (left-edge for onset, right-edge for coda) differing significantly from both vowel-adjacent edge and c-center, the latter two did not differ significantly from each other (V-remote edge vs. c-center: p=.047; V-remote vs. V-adjacent edge: p=.016). The significant interaction arises due to a different behavior of the landmarks c-center and V-adjacent edge for the two positions. While in onset position, c-center and V-adjacent edge do not differ from each other, in coda, c-center is more variable compared to the V-adjacent edge. Two paired-sampled t-tests, run separately for onset and coda, confirm that c-center and V-adjacent edge differ significantly from each other for onset, but not for coda (coda: $t(3)$=-.60, p=.59; onset: $t(3)$=3.17, p=.05).
Overall, the data conform only in parts to the predictions of the gestural syllable model. For one, it was predicted that for onset, c-center should be the landmark with the lowest variability, while for coda it should be left-edge (V-adjacent edge). For coda, this prediction is borne out, but not for onsets. Both onset and coda share the characteristic that the V-adjacent edge is least variable, while the V-remote edge is most variable. While the c-center landmark is not the least variable landmark for onset (against the predictions of the gestural syllable model) it is nonetheless the patterning of the c-center landmark that significantly differentiates onset and coda position.

Table 2: Means and standard deviations of lag SD by Position and Landmark.

	LANDMARK		
Position	*c-center*	*V-adjacent edge*	*V-remote edge*
Onset	9.4 (3.7)	9.6 (3.9)	11.9 (3.1)
Coda	11.6 (1.1)	10.0 (1.7)	16.3 (1.3)

Summarizing the results so far, the data have rendered mixed results. For onsets, we observe a shift of the vowel-adjacent consonant towards the anchorpoint as onset complexity increases. The stability analysis does not identify the c-center as the uniquely most stable landmark, yet it is the relative c-center variability (relative to the two other landmarks) that differentiates onset and coda. For onsets, c-center variability does not differ significantly from V-adjacent edge variability, but for codas, the difference is significant. For codas, results are consistently as predicted: the timing of the vowel-adjacent consonant does not change as a function of coda complexity, and left-edge (V-adjacent edge) is the most stable landmark. Interestingly, the shift analysis for the vowel-adjacent consonant revealed a Set effect for onsets, mainly due to the /pl-/ cluster, but not for codas. For the vowel-remote consonant, both onset and coda showed significant Set effects, with the Set effects for onsets being more varied and more pronounced.

3.2.4 Overlap analysis

Our next analysis concerns the degree of overlap in onset and coda clusters. This allows us to investigate how the internal structure of the clusters may interact with timing relations in the two syllable positions. If vowel-remote consonant differences that became apparent in onset arise from differences in overlap, /pl-/ and /km-/ should overlap less than the other clusters. This would also be in line with Bombien (2011) reporting that voiceless clusters in German overlap less than voiced clusters. /sk-/ patterned in the shift analyses with /bl-, gm-/ and would thus be expected to exhibit similar degree of overlap to these clusters. Bombien found that /f-/ initial clusters overlapped more than /p-, k-/ initial clusters, so from that perspective we might also expect a higher degree of overlap for /sk-/.

Figure 3 shows the means across subjects for both the absolute and the normalized overlap values. The larger the values, the less overlap. First, we observe an overall difference in overlap as a function of cluster position, that is, onset versus coda. The mean onset overlap value comes to .21, SD=.16; the mean coda overlap value is .05, SD=.19. An ANOVA testing for an overall difference in overlap between onset and coda on the normalized overlap values rendered significant results (random factor Subject, fixed factor Cluster Position (onset vs. coda), $F(1, 3)=27.43$, $p=.014$).

Cluster type effects were assessed on the basis of univariate ANOVAs on the overlap values separately for onset and coda. For coda the fixed factor was Cluster Type (/-lm, -lp, -ks, -kt, -bt/) and random factor Subject. The ANOVA failed to reject the null hypothesis (normalized values: $F(4,12)<1$, $p=.62$; absolute values: $F(4,12)< 1$, $p=.52$), showing that coda clusters do not differ significantly in their overlap patterns as a function of cluster composition. For onsets, likewise with random factor Subject and fixed factor Cluster Type (/bl-, pl-, gm-, km-, sk-/), the results were highly significant for absolute ($F(4, 12)=25.3$, $p<.001$) and normalized values ($F(4,12)=19$, $p<.001$). A Bonferroni posthoc test on the absolute values showed that /km-/ differed significantly from all other clusters. For the normalized values, the posthoc test showed that /sk-/ differed from /bl-/ and /km-/ at the .05 level. These results overall confirm that /km-/ is the least and /sk-/ the most overlapped pattern.

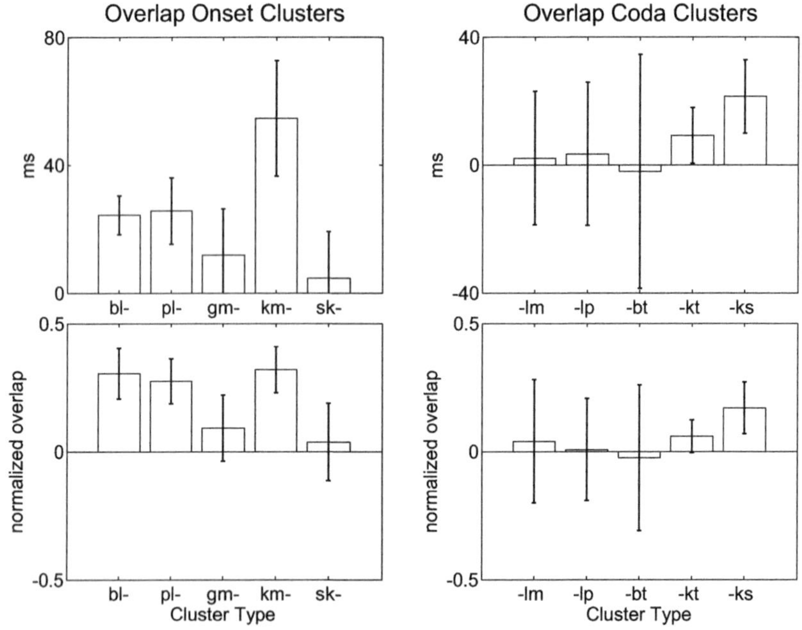

Figure 3: Overlap for onset and coda clusters for absolute (top panels) and normalized (bottom panels) values. Larger values mean less overlap, negative values mean that C2 has reached its target before C1 is released.

We conclude the data analysis section by looking at the overlap patterns as a function of voicing and place order. These analyses are restricted to onsets; for coda the dataset is too unbalanced to allow for a deeper investigation of these effects. Figure 4 shows the overlap values as boxplots for both absolute and normalized values, with the data averaged by voicing of C1 on the left and by place order on the right.

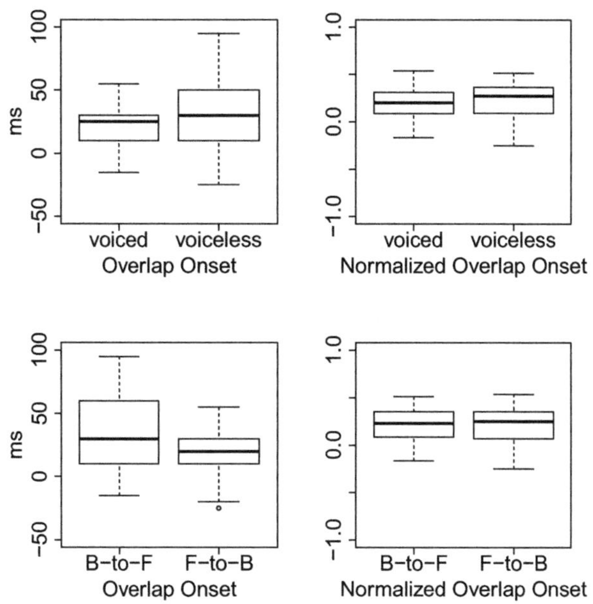

Figure 4: Absolute and normalized onset overlap values, data averaged by voicing of C1 at the top and by place order at the bottom.

For the voicing analysis, a linear mixed model ANOVA rendered significance only for the absolute (F=10.1, p=.002) but not the normalized values (F<1).[3] Overlap for voiced onset clusters shows, for the absolute values, a trend to be smaller than overlap in voiceless clusters, in agreement with Bombien's results for German. This effect is, however, carried entirely by the /gm-, km-/ opposition, /sk-/ as a voiceless cluster shows the smallest amount of overlap and the difference between

3 A linear mixed model ANOVA was chosen since this test statistic deals well with unbalanced datasets. Since the calculation of the degrees of freedom in a mixed model is unclear, p-values were determined using Markov Chain Monte Carlo sampling, following Baayen (2008) and as implemented in the languageR package.

/bl-/ and /pl-/ is not very pronounced at all (see Figure 3). For the place order effect for onsets, for the absolute values, we see an order effect in that back-to-front clusters are less overlapped than the reverse order, in agreement with the previous literature. A mixed linear model ANOVA with random factor Subject and fixed factor Order (back-to-front, front-to-back) was significant $F=18.37$ $p=.0002$; for the normalized values, there was no significant difference ($F<1$). The discrepancy between normalized and absolute overlap values arises due to systematic differences in cluster duration with back-to-front clusters having a longer duration.

Overall, the overlap analysis revealed that onset consonants with each other compared to coda consonants. Codas show no significant cluster-type effect, for onsets /sk-/ shows the most and /km-/ the least overlap. Back-to-front clusters are on average less overlapped than front-to-back clusters. Predictions derived from the vowel-remote consonant shift values were partially confirmed. Overall the difference in shift for /pl-, km-/ can be attributed to these clusters showing less overlap than their voiced counterparts. However, /pl-/ patterns more closely with /bl-/, the difference between /gm-/ and /kl-/ is much bigger. /sk-/ displays the most overlap and the least vowel-remote consonant shift.

4 Discussion

The experiment reported here tested the articulatory organization of German syllable onset and coda clusters. The aim was to investigate for one, whether the German data would adhere to the predictions made by the gestural theory of syllable structure, and secondly the interaction between syllable position conditioned timing and the internal composition of clusters.

For codas, the results have fully confirmed the predictions put forward by Browman and Goldstein (1988): the timing of the vowel-adjacent consonant is the same irrespectively of coda complexity or of coda composition. The left-edge (V-adjacent edge) of the coda cluster is the most stable measurement point with respect to the vowel; there is no evidence for a global coordination of coda clusters in the sense of a c-center effect. Set effects only pertained to the vowel-remote consonant but were overall weak compared to onsets; also overlap patterns showed no cluster type effects for coda. These data support the idea put forward in the gestural model that onset clusters are organized quite differently from coda clusters. The deeper implications of this view for phonological analysis have remained largely unexplored so far, apart from the work of Nam (2007a,b) on anti-phase coupling being a phonetic correlate of moraic weight, as mentioned in the Introduction.

As to coda /l/ clusters, the data support the notion that the unexpected variability in vowel-coda timing found by Marin and Pouplier (2010) for American English /l/-clusters may be due to the dorsal gesture of English /l/. German coda /l/ clusters patterned no differently from the other clusters and it is usually assumed that German /l/ has either no retraction gesture at all, or that any dorsal gesture, if present, plays only a minor role (Recasens et al., 1998). Therefore the dorsal retraction gesture of English /l/ may have conditioned the Marin and Pouplier results. There have been a variety of different proposals on how to model the syllable affiliation of the dorsal gesture of English /l/ (Carter, 2003; Goldstein et al., 2008; Scobbie and Pouplier, 2010). While taking up that discussion will lead too far astray here, generally these data point to the significance of articulatory synergies in consonant-vowel timing having been underestimated so far. Future research on liquid /l, r/ clusters cross-linguistically should be informative in this respect.

The onset timing patterns differed significantly from the coda timing patterns, providing yet another piece of evidence for syllabic structure being expressed in articulatory timing. Looking in more detail at the onset results, a somewhat varied picture emerges from the current data: First of all, the predictions of the gestural syllable model are confirmed in the form of a significant shift of the vowel-adjacent consonant towards the vowel with increasing onset complexity. Yet there was a significant Set effect for the vowel-adjacent consonant due to /pl-/ showing no such shift. Also the timing of the vowel-remote consonant showed a significant Set effect for onsets: the voiceless C1 clusters /km-, pl-/ are characterized by a greater vowel-remote consonant shift compared to the other clusters.

In terms of overlap, /sk-/ displays the most overlap and the shift patterns are exactly as predicted by c-center theory. For the clusters /km-, gm-/ the vowel-adjacent consonant shift was observed as expected, but

the clusters differ quite a bit in terms of the vowel-remote consonant. This is reflected in the overlap patterns as well: /km-/ exhibits the least overlap of all clusters and also the biggest ratio for the vowel-remote consonant. This means that the difference in overlap to other clusters is achieved mainly by extending the left-edge of the onset cluster. Note that in terms of the remote-consonant shift, /km-, pl-/ on the one hand, and /gm-, bl-/ on the other hand pattern similarly, suggesting an effect of voicing. This is partially supported by the overlap analysis: voiceless clusters are overall less overlapped compared to the voiced clusters. Yet this effect is mainly driven by /km-, gm-/ and to a lesser degree by differences between /pl-, bl-/; /sk/ even patterns opposite to the overall statistical trend. /pl-/ seems to have a different coordination to the vowel, the (lack of a) shift of the vowel-adjacent consonant is comparable to coda clusters (not the overlap pattern though): it looks like there is an interaction of voicing with a front-to-back effect. /pl-/, as a front-to-back cluster is relatively more overlapped than /km-/ as a back-to-front cluster. As voiceless C1 stop clusters, both /pl-/ and /km-/ show overall less overlap compared to the voiced C1 stop clusters and compared to the fricative initial cluster. These overlap results agree with Bombien's (2011) findings for German; unfortunately, he did not investigate onset-vowel timing, thus no further comparison of the results is possible.
An interesting suggestion which may prove relevant to understanding overlap patterns involving nasals comes from Vallée et al. (2009). The authors conjecture that for plosive+nasal sequences the high intraoral pressure build-up during the obstruent counteracts the lowering of the velum[4], possibly being one of the factors responsible for a cross-linguistic preference for nasal+plosive sequences of plosive+nasal sequences (irrespective of syllable boundary). Conceivably, the effect of aerodynamic factors on velum timing would concomitantly be reflected in the coordination of the labial/lingual gesture of the nasal, conditioning relatively little overlap in stop+nasal clusters as is the case here for /km-/. Even the difference between /gm-/ and /km-/ observed for the present data

4 The authors base their hypothesis on EMA data for VCV utterances reported in the paper. They observe that the velum continues to rise during the closure of plosives. This is interpreted as a form of cavity enlargement caused by high intraoral pressure build-up during the plosive, i.e. the velum is being pushed up by aerodynamic effects. The effect is more pronounced for voiceless compared to voiced plosives.

would be in line with this reasoning: intraoral pressure for a voiced obstruent is weaker than for a voiceless one, and indeed /gm-/ shows more overlap compared to /km-/. Generally, extending our at present relatively limited knowledge about velum timing and aerodynamic factors is bound to lead to a more comprehensive understanding of cluster timing. The idea mentioned in the Introduction that codas would exhibit a greater variety of patterning because they have more degrees of freedom compared to onsets could not be confirmed in the current data. Overall, Set effects were stronger for onsets compared to codas. If there is only sequential coupling in codas, we can expect that the vowel-remote consonant of the coda exerts no influence on vowel-consonant timing. Hence the timing of V-C1 is very stable, and no Set effects arise. For onsets, all consonants are coupled to the vowel as well as to each other, hence there is more potential for an interaction between cluster timing and syllable position timing. It has been argued that differences among clusters in overlap may arise for perceptual reasons, even though this has been not uncontested (Chitoran and Goldstein, 2006; Kühnert et al., 2006). Onsets are important for lexical access, hence it may not be surprising that we find more overlap differences (and hence more Set effects for onset-vowel timing) for onsets compared to coda. Arguably perceptual recoverability has to be ensured to a greater degree in onset compared to coda and thus might exert a greater influence on articulatory timing. Relatedly, Bombien (2011) hypothesizes that perceptual factors condition differences in overlap between /kn-/ and /kl-/ clusters in German (though see above for Vallée's proposal on the shaping role of aerodynamics). Yet Chitoran and Goldstein (2006) point out that their earlier, perceptually-based interpretation of the place order effect in Chitoran et al. (2002) might not hold after all: place order effects are also found for clusters in which perceptual recoverability is not at issue for either order. More direct experimental evidence is called for in order to understand the role of perceptual factors in consonant timing[5].

5 Bombien and Hoole (2011) have recently presented pilot endoscopy data on the role of the laryngeal gesture in onset clusters (see also Hoole, 2006). These data suggest that the laryngeal gesture participates in the c-center effect, which in turn implies that the behavior of the supra-laryngeal gestures cannot be fully understood without taking the laryngeal gesture into account. As is the case for velum timing in nasals and aerodynamics generally, laryngeal timing will be an important area of future research

Coming back to the data at hand, how can interactions between C-C timing in a cluster and overall cluster-vowel timing be modeled? Goldstein et al. (2008) have proposed two basic mechanisms by means of which microscopic cluster- and speaker-specific variation in timing can be accounted for while maintaining macroscopic in-phase coordination pattern for onsets (codas are not part of that paper). For one, there may be differences in coupling strength. Assuming greater coupling strength between C2-V than between C1-V in a C1C2V cluster would result in a greater tendency for C2 to be synchronous to the vowel, and concomitantly in a greater leftward shift of C1 compared to the rightward shift of C2. The variation in coupling strength is assumed to be a natural by-product of a self-organizing system; it may vary between speakers and onset types. Macroscopically, however, syllabic organization in onset is still hypothesized to be characterized by in-phase coupling; on average the vowel-adjacent consonant is expected to shift towards the anchorpoint with increasing complexity in onsets but not for codas. Secondly, the authors propose that further cluster-specific timing effects may arise if not all gestures of an onset cluster are coupled to the vowel; different onset types may differ in their coupling topologies. The authors argue that the place order effect in Georgian may arise due to either the closure or release phase of the consonant being coupled in-phase to the vowel. This builds on Nam's recently developed version of gestural theory in which the closure and release phases of consonants are modeled as separate gestures (Browman, 1994; Nam, 2007a). Conceivably, the interaction of C1 voicing and remote consonant shift we observed for our onset clusters could be modeled in a similar fashion, yet how to accommodate the difference between /pl-/ and /km-/ in the current data is not immediately clear.

The two mechanisms proposed by Goldstein et al. (2008) render the gestural syllable model a very powerful one, likely at the expense of predictive power. At the same time, it opens up the possibility for syllabic constituency and syllable affiliation to be a gradient phenomenon through continuous variation in coupling strength and also through different coupling topologies allowing, for instance, for not all gestures of an onset to participate in all coupling relations. Yet it will be a challenge

predestined to enhance our understanding of syllable and cluster timing.

to tease apart what kinds of timing patterns best be modeled on the basis of coupling strength versus coupling topology differences. Goldstein et al. argue that consistency across speakers may be a criterion for identifying coupling topology differences, coupling strength should vary more gradiently between speakers. At this point the basic assumption is maintained that consonant-vowel coupling in onsets is strictly in-phase and that any syllable position timing effects can be modeled on the basis of in-phase and anti-phase coupling relations only. The reason to strictly allow only two phasing patterns lies in the commitment to tie linguistic and physiological markedness together. This way, coupling relations provide a basic markedness metric: the more anti-phase coupling relations, the more 'marked' a cluster is hypothesized to be (Nam, 2007a). Such predictions should then be testable against acquisition data or patterns of sound change. The data presented here do not follow the assumption that deviations from the preferred coupling mode are inherently marked physiologically as well as phonologically; there is no immediate evidence that in German the markedness status of clusters varies as a function of voicing or place order[6]. However, for the view that /kn-/ clusters in German are more marked than /kl-/, see Bombien (2011). How these patterns could be modeled in terms of coupling relations and to tease apart the manifold factors influencing articulatory timing therefore remains an important topic for future research.

In sum, while there may be a greater range of factors contributing to intergestural timing relations than originally included in the gestural model of syllable structure, the most important insight that has emerged from the articulatory work on syllable structure over the past 30 years is that syllabic structure is expressed in (or, is epiphenomenal to) intergestural timing relations. The syllable is part of a larger prosodic hierarchy, and complex timing interactions between prosodic levels can be expected, just as much as a language's rhythmic structure might affect articulatory timing within the syllable (Saltzman et al., 2008; Shaw et al., 2009; Smith, 1995). Also the role or synergistic effects that the liquid data point to warrant further investigation.

6 It should be mentioned here that /km-/ generally does not exist in German; it only occurs in the word *Khmer*, the name of the people of Cambodia.

Thus detailed combined empirical and modeling studies are called for in order to understand how multiple levels of timing may interact to give rise to universal, language- and cluster-specific aspects of articulatory timing.

5 Acknowledgements

This work was supported by grant PO 1269/1-1 of the Deutsche Forschungsgemeinschaft. Thank you to my colleagues in Munich as well as to the organizers and participants of the Planning and Dynamics Summer School for many interesting discussions. Manfred Pastätter, Aleksandra Bigaji and Susanne Waltl have been of much assistance during data collection and analysis.

References

Baayen, R. H. (2008). *Analyzing Linguistic Data: A Practical Introduction to Statistics Using R.* Cambridge University Press, Cambridge.

Bombien, L. (2011). *Segmental and prosodic aspects in the production of consonant clusters.* PhD thesis, Institute of Phonetics and Speech Processing, Ludwig-Maximilians Universität, Faculty of Languages and Literatures, Munich, Germany. http://edoc.ub.uni-muenchen.de/12840/1/Bombien_Lasse.pdf.

Bombien, L. and Hoole, P. (2011). Articulatory overlap in French and German mixed-voicing clusters. *Paper presented at the 9th International Seminar on Speech Production, Montréal, Canada.*

Bombien, L., Mooshammer, C., Hoole, P., and Kühnert, B. (2010). Prosodic segmental effects on EPG contact patterns of word-initial German clusters. *Journal of Phonetics,* 38(3):388–403.

Browman, C. P. (1994). Lip aperture and consonant releases. In Keating, P. A., editor, *Phonological Structure and Phonetic Form. Papers in Laboratory Phonology III,* pages 331–353. Cambridge, Cambridge University Press.

Browman, C. P. and Goldstein, L. (1988). Some notes on syllable structure in Articulatory Phonology. *Phonetica,* 45(2-4):140–155.

Browman, C. P. and Goldstein, L. (1995). Gestural syllable position effects in American English. In Bell-Berti, F. and Raphael, L. J., editors, *Producing Speech: Contemporary Issues,* pages 19–33. AIP Press, Woodbury NY.

Browman, C. P. and Goldstein, L. (2000). Competing constraints on intergestural coordination and self-organization of phonological structures. *Bulletin de la Communication Parlée*, 5:25–34.

Butcher, A. (2006). Australian Aboriginal languages: Consonant-salient phonologies and the 'place of ariculation' imperative. In Harrington, J. and Tabain, M., editors, *Speech Production: Models, Phonetic Processes and Techniques*, pages 187–210. Psychology Press, New York.

Byrd, D. (1995). C-centers revisited. *Phonetica*, 52:285–306.

Carter, P. (2003). Extrinsic phonetic interpretation: Spectral variation in English liquids. In Local, J., Ogden, R., and Temple, R., editors, *Papers in Laboratory Phonology VI: Phonetic Interpretation*, pages 237–252. Cambridge University Press, Cambridge.

Chitoran, I. and Goldstein, L. (2006). Testing the phonological status of perceptual recoverability: Articulatory evidence from Georgian. *Poster presented at the 10th Conference on Laboratory Phonology, Paris.*

Chitoran, I., Goldstein, L., and Byrd, D. (2002). Gestural overlap and recoverability: Articulatory evidence from Georgian. In Gussenhoven, C., Rietveld, T., and Warner, N., editors, *Papers in Laboratory Phonology 7*. Mouton de Gruyter, Berlin.

Fowler, C. (1980). Coarticulation and theories of extrinsic timing. *Journal of Phonetics*, 8:113–133.

Giles, S. B. and Moll, K. L. (1975). Cinefluorographic study of selected allophones of English /l/. *Phonetica*, 31:206–227.

Goldstein, L., Byrd, D., and Saltzman, E. (2006). The role of vocal tract gestural action units in understanding the evolution of phonology. In Arbib, M., editor, *From Action to Language: The Mirror Neuron System*, pages 215–249. Cambridge University Press, Cambridge.

Goldstein, L., Chitoran, I., and Selkirk, E. (2007). Syllable structure as coupled oscillator modes: Evidence from Georgian vs. Tashlhiyt Berber. In *Proceedings of the XVI International Congress of Phonetic Sciences, Saarbrücken, Germany*, pages 241–244.

Goldstein, L., Nam, H., Saltzman, E., and Chitoran, I. (2008). Coupled oscillator planning model of speech timing and syllable structure. In *Proceedings of the 8th Phonetic Conference of China and the International Symposium on Phonetic Frontiers, Beijing*.

Hermes, A., Grice, M., Mücke, D., and Niemann, H. (2008). Articulatory indicators of syllable affiliation in word initial consonant clusters in Italian. In *Proceedings of the 8th International Seminar of Speech Production, Strasbourg*, pages 433–436.

Honorof, D. and Browman, C. P. (1995). The center or the edge: How are consonant clusters organized with respect to the vowel? In *Proceedings of the XIIIth International Congress of the Phonetic Sciences, Stockholm*, volume 3, pages 552–555.

Hoole, P. (2006). Experimental Studies of Laryngeal Articulation. Habilitationsschrift, Institute of Phonetics and Speech Processing, Ludwig-Maximilians Universität, Faculty of Languages and Literatures, Munich, Germany.

Hyman, L. (2008). Universals in phonology. *Linguistic Review*, 25(1/2):83–137.

Hyman, L. (2011). Does Gokana really have no syllables? Or: What's so great about being universal? *Phonology*, 28:55–85.

Iskarous, K., Shadle, C., and Proctor, M. (2011). Articulatory-acoustic kinematics: The production of American English /s/. *Journal of the Acoustical Society of America*, 129(2):944–954.

Kelso, J. A. S. (1995). *Dynamic Patterns. The Self-Organization of Brain and Behavior.* MIT Press, Cambridge MA.

Kelso, J. A. S., Saltzman, E. L., and Tuller, B. (1986). The dynamical perspective on speech production: Data and theory. *Journal of Phonetics*, 14:29–59.

Kühnert, B., Hoole, P., and Mooshammer, C. (2006). Gestural overlap and c-center in selected French consonant clusters. In *Proceedings of ISSP '06-7th International Seminar on Speech Production, Brazil.*

Löfqvist, A. and Gracco, V. L. (1999). Interarticulator programming in VCV sequences: Lip and tongue movements. *Journal of the Acoustical Society of America*, 105(3):1864–1876.

Marin, S. (2011). Organization of complex onsets in Romanian. In *Proceedings of the 9th International Seminar on Speech Production, Montréal, Canada*, pages 179–186.

Marin, S. and Pouplier, M. (2010). Temporal organization of complex onsets and codas in American English: Testing the predictions of a gestural coupling model. *Motor Control*, 14(3):380–407.

Nam, H. (2007a). *Gestural coupling model of syllable structure.* PhD thesis, Yale University.

Nam, H. (2007b). Syllable-level intergestural timing model: Split-gesture dynamics focusing on positional asymmetry and moraic structure. In Cole, J. and Hualde, I., editors, *Papers in Laboratory Phonology 9*, pages 483–506. Mouton de Gruyter, Berlin.

Nam, H., Goldstein, L., and Saltzman, E. (2009). Self-organization of syllable structure: A coupled oscillator model. In Pellegrino, F., Marisco, E., Chitoran, I., and Coupé, C., editors, *Approaches to Phonological Complexity*, pages 299–328. Mouton de Gruyter, Berlin.

Nam, H. and Saltzman, E. (2003). A competitive, coupled oscillator model of syllable structure. In *Proceedings of the XVth International Congress of the Phonetic Sciences, Barcelona, Spain*, pages 2253–2256.

Öhmann, S. E. (1966). Coarticulation in VCV utterances: Spectrographic measurements. *Journal of the Acoustical Society of America*, 39(1):151–168.

Öhmann, S. E. (1967). Numerical model of coarticulation. *Journal of the Acoustical Society of America*, 41:310–320.

Pouplier, M. and Beňuš, S. (2011). On the phonetic status of syllabic consonants: Evidence from Slovak. *Journal of Laboratory Phonology*, 2(2).

Recasens, D., Pallarès, M. D., and Fontdevila, J. (1997). A model of lingual coarticulation based on articulatory constraints. *Journal of the Acoustical Society of America*, 102(1):544–561.

Recasens, D., Pallarès, M. D., and Fontdevila, J. (1998). An electropalatographic and acoustic study of temporal coarticulation for Catalan dark /l/ and German clear /l/. *Phonetica*, 55:53–79.

Saltzman, E. and Munhall, K. G. (1989). A dynamical approach to gestural patterning in speech production. *Ecological Psychology*, 1:333–382.

Saltzman, E., Nam, H., Krivokapic, J., and Goldstein, L. (2008). A task-dynamic toolkit for modeling the effects of prosodic structure on articulation. In Barbosa, P. and Madureira, S., editors, *Proceedings of the Speech Prosody 2008 Conference, Campinas, Brazil*, pages 175–259.

Scobbie, J. and Pouplier, M. (2010). The role of syllable structure in external sandhi: An EPG study of vocalisation and retraction of word-final English /l/. *Journal of Phonetics*, 38(2):240–259.

Shaw, J., Gafos, A., Hoole, P., and Zeroual, C. (2009). Temporal evidence for syllabic structure in Moroccan Arabic: Data and model. *Phonology*, 26:187–215.

Smith, C. (1995). Prosodic patterns in the coordination of vowel and consonant gestures. In Connell, B. and Arvaniti, A., editors, *Phonology and Phonetic Evidence. Papers in Laboratory Phonology IV*, pages 205–222. Cambridge University Press, Cambridge.

Vallée, N., Rossato, S., and Rousset, I. (2009). Favoured syllabic patterns in the world's languages and sensorimotor constraints. In Pellegrino, F., Marisco, E., Chitoran, I., and Coupé, C., editors, *Approaches to Phonological Complexity*, pages 111–139. Mouton de Gruyter, Berlin.

Waltl, S. and Marin, S. (2010). Temporal organization of three-consonant onset clusters in American English. *Poster presented at Laboratory Phonology 12, Albuquerque, New Mexico*.

6 Appendix

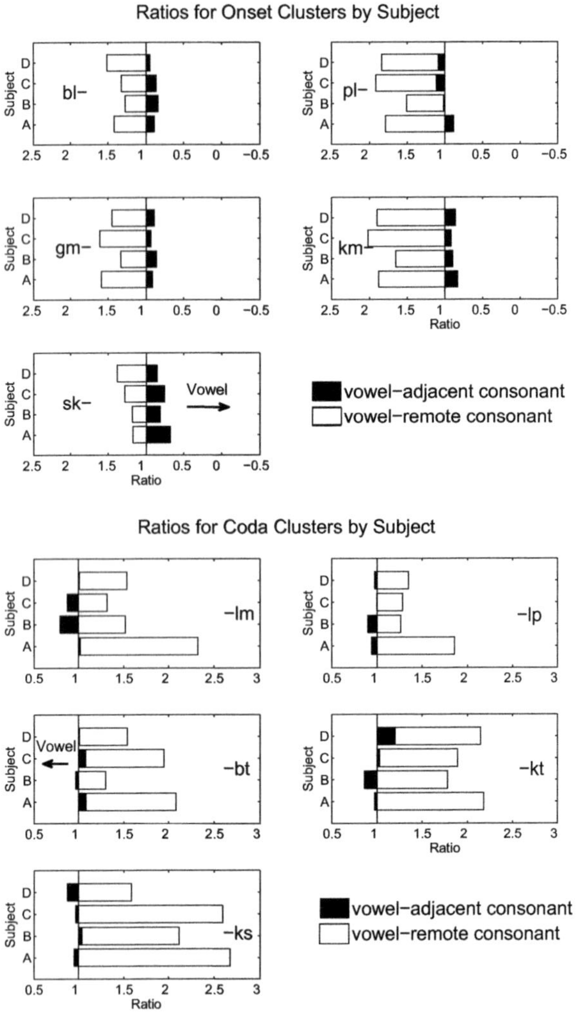

Figure 5: Ratios for onset and coda clusters by set and by subject. Ratios <1 mean that the vowel-adjacent consonant has shifted closer to the anchorpoint between singleton and cluster conditions. Onsets are shown at the top, codas at the bottom.

Producing spoken sentences: The scope of incremental planning

LINDA WHEELDON

Abstract: The production of spoken sentences involves the generation of a number of levels of representation: a conceptual representation for the message we wish to convey, a grammatical representation that determines an appropriate word order for that message, and phonological and phonetic representations to guide articulation. In normal speech, these representations can be generated and articulated at rates of several words per second. To account for such processing speed, models of sentence production propose that speech is planned incrementally, so that the articulation of early parts of an utterance occurs in parallel with the planning of upcoming segments. However, exactly how processing at different levels is co-ordinated remains a matter of dispute. In particular, there is disagreement about how much of an utterance must be generated at a particular level of representation before processing at the next level can begin. The focus of this paper is on the timing of early conceptual and grammatical encoding processes. A series of experiments is reviewed, which used reaction-time methodologies to investigate the production of sentences in English and Japanese. The aim of the experiments was to determine the scope of advanced planning prior to sentence onset and to investigate the relationship between conceptual and grammatical processes.

1 Introduction

In order to produce sentences we must translate some non-linguistic idea into an articulated utterance. All models of speech production postulate that this translation process occurs in a number of successive steps (Bock and Levelt, 1994; Garrett, 1980a,b; Levelt, 1989, 1992; Pickering and Branigan, 1998; Chang, 2002; Chang et al., 2006; Ferreira and Slevc, 2007). The starting point is a conceptual structure for an utterance that details the information the speaker wants to convey. This representation is usually called the message (Levelt, 1989). There is very little agreement about how messages are structured. However, the current view is that messages are non-linear and must at least contain conceptual category information and have a thematic structure with concepts assigned to thematic roles.

So for example, the message for the sentence *Anne kissed Peter* would comprise an agent-Anne performing an action-kiss on a patient-Peter. Arguably, the message must contain all the information required by a given language to form a legal utterance e.g., mood, focus, time etc. (Levelt, 1989). The message triggers grammatical encoding processes, which select the appropriate lexical items and generate a syntactic structure to fix their linear order. Finally, the phonological and phonetic structure of the utterance must be generated to guide articulation. This chapter will focus on planning during conceptual and grammatical encoding. The main issue to be addressed concerns the way in which these processes proceed over time, and in particular how much processing occurs prior to the onset of articulation.

1.1 Incremental processing

The speed with which we can articulate complex sentences makes it unlikely that the processing of each component level of representation is completed for the entire sentence before processing at the next begins. Instead, most current models of language production propose that processing at all levels occurs in an incremental fashion (e.g., Kempen and Hoenkamp, 1987; Levelt, 1989, 1992). In Levelt's (1989) blueprint for the speaker, utterances are produced in a piecemeal fashion, with early parts of the utterance being articulated while we plan upcoming parts. For example, if a speaker wished to produce the sentence *Rosa and James danced together last night*, prior to articulation they would have to build the conceptual, grammatical and phonological structures they needed. If they did this incrementally they might first retrieve the information relating to the agents, *Rosa and James*. While the agent information was being grammatically encoded, the speaker might conceptualise the action information *danced together*, and during the articulation of the phrase *Rosa and James* the speaker could simultaneously grammatically encode the action and conceptualise the time information *last night*, and so on. In such an incremental system, some conceptual processing must have occurred before grammatical processing can begin, but different pieces of the same utterance can be conceptually and grammatically processed in parallel.

Levelt (1989) argues that an incremental production system is attractive for a number of reasons. It can explain the fluency of speech because it allows the fast release of formulated chunks of the utterance for articulation and spreads the processing load efficiently across several different processors. Incremental processing also reduces the need for the temporary storage of completed chunks of the utterance thereby reducing processing costs. Nevertheless, short-term storage capacity could sometimes be necessary as the order in which the message chunks are released might not be the same as the order required by grammatical encoding processes. For example, the sentence *Rosa and James last night danced together* is not grammatical in English. Therefore, any model of sentence production that outputs language in this piecemeal fashion must also explain how the system determines the correct order of chunks for output. We will return to this issue in section 2.3.

1.2 The scope of advanced planning

Any detailed incremental model of language production must specify, for each processing level, the minimal chunk of information it constructs and delivers as output. Of course planning increments for particular levels of processing will vary in a language dependent way as languages have different backward dependencies that may affect the lower limit of processing scope. For example, in many languages the form of a determiner (e.g., *the*) is dependent on the grammatical gender of the noun it refers to (e.g., *das Auto*, the car/*die Blume*, the flower). This means that a speaker would need to retrieve the noun before they could select the correct determiner. Languages also have colocational dependencies between words that can affect word choice in a backward dependent way e.g., in English it is grammatical to say things like *sink into oblivion* or *fall into disuse* but do not *fall into oblivion* or *sink into disuse* (see Smith, 2000, for a discussion). Such idiomatic phrases generate similar amounts of structural priming as non-idiomatic phrases (Konopka and Bock, 2008) suggesting that their structure is planned on-line during production in the same way, rather than being stored as lexical items.

It is also possible, of course, that the scope of advanced planning might vary in a context or speaker dependent way. There are some findings that suggest we can alter our planning scope to a limited extent under different conditions of time pressure (Ferreira and Swets, 2002) or due to variations in some forms of cognitive load (Wagner et al., 2010) and working memory load (Slevc, 2011). Moreover, individual differences in working memory have been shown to affect processing scope in language comprehension (Swets et al., 2007), and such factors are also likely to influence advanced planning scope in production. The research we describe below does not aim to address these issues. Instead we asked random samples of normal speakers to generate fluent sentences, beginning as quickly as possible. The scope of advanced planning observed under these conditions is arguably optimal for speed and fluency and, as we argue below, provides important constraints on cognitive models of language production.

There is still a great deal of disagreement about exactly how big the planning units are at different levels of processing. It is, of course, not necessary that the scope of processing remains the same at each level. Indeed many models propose that each level has a different processing scope, often with scope decreasing as processing moves closer towards articulation (e.g., Bock and Levelt, 1994; Garrett, 1980a,b; Levelt, 1989). A number of different proposals exist in the literature. Wundt (1900) argued that conceptually a clause must be planned which can then be grammatically encoded in phrasal chunks. In the model proposed by Garrett (1980a,b) and developed by Bock and Levelt (1994), grammatical encoding is lexically driven and requires verb selection. According to this model, there is a clausal scope for lexical access; a speaker retrieves all the open class words for a clause and assigns them to grammatical functions (like subject/or object) before building a syntactic structure. More recently researchers have proposed more tightly incremental word-by-word processing (Griffin, 2001; Levelt and Meyer, 2000; Meyer et al., 1998).

Evidence exists for all of the proposed processing scopes. Planning pauses in speech have been shown to occur more frequently between clauses than clause internally (Butterworth, 1980; Goldman Eisler, 1968). Speech error data have also been used to claim that the words for a whole clause are retrieved prior to speech onset. Word exchange errors such as *this spring has a seat in it* suggest that the exchanging words *spring* and *seat* are retrieved in parallel Garrett (1980a). Similarly, subject-verb agreement errors such as those shown in (1) provide evidence for the clause as a unit of processing. These errors are often caused by the verb agreeing erroneously with a local noun (e.g., *posters are*) rather than the subject noun (e.g., *The slogan is*). Such errors are more likely to occur when the local noun is in the same clause as the verb (1.a) than in a different clause (1.b), again suggesting that elements of a clause are processed in parallel (Bock and Cutting, 1992).

1. a) The slogan on the posters *are* really effective

   b) The boy [that likes the snakes] *are* really happy

It remains unclear, however, at which level of representation the clause functions as a processing unit. The effects described above could occur during conceptual, rather than grammatical processing.
Experimental evidence exists for tighter incremental planning. For example, Schriefers et al. (1998) investigated whether verb retrieval was necessary prior to sentence onset. In their study, German speakers produced descriptions of pictured actions like *The man empties the bucket.* Different grammatical structures were elicited using a sentence completion task, as in (2). A subject-verb-object (SVO) order was elicited in a main clause (2.a). Lead-in phrases were used to elicit different word orders with the same picture; SOV in a subordinate clause (2.b) and VSO following an adverbial (2.c). The critical manipulation was the position of the verb in the sentence.

2. a)	*-Der Mann* ***leert*** *den Eimer* The man empties the bucket
b) *Auf dem nächsten Bild sieht man wie* On the next picture one sees how	*-der Mann den Eimer* ***leert*** the man the bucket empties
c) *Und auf dem nächsten Bild* And on the next picture	*-**leert** der Mann den Eimer* empties the man the bucket

At picture onset, speakers heard and saw distractor verbs, which were semantically related (e.g., *empty*) or unrelated (e.g., *write*) to the verb in the sentence they would produce. In simple picture naming tasks, a semantically related distractor causes interference and slows naming latency (Schriefers et al., 1990). In this experiment, semantic interference slowed sentence production latencies but only when the verb occurred sentence initially (Example 2.c), indicating that the verb had been retrieved prior to sentence onset. When the verb occurred later in the sentence (2.a and 2.b), onset latencies were unaffected by the semantically related distractors. This finding provides strong evidence that, unless it is in sentence initial position, the verb need not be accessed before speech onset.

Evidence for tightly incremental word-by-word processing has come from studies using eye-tracking technology to record the gaze patterns of speakers while they name pictured objects in noun phrases such as *the hat and fork* (e.g., Griffin, 2001; Meyer et al., 1998; Levelt and Meyer, 2000). The looking patterns derived from these studies are very regular. On the majority of trials speakers fixated on the objects in their order of mention and their shift of gaze to the next picture was closely coordinated with articulation, occurring just before the articulation of the first object's name. The amount of time spent looking at an object was affected by lexical and phonological properties of its name, such as word frequency and word length. Speakers also rarely looked ahead at objects to be named later although some peripheral processing of immediately adjacent objects can occur (e.g., Morgan and Meyer, 2005). These findings suggest that we plan each item to the level of phonological encoding before moving the eyes to the next object to be named, with planning progressing only slightly ahead of articulation. However, these experiments usually involved the production of one sentence structure to one fixed pattern of pictures and it is therefore not clear what they tell us about early conceptual and grammatical planning processes. Eye tracking studies, which have elicited varied sentence structures, report that some aspects of the picture arrays or scenes receive an initial scan prior to gaze returning to the initial object to be named. From then on gaze duration and shift is tightly locked to onset of articulation (Griffin and Bock, 2000). Griffin and Bock (2000) have proposed that during the initial fixation, the conceptual content of the utterance is determined prior to the formulation phase during which words are accessed incrementally and phrase structure is built.

2 Testing processing scope during spoken sentence production

2.1 Evidence for a phrasal processing scope

We turn now to a series of experiments conducted by myself and colleagues, which were designed to investigate the scope of advanced planning during spoken sentence production. In particular, we were interested in how much of a sentence a speaker plans before beginning to speak. The experiments therefore use speech onset latencies as the dependent measure. The first experiment was an extension of a study by Levelt and Maassen (1981), who demonstrated that sentence onset latencies were longer for coordinate noun phrases (e.g., *The circle and the square move up*) than for coordinate sentences (e.g., *The circle moves up and the square moves up*). This finding suggests that speakers did not plan the whole of the utterance prior to speech onset, as the coordinate sentences are more complex than the coordinate noun phrases. However, this study is ambiguous as to the scope of the processing unit, which could be the initial phrase or the initial clause.

Smith and Wheeldon (1999) (Experiment 1) designed an experiment to test between lexical, phrasal and clausal processing scopes for sentence production. In our experiment, speakers described arrays of moving pictures from left-to-right and their sentence production latencies were measured. On the critical trials the visual displays elicited two kinds of single clause sentences (see Figure 1). The sentences in Figure 1 do not differ in their total structural complexity and are perfectly matched for lexical complexity. They differ, however, in the complexity of their initial phrase, with one sentence beginning with a coordinate noun phrase (NP) and the other with a simple NP. We were interested in how quickly speakers started to articulate these sentences. There are a number of possibilities: speakers could retrieve the first content word prior to articulation, in which case production latencies for the two sentence types should not differ. Alternatively they could plan the entire clause prior to articulation and again production latencies should not differ. However, if speakers prefer to process the initial phrase prior to articulation, then they should take longer to begin the sentences with initial coordinate NPs than the sentences with initial simple NPs.

Initial coordinate NP The dog and the hat move above the fork

Initial Simple NP The dog moves above the hat and the fork

Figure 1: A picture array from Smith and Wheeldon (1999) and examples of the experimental sentences it was designed to elicit

On each trial, the three pictures were presented simultaneously and began to move immediately either up or down. The movement covered 2.5cm of the screen and was completed in 600ms. The pictures were removed from screen 500ms after response completion and there was a two second inter trial interval. A set of 92 different pictured objects were used and many filler trials were included, with different numbers of pictures and sentence structures, to maximise visual, conceptual and syntactic variability from trial to trial.

In this experiment (and the other experiments discussed below), about 30 participants were tested. They were asked to begin to produce the sentences as quickly as possible without making errors, pauses or hesitations. These instructions reduce variation in the data and encourage speakers to generate their preferred minimal amount of structure prior to speech onset. As we were interested in how speakers produce error free, fluent sentences, all trials with errors and disfluencies were excluded from the analyses of the sentence production latencies.

We observed significantly longer latencies (77ms) to sentences beginning with a coordinate NP than to sentences beginning with a simple NP. This finding is not consistent with a lexical processing scope. Speakers could have initiated sentence production having retrieved the first noun in both sentence types. Instead however, the latencies show that they dedicated more processing time to the initial coordinate NPs than the initial simple NPs. For the same reason, this finding is not consistent with a clausal processing scope as more time is dedicated to elements within the first phrase than to the rest of the clause prior to speech onset. However, this experiment does not reveal at which level of processing a phrasal scope is operating, as the coordinate NP is visually, conceptually, grammatically and phonologically more complex than the simple NP. Further experiments suggest that visual complexity does not contribute significantly to the effect, as the latency difference is not observed when speakers simply name the moving pictures from left-to-right (Wheeldon and Meyer, 2005). Therefore the visual tracking of single or double picture movements does not contribute to the effect. The translation of a visual scene into a spoken sentence is therefore an essential component of the effect.

The issue of phonological complexity is more difficult to deal with. Sentences are produced with rhythm and intonation i.e., prosodic structure, and these structures often coincide with syntactic units. Therefore effects of prosodic and syntactic units are difficult to disentangle. However, there is good evidence the scope of phonological encoding prior to speech onset is at most a single phonological word - a unit that can be larger than a lexical word but with a single stressed syllable (Levelt, 1989; Levelt et al., 1999; Wheeldon and Lahiri, 1997, 2002). The initial phonological word is indeed bigger in the coordinate sentences e.g., [the dog and the]$_\omega$ than the simple sentences e.g. [the dog]$_\omega$, although effects of phonological complexity are usually much smaller (15-20ms) than the effects we have observed (Wheeldon and Lahiri, 1997, 2002). Moreover the effect remains when sentences are matched for phonological structure (Allum and Wheeldon, 2007) (Experiment 1, discussed below).

In addition, it remains possible that the processing scope is not phrasal but lexical and that speakers simply prefer to retrieve the first two content words of a sentence before they begin to speak. The second content word of the simple NP sentences is always the verb "moves" whereas the second content word in the complex NP sentences is a different picture name on each trial. The retrieval of the first two content words of the sentences beginning with the simple NPs would, therefore, be easier than for sentences beginning with complex NPs. To rule out both of these possibilities, Allum and Wheeldon (2007, Experiment1) replicated the experiment in Japanese (see also Martin et al., 2004). We used coloured picture displays to elicit simple and coordinate sentences. Unlike English, the verb final properties of Japanese allow the subject and a complement to take the first two positions in a sentence, as can be seen in the example sentences in (3). Japanese is a topic-comment language and the topic is marked by the particle *wa*. This means that from left-to-right, the Japanese sentences are perfectly matched for lexical and phonological complexity. Nevertheless, Japanese speakers were significantly slower to initiate the coordinate NP sentences than the simple NP sentences (by 32ms). The finding replicates the English experiment described above and provides strong support for the claim that the latency effect is due to the structure of the sentence initial phrase rather than to differences in lexical and/or phonological structure.

3. a) [INU to BOUSHI wa] FOOKU no ue ni arimasu
[Dog and hat TOP] fork above are
The dog and the hat are above the fork

b) [INU wa] BOUSHI to FOOKU no ue ni arimasu
[Dog TOP] hat and fork above is
The dog is above the hat and the fork

2.2 Conceptual or grammatical units?

The experiments reviewed so far provide evidence that a phrasal scope operates at some early conceptual or grammatical level of processing during sentence production. However, the sentences tested so far cannot reveal at which level of processing this scope operates. This is because they don't allow us to distinguish between different grammatical and conceptual structures. Both the simple and the coordinate sentence initial NPs in our sentences correspond to two major grammatical units: the subject phrase and the head of the subject phrase. They also correspond to a major conceptual unit: the theme or actor.

In order to distinguish between the grammatical options, Allum and Wheeldon (2007, Experiment 2) tested whether the entire subject phrase is the preferred minimal scope of processing prior to speech onset. In this experiment two sentence types were compared (see Example (4) below). The subject phrase in sentence (4.a) again comprises a coordinate NP with both nouns acting as hierarchically equal heads. In sentence

(4.b) the subject phrase is more complex, comprising a head noun phrase and a modifying prepositional phrase (PP).

4. a) Coordinate NP sentences [The fork and the dog] are blue

   b) PP sentences [The fork above the dog] is blue

If the planning scope is the first complete verb argument phrase (i.e., the whole subject phrase), then speech onsets for the two sentence types should be similar, or perhaps longer for the PP sentences, due to their greater syntactic complexity. If the planning scope can span a unit smaller than a whole verb argument phrase, such as the head of the subject phrase, then latencies to the coordinate NP sentences should be longer than to PP sentences. We found that latencies to coordinate NP sentences were significantly longer (by 102ms) than latencies to the PP sentences. This finding provides evidence that speakers did not encode the whole of a subject phrase prior to articulation but instead planned a smaller unit such as the head of the subject phrase.
However, we still do not know if the planning unit is determined by conceptual or grammatical factors. Is the planning unit equal to a major conceptual unit (e.g. the theme) or simply the first grammatical phrase to be produced? English is a head-initial language, which means that the head of the subject phrase comes first. The head of the subject phrase also plays a central thematic role - as the agent or theme of the message. So for English, conceptual and grammatical units are confounded. In contrast, Japanese is a head-final language, therefore within the subject phrase, subsidiary phrases occur before the subject head. For example, in the Japanese sentence *the fork above the dog is blue* the modifying PP *above the dog* precedes the subject head *the fork*. Allum and Wheeldon (2007) used the head-final characteristics of Japanese to determine whether processing scope corresponds to the sentence initial grammatical phrase or the head of the subject phrase and theme (Experiment 3). In this experiment, we again used colour coded pictures to elicit the sentences we wanted. In these sentences we progressively extended the initial PP relative to the head phrase, while keeping the overall subject phrase length the same (see Example 5).

5. a) KANI no ue no YAKAN to TSUKUE to PANDA wa aka DESU
[crab above] kettle and desk and panda TOP red ARE
The kettle and the desk and the panda above the crab are red

b) KANI to YAKAN no ue no TSUKUE to PANDA wa aka DESU
[crab and kettle above] desk and panda TOP red ARE
The desk and the panda above the crab and the kettle are red

c) KANI to YAKAN to TSUKUE no ue no PANDA wa aka DESU
[crab and kettle and desk above] panda TOP red IS
The panda above the crab and the kettle and the desk is red

If Japanese speakers can initiate articulation having processed the first grammatical phrase then sentence production latencies should increase as the length of the PP increases (from 5.a to 5.c). However, if they have to process up to the head of the subject phrase, a major thematic unit, then latencies to all sentence types should not differ as the subject phrases in all sentences are matched for overall length and complexity. We found that sentence onset latencies increased by approximately 50ms with each noun added to the sentence initial PP. This result suggests that the initial syntactic phrase is more thoroughly processed at some stage than the whole subject phrase.

The experiments described so far allow us to draw a number of conclusions. First, the scope of the process we are tapping into is not the whole subject phrase or theme. Instead, speakers can initiate sentence production having processed a sentence initial phrase. Moreover, sentence onset latency is determined by the size of this initial phrase irrespective of the thematic or grammatical role it plays in the sentence to be produced; similar effects are observed in Japanese and English, despite differences between the two languages in the ordering of head and subsidiary phrases. Critically, these ordering differences are determined by *grammatical convention* alone and do not mirror the conceptual saliency of the information. It would be odd to suggest that the information in a subsidiary preposition phrase was conceptually more salient to Japanese speakers than the topic of the sentence. These findings therefore suggest that the locus of the effect is in the process of *grammatical* encoding.

2.3 The scope of lexical access

We turn now to the question of the scope of lexical access. Does the phrasal scope we have shown so far determine the scope of lexical access prior to articulation? This is an important question as the answer has consequences for the modeling of grammatical encoding processes. Critically, if the scope of grammatical encoding is a phrase and this scope controls lexical access in advance of articulation then how does a non-linear conceptual message ensure the correct order of lexical access for output?

In traditional, lexically-driven models, the order of lexical activation is driven by the conceptual weighting of lexical concepts (Bock and Levelt, 1994; Levelt, 1989, 1992; Pickering and Branigan, 1998). So for example, in a given thematic structure, the agent or theme might be the most salient concept. This would cause its associated lexical item to become most highly activated and therefore be assigned to the subject role in the sentence to be produced. Once this grammatical function assignment has occurred, syntactic structure can be built in an incremental fashion. For example consider again the sentence *Anne kissed Peter*. If the agent *Anne* was conceptually most salient then the lexical representation of *Anne* would become highly active and be assigned the subject role, resulting in an active sentence. However, if for some reason the patient *Peter* was conceptually most salient, then its lexical representation would receive the most activation causing it to be assigned the subject role, resulting in the passive sentence *Peter was kissed by Anne*.

However, conceptual weighting cannot explain the ordering of activation of lexical items for a sentence initial modifying phrase (e.g., *above the dog*). In this situation, no clear conceptual weighting factor such as salience, animacy or focus is in operation. The required order of activation is based on a purely grammatical convention. So if, prior to utterance onset, lexical access occurs only for an initial subsidiary phrase, then it must be possible for syntactic processes to interact directly with conceptual processes to ensure the correct order of activation of lexical items. Data showing a phrasal scope of lexical access can, therefore, provide evidence against a lexically mediated approach to the generation of syntax and for an approach that allows word ordering prior to lexical access.

Recently models have been proposed that allow syntactic structure to be generated based on thematic structure without reference to lexical content (Chang, 2002; Chang et al., 2000, 2006). In these models, the process of lexical selection is kept completely separate from syntactic sequencing decisions. The selected lexical concepts activate their associated lexical items but this activation process is blind to the thematic role of the lexical concept. This means that the word for the concept *Anne* will be activated in the same way regardless of the thematic role it plays in the message. The most appropriate word order is determined by the thematic structure and the speakers acquired syntactic knowledge. In this model, therefore, syntactic structure can be generated prior to, and independently of, lexical access.
Allum and Wheeldon (2009) argued that if the scope of grammatical encoding defines the scope of lexical access, then in the PP subject phrases only the first noun should be retrieved prior to speech onset for both Japanese and English speakers - irrespective of the role it plays in the sentence. We tested this claim using a picture preview technique. The sequence of events on each trial is shown in Figure 2.

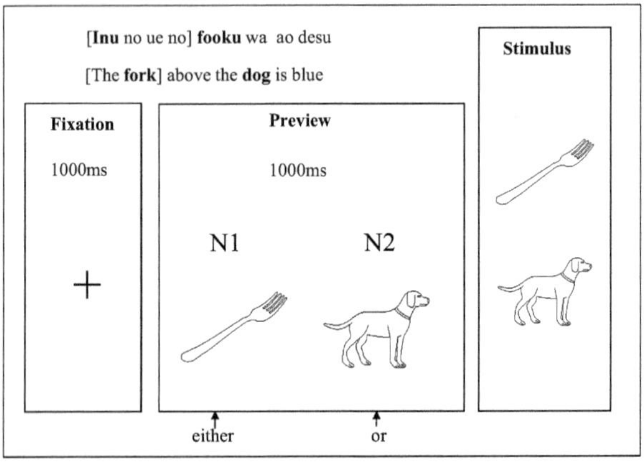

Figure 2: Sequence of events on a picture preview trial (Allum and Wheeldon, 2009).

On each trial, speakers first saw a fixation cross. This was replaced for one second by either a blank screen or by one of the pictures subjects would have to use in the sentence they were about to produce. Finally subjects saw the visual display they should describe and their speech onset latencies were recorded. Pictures were previewed on one third of all trials and speakers knew that the previewed picture would always occur in the upcoming sentence to be produced. Again a large number of filler trials were used to vary the syntactic structures produced as well as the visual and sentence positions of the previewed pictures. We reasoned that, if during the production of the target sentences, the preview picture name was retrieved prior to speech onset, then we should see a preview benefit in the sentence production latencies. In other words, if you need to retrieve the word *fork* before you can start your sentence, then having already retrieved its name during the preview period should speed you up. The target sentences included a simple subject phrase head and a subsidiary PP (see Figure 2). Pictures were previewed in the first or the second phrase of the target sentences and the same experiment was run in both English and Japanese. The results are summarised in Table 1. As can be seen, sentence production latencies were significantly faster when the sentence initial picture was previewed. However, there was no significant facilitation due to the preview of a picture that occurred in the second phrase. This pattern of results was the same for English and Japanese speakers.

Table 1: The results of Allum and Wheeldon (2009), Experiments 4 and 5: Picture preview in prepositional phrase sentences in English and Japanese. Mean RTs and percentage error rates (in parentheses) are shown for the three Picture preview conditions, as is the difference between unpreviewed and previewed conditions. Significant effects are marked with an asterisk.

	JAPANESE		ENGLISH	
Condition	RT (%err)	RT Diff	RT (%err)	RT Diff
No Preview	916 (5.2)		1080 (8.3)	
Preview (N1)	740 (5.5)	176*	992 (6.7)	88*
Preview (N2)	908 (7.0)	8	1084 (8.7)	-4

This pattern of results mirrors that of the scope experiments reviewed in the previous section, in that it is consistent with the claim that only the

lexical items for the first phrase of a sentence need to be retrieved prior to speech onset. However, it is possible that this is a purely methodological effect. Perhaps previewing non-initial information simply has the effect of confusing speakers thereby slowing them down and masking any preview benefit for the second noun. Alternatively, if the second noun to be produced is highly active due to preview, it might compete with the first noun to be produced for selection, again slowing sentence onset latencies.
However, if the scope of lexical access is really determined by phrase structure then we should see a different pattern of preview effects for coordinate NP sentences (Example 6), which should show a facilitatory effect of preview for both first and second nouns.

6. a) [Inu to fooku wa] ao desu

   b) [The dog and the fork] are blue

The results of the coordinate NP experiments are shown in Table 2. The pattern of results is very different to that for the prepositional phrase sentences.

Table 2: The results of Allum and Wheeldon (2009), Experiments 1 and 3: Picture preview in coordinate NP sentences in English and Japanese. Mean RTs and percentage error rates (in parentheses) are shown for the three Picture preview conditions, as is the difference between unpreviewed and previewed conditions. Significant effects are marked with an asterisk.

	JAPANESE		ENGLISH	
Condition	RT (%err)	RT Diff	RT (%err)	RT Diff
No Preview	1084 (8.0)		955 (11.2)	
Preview (N1)	962 (7.0)	122*	835 (6.7)	120*
Preview (N2)	1036 (7.5)	48*	895 (6.9)	60*

Now there is a significant facilitation of sentence production latencies due to preview of both first and second nouns and once again the results for Japanese and English speakers are very similar. The preview effect for initial nouns is significantly larger than that for second nouns, showing an added benefit of preview for words to be produced first. Critically, however, the second noun also shows a preview benefit when it occurs in the first coordinate NP of the sentence. Together, the preview experiments provide evidence that speakers retrieve the nouns for the first phrase of a sentence before they begin to produce it.

The final experiment I want to describe was designed to rule out an alternative explanation for the findings of the preview experiments described above. In these experiments, the required sentence structures were elicited using displays in which the phrase constituency of the pictured objects was determined by colour grouping. Colour is a very salient perceptual feature. Is it possible therefore, that the preview effect was determined by colour grouping rather than by grammatical grouping? We were able to test this possibility in Japanese because this language has two different forms of coordination. The experiments described so far made use of *To..wa* coordination, as in Example 6 above. *To* typically binds the two items closely as a set and *wa* often functions contrastively. The coordinated items are therefore bound as a unit and contrasted with other items. Alternatively, it is possible in Japanese to use *mo..mo* or a 'listing' coordination as in Example 7 below. This form of coordination has a looser binding both conceptually and syntactically and is not contrastive in function.

7. [Inu mo fooku mo] ao desu
   The dog and the fork are blue

The items in the *mo..mo* coordination play the same thematic role as in the *to..wa* coordination but the concept is different. In the sentence *Keio University and Waseda University are excellent* the *to..wa* coordination would imply that these universities are both excellent in contrast to others. The *mo..mo* coordination would imply that these two Universities are excellent as well as other universities. The two kinds of coordination also have different effects on the scope of application of adjectives. In the sentence *The red chair and the desk are made of wood* the *to..wa* coordination would extent the colour adjective to apply to the second noun whereas the *mo..mo* coordination would not. These differences led us to think that the two forms of coordination might also differ in their scope of lexical access with the two constituent simple NPs in the *mo..mo* coordination behaving as separate units. We therefore reran the Japanese coordinate NP preview experiment but simply asked speakers to use *mo..mo* coordination. Importantly, however the same colour coded visual display was used to elicit the *mo..mo* coordination as had been used to elicit the *to..wa* coordination. The results can be seen in Table 3.

Table 3: The results of Allum and Wheeldon (2009), Experiment 2: Picture preview in mo…mo coordinate NP sentences in Japanese. Mean RTs and percentage error rates (in parentheses) are shown for the three Picture preview conditions, as is the difference between unpreviewed and previewed conditions. Significant effects are marked with an asterisk.

Condition	RT (%err)	RT Diff
No Preview	1006 (4.7)	
Preview (N1)	934 (3.9)	72*
Preview (N2)	1036 (2.3)	-30

Mo..mo coordination yielded a very different pattern of results to *to..wa* coordination despite the use of visually identical displays to elicit the sentences. First noun preview again significantly speeded sentence production latencies compared to no preview. However, second noun preview slowed sentence production latencies, although not significantly. This pattern of results provides strong support for our claim that syntactic rather than visual grouping determines the scope of lexical access during sentence production.

3 Conclusion

The series of experiments I have reviewed provide evidence in support of a number of claims about the scope of advanced planning during spoken sentence production. First, they provide strong evidence that language production is incremental. All of the experiments show that more processing time is devoted to the beginning of an utterance prior to speech onset, than to the utterance as a whole. These experiments also provide information about the nature of the minimal unit speakers prefer to plan before beginning their utterances. This unit proved to be a phrasal chunk, which did not correspond to a minimal syntactic phrase such as the first noun phrase of a coordinate NP. The experiments show repeatedly, that speakers preferred to process the whole of a coordinate NP prior to speech onset, as latencies to sentences beginning with coordinate NPs were consistently slower than latencies to sentences beginning with simple NPs. The data also show that the processing unit does not necessarily correspond to a major grammatical unit such as the subject phrase or its head element. Nor does it correspond to a major thematic unit such as agent or theme. The Japanese experiments demonstrate that speakers can initiate their utterance having processed a sentence initial prepositional phrase, which plays a subordinate role both thematically and grammatically. It is not necessary to access the lemma for the head of the subject phrase prior to speech onset. Crucially, the sentence initial placement of the preposition phrase in Japanese is a *grammatical* convention determined by the head-final syntax of the language. We therefore argued that the phrasal scope of processing we observed operates at the level of grammatical encoding. Nevertheless, it remains problematic to find a satisfactory definition for the processing unit our experiments have identified (see Allum and Wheeldon, 2007, for a discussion). Although the evidence suggests that the unit operates at the level of grammatical encoding, its definition seems to require some reference to thematic structure as there is no clear syntactic definition. The unit is not a minimal syntactic phrase which would be a simple NP (e.g., *The dog*) in all of the sentences we have tested. Instead, it seems to be a phrasal unit corresponding to a thematic unit in the message - not necessarily a verb-argument role but perhaps minimal thematic unit such as a modifier. The experiments testing the different forms of coordination in Japanese manipulated the degree of both conceptual and syntactic binding. It remains unclear how each of these levels of structure contribute to different effects observed for the two forms.

Our experiments also provide information about the relationship between conceptual and grammatical encoding. The picture preview experiment tested the scope of lexical access prior to sentence onset. These experiments provided evidence to suggest that the phrasal scope, identified in previous experiments, determines the extent of lexical access prior to articulation. This finding is critical for the modelling of sentence production as it supports a model in which syntactic linearization processes precede lexical access processes, with the former guiding the latter.

References

Allum, P. and Wheeldon, L. R. (2007). Planning scope in spoken sentence production: The role of grammatical units. *Journal of Experimental Psychology: Learning Memory and Cognition*, 33(4):791–810.

Allum, P. and Wheeldon, L. R. (2009). Scope of lexical access in spoken sentence production: Implications for the conceptual-syntactic interface. *Journal of Experimental Psychology: Learning Memory and Cognition*, 35(5):1240–1255.

Bock, J. K. and Cutting, J. C. (1992). Regulating mental energy: Performance units in language production. *Memory and Language*, 31:99–127.

Bock, J. K. and Levelt, W. J. M. (1994). Language production: Grammatical encoding. In Gernsbacher, M., editor, *Handbook of Psycholinguistics*, pages 945–984. Academic Press, New York.

Butterworth, B. (1980). Evidence from pauses in speech. In Butterworth, B., editor, *Language Production: Vol.1. Speech and Talk*, pages 155–176. Academic Press, London.

Chang, F. (2002). Symbolically speaking: A connectionist model of sentence production. *Cognitive Science*, 26:609–651.

Chang, F., Dell, G. S., Bock, J. K., and Griffin, Z. M. (2000). Structural priming as implicit learning: A comparison of models of sentence production. *Journal of Psycholinguistic Research*, 29:217–229.

Chang, F., Dell, G. S., and Bock, K. (2006). Becoming syntactic. *Psychological Review*, 113:234–272.

Ferreira, F. and Swets, B. (2002). How incremental is language production? Evidence from the production of utterances requiring the computation of arithmetic sums. *Journal of Memory and Language*, 46:57–84.

Ferreira, V. S. and Slevc, L. R. (2007). Grammatical encoding. In Gaskell, M. G., editor, *The Oxford Handbook of Psycholinguistics*, pages 453–470. Oxford University Press.

Garrett, M. F. (1980a). Levels of processing in sentence production. In Butterworth, B., editor, *Language Production: Vol.1. Speech and Talk*, pages 177–220. Academic Press, London.

Garrett, M. F. (1980b). The limits of accommodation: Arguments for independent processing levels in sentence production. In Fromkin, V. A., editor, *Errors in Linguistic Performance: Slips of the Tongue, Ear, Pen and Hand*, pages 263–271. Academic Press, New York.

Goldman Eisler, F. (1968). *Psycholinguistics: Experiments in Spontaneous Speech.* Academic Press, New York.

Griffin, Z. M. (2001). Gaze durations during speech reflect word selection and phonological encoding. *Cognition*, 82:B1–B14.

Griffin, Z. M. and Bock, K. (2000). What the eyes say about speaking. *Psychological Science*, 11:274–279.

Kempen, G. and Hoenkamp, E. (1987). An incremental procedural grammar for sentence formulation. *Cognitive Science*, 11:201–258.

Konopka, A. E. and Bock, J. K. (2008). Lexical or syntactic control of sentence formulation? Structural generalizations from idiom production. *Cognitive Psychology*, 58:68–101.

Levelt, W. J. M. (1989). *Speaking: From Intention to Articulation.* MIT Press, Cambridge MA.

Levelt, W. J. M. (1992). Accessing words in speech production: Stages, processes and representations. *Cognition*, 42(1-3):1–22.

Levelt, W. J. M. and Maassen, B. (1981). Lexical search and order of mention in sentence production. In Klein, W. and Levelt, W. J. M., editors, *Crossing the Boundaries in Linguistics*, pages 221–252. Reidel, Dortrecht.

Levelt, W. J. M. and Meyer, A. S. (2000). Word for word: Multiple lexical access in speech production. *The European Journal of Cognitive Psychology*, 12(4):433–452.

Levelt, W. J. M., Roelofs, A., and Meyer, A. (1999). A theory of lexical access in speech production. *Behavioural and Brain Sciences*, 22:1–75.

Martin, R. C., Miller, M., and Vu, H. (2004). Lexical-semantic retention and speech production: Further evidence from normal and brain-damaged participants for a phrasal scope of planning. *Cognitive Neuropsychology*, 21(6):625–644.

Meyer, A. S., Sleiderink, A. M., and Levelt, W. J. M. (1998). Viewing and naming objects: Eye movements during noun phrase production. *Cognition*, 66:B25–B33.

Morgan, J. L. and Meyer, A. S. (2005). Processing of extrafoveal objects during multiple-object naming. *Journal of Experimental Psychology: Learning, Memory, and Cognition*, 31:428–442.

Pickering, M. J. and Branigan, H. P. (1998). The representation of verbs: Evidence from syntactic persistence in language production. *Journal of Memory and Language*, 39:633–651.

Schriefers, H., Meyer, A. S., and Levelt, W. J. M. (1990). Exploring the time course of lexical access in language production: Picture-word interference studies. *Journal of Memory and Language*, 29:86–102.

Schriefers, H., Teruel, E., and Meinshausen, R. M. (1998). Producing simple sentences: Results from picture-word interference experiments. *Journal of Memory and Language*, 39:609–632.

Slevc, L. R. (2011). Saying what's on your mind: Working memory effects on sentence production. *Journal of Experimental Psychology: Learning, Memory, & Cognition*, 37(6):1503–1514.

Smith, M. and Wheeldon, L. R. (1999). High level processing scope in spoken sentence production. *Cognition*, 73:205–246.

Smith, M. C. (2000). Conceptual structures in language production. In Wheeldon, L., editor, *Aspects of Language Production*, pages 331–374. Psychology Press, Hove.

Swets, B., Desmet, T., Hambrick, D. Z., and Ferreira, F. (2007). The role of working memory in syntactic ambiguity resolution: A psychometric approach. *Journal of Experimental Psychology: General*, 136:64–81.

Wagner, V., Jescheniak, J. D., and Schriefers, H. (2010). On the flexibility of grammatical advance planning during sentence production: Effects of cognitive load on multiple lexical access. *Journal of Experimental Psychology: Learning, Memory, and Cognition*, 36:423–440.

Wheeldon, L. R. and Lahiri, A. (1997). Prosodic units in speech production. *Journal of Memory and Language*, 37:356–381.

Wheeldon, L. R. and Lahiri, A. (2002). The minimal unit of phonological encoding: prosodic or lexical. *Cognition*, 85:B31–B41.

Wheeldon, L. R. and Meyer, A. (2005). Planning sentence structure: Speech latency and gaze patterns during the production of word lists and sentence. In *Paper presented at the 4th Workshop on language production. Maastricht.*

Wundt, W. (1900). *Die Sprache.* Kroner, Leipzig.

Utterance preparation and stress clash: Planning prosodic alternations

SAM TILSEN

Abstract: Models of speech planning and production allow for the prosodic structure of an utterance to be only partially built when the utterance is produced. Previous studies have found evidence that higher-level prosodic units exert a stronger influence in relatively prepared speech compared to unprepared speech. A related issue is whether prosodic alternations are likewise influenced by preparation. This chapter reviews phonological and phonetic treatments of a clash-driven prosodic alternation known as the "rhythm rule", and reports on a preliminary analysis of an experimental study. The experiment tested the hypothesis that the extent to which an utterance has been prepared will affect the magnitude of prominence reduction that typically occurs in the rhythm rule. Durational decreases due to clash were observed only in prepared utterances; in unprepared speech clash unexpectedly resulted in an increase in segmental durations. These results suggest that variation due to prosodic alternations is substantially influenced by the extent to which an utterance has been prepared, and hence provide a new direction for exploration of the interaction between prosody and time-constraints on planning.

1 Introduction

Phonological representations tend to promote the assumption that prosodic structure is fully built prior to the initiation of an utterance. This may be due to emphasis placed on changes that occur in deriving surface forms from underlying ones, as well as the relatively static nature of the representations themselves. Here "prosodic structure" is construed broadly to include the organization of prosodic boundaries and relations of relative prominence. Prominence is associated with individual syllables and is expressed with a combination of acoustic variables, particularly duration and fundamental frequency (F0). Phonological factors such as metrical accent (or stress), intonational pitch accent, and prosodic boundaries, all contribute to prominence.

Some utterances may be quite short and consist of only a single word, syllable, or even a lone gesture; however, for current purposes, it is desirable to consider longer utterances consisting of multiple words. There is a tendency in conversational speech for words in such utterances to be grouped into phrases, and this grouping is often associated with prosodic patterns involving metrical and/or intonational pitch accent. Importantly, when grouping of words into higher-level prosodic phrasal units occurs, there is a potential for alternations in how stress and pitch accent are realized in a given word, compared to how they are realized when the word is produced in isolation. Assuming that most phrases are not lexically stored, these alternations must be computed on-line, either prior to or during production. While it is possible for boundary organization and prominence to be fully determined prior to the production of a phrase, current models of speech production allow for variation in the extent to which prosodic structure is built. This paper will explain how two types of speech production models - incremental and dynamical models - predict variation in prosodic structure to arise from the amount of time available for utterance preparation. Specifically, the focus here is on a prosodic alternation known as the "rhythm rule." This alternation involves a difference in the prominence pattern of a word when it followed by another word with initial prominence, e.g. "se.ven.TEEN ga.ZELLES" vs. "SE.ven.teen GEC.kos". Examples 1-3 below illustrate the rhythm rule in several contexts. In examples 1a, 2a, and 3a, the primary stress in the underlined word falls on the final syllable, with secondary stress falling on a preceding syllable. Here there is no application of the rhythm rule since the initial syllable of the following word is unstressed. In contrast, examples 1b, 2b, and 3b illustrate how primary stress occurs earlier in the word (marked in bold) when it is followed by a word with initial stress. Various phonological approaches to representing this alternation are considered in section 1.2. There are two general requirements for the alternation to occur: first, the words participating in the rhythm rule (the bracketed words in examples 1-3), must be grouped together into a prosodic phrase, and second, there must be a stress or pitch accent "clash", where juxtaposition of isolation forms of the words gives rise to a pattern of adjacent primary stresses or pitch accents within the phrase.

1. a. I saw [thir.TEEN gi.RAFFES]. b. I saw [THIR.teen GHOSTS].

2. a. [si.a.MESE ca.TA.strophes] are rare. b. [SI.a.mese CAR.ni.vals] are common.

3. a. You like [Ten.nes.SEE a.PART.ments]. b. You like [TEN.nes.see AP.ples].

An experimental study was conducted to explore whether the rhythm rule is manifested differently in prepared speech compared to unprepared speech. Because models of production posit that utterances can be initiated without fully determined prosodic structure, it is possible that the phonetic manifestations of the rhythm rule may differ between utterances that have been planned to a greater or lesser extent. A preliminary analysis of experimental results is presented, which shows that changes in relative syllable prominence associated with the rhythm rule are influenced by the extent to which an utterance has been prepared. In other words, whether speakers produce an utterance as soon as they are able to, or delay production for a brief period of time, influences whether prosodic alternations occur. This result suggests that future studies of prosody and articulation take into account the temporal dynamics of utterance preparation.

1.1 Prosodic structure in models of speech planning

Most models of speech planning and production allow for utterances to be produced with incompletely built prosodic structure. Both incremental and dynamical models are discussed here in order to familiarize the reader with different approaches to deriving preparation-related predictions. In incremental models, structure can be reformed iteratively during utterance planning; as more lexical information is retrieved from memory, processing modules are able to construct more detailed representations and potentially alter those representations. Utterances can be produced before all potentially relevant information has had an opportunity to influence the structural representations computed by the processors. Dynamical models of planning associate structural units with "planning systems", which are modeled by real-time continuous variables. These variables can interact with each other through coupling, and the interactions can result in changes that influence the magnitudes and durations of articulatory gestures. The process of fully activating units takes some time, and the effects of their interactions emerge over time, hence the system of dynamical variables requires some time to reach a steady state. If an utterance is produced before planning systems have fully stabilized, prosodic structure and alternations may be only partially realized.

Levelt (1989) and Levelt et al. (1999) present an incremental model of speech planning which is quite comprehensive in that it accommodates a range of segmental and prosodic phenomena. In the model, metrical structure is retrieved at an early stage from lexical entries. This occurs in a metrical spell-out routine, which accesses lexically stored information regarding the number of syllabic peaks in a word and the location of word accent (primary stress). Metrical spell-out provides input to a prosody generator, in parallel with segmental spell-out. The prosody generator computes phonetic parameters that serve as input to phonetic spell-out; these phonetic parameters include duration, intensity, and pitch for a given syllable frame, and they are computed based upon the structural representations of metrical stress, pitch accent, and prosodic boundaries that are available to and computed by the prosody generator (Levelt, 1989, p. 367). To accommodate prominence alternations in the rhythm rule context, the prosody generator is able to "look ahead" to the metrical structure of following words and compute a change in prosodic structure. The lookahead process must also take into account prosodic phrase structure, in order to avoid triggering metrical alternations when a clash straddles a phrase boundary.

The rhythm rule is categorical but not obligatory in the Levelt (1989) model. Information regarding the metrical pattern of the upcoming word may not be available when the prosody generator computes phonetic parameters, "because of a high speech rate, or for some other reason" (Levelt, 1989, p. 374). The model thus makes the following prediction: the rhythm rule either will or will not be implemented, depending upon whether information regarding the metrical structure of the upcoming word is available when the prosody generator computes phonetic parameters for a given word and outputs them to phonetic spell-out. In either case, the phonetic outcome is dependent upon whatever partially-built metrical structure is available for input to the prosody generator when it computes its output phonetic parameters.

Dynamical planning models also allow for utterances to be produced with incompletely built prosodic structure. Although less comprehensive in scope than the incremental model of Levelt (1989), several models have extended the task-dynamic framework of articulatory phonology (Browman and Goldstein, 1992; Saltzman and Munhall, 1989) to incorporate prosodic planning dynamics. These models are based upon hierarchical networks of coupled oscillators. In these approaches prosody-related patterns of duration and relative timing in production arise from changes in frequency-locking or strength of phase-coupling between syllables, feet, and prosodic phrases, in some cases in conjunction with the presence of special prosodic gestures that slow the production system (Byrd and Saltzman, 2003; Saltzman et al., 2008; Tilsen, 2009). The framework developed in Tilsen (2011a,b) allows for both phase-coupling and amplitude-coupling between oscillatory planning systems at various levels of the prosodic hierarchy. Amplitude-coupling forces influence the relative activations of syllable and gestural planning systems, which in turn can influence gestural magnitudes and durations. Due to interactions between amplitude-coupling forces and relative phase, these forces can promote rhythmic alternation of syllable prominence (Tilsen, 2011b). Crucially, the coupling forces take some time to exert a maximal effect. This allows for the possibility that utterances produced with a relatively short period of time for planning may not exhibit fully stabilized prosodic dynamics.

The potential for speech to be produced when prosodic planning systems have not fully stabilized is similar to incomplete building of structure; however, there is a potentially important conceptual distinction to be drawn. The dynamical notion of structure building assumes a gradient view of structure in which prosodic "units", such as stress or pitch accents, are dynamical systems that exhibit continuous variation in activation over time. This differs from the more reified metaphor of a grid in which prominence-objects are stacked in association with syllable slots and tone-units are associated to those slots. Incremental processing favors viewing structure as a composition of objects in space, since it relies fundamentally on the concept of retrieval of information from memory. The things that are retrieved are countable, e.g., a metrical pattern is a number of syllable peaks; changes in the pattern are formulated by rules that move or alter structural objects such as grid marks or pitch accents. In contrast, the dynamical conception of what is "retrieved" from memory involves a pattern of relative activation and phase, along with coupling forces; subsequent changes to the pattern ("structure building") arise from the intrinsic dynamics of systems and their coupling interactions (see Tilsen, 2011a,b, for detailed illustrations of the approach). The current experiment does not aim to resolve between these competing views of speech planning, but the discussion in section 4 will consider whether the two approaches make differing predictions regarding the effects of preparation.

1.2 Experimental evidence for an influence of preparation

There are several studies which suggest that that the amount of time available for utterance preparation has an influence on the organization of prosodic structure. Numerous experiments by Sternberg et al. (1978, 1988) have shown that in prepared utterances the number of feet (or stress groups), i.e., the "length of the utterance", has a linear effect on the reaction time (RT) to initiate the utterance. They interpreted this effect to arise from a series of selection and execution processes. The selection process draws units from a motor program buffer and the execution process produces the associated motor commands. All feet in an utterance are stored as separate units in the buffer. The more units that occupy the buffer, the longer it takes to select the first unit in the utterance, and hence RT increases linearly with the number of feet in the buffer. Previously selected units remain in the buffer, so that all selection processes during an utterance are affected equally. The durations of produced units depend on the time-courses of both selection and execution processes; hence foot durations increase linearly with utterance length, because the selection of each foot will take longer if there are more of them. As a direct consequence of this, utterance length has a nonlinear effect on the duration of the utterance as a whole: the effect of utterance length on the selection of each foot is multiplied by the length of the entire utterance, i.e., the number of feet in the utterance.

More recently, similar effects have been observed in association with the number of prosodic words in an utterance. Wheeldon and Lahiri (1997) conducted a study in Dutch that suggests preparation time plays a key role in influencing the building of prosodic structure. Their study examined the effect of the number of prosodic words in an utterance on the RT to initiate the utterance. They compared utterances with two and three prosodic words in which the number of syllables was held constant. Analogous example utterances in English are "I seek the water" (two prosodic words) and "I seek fresh water" (three prosodic words). The contrast derives from the propensity for the determiner to cliticize to the prosodic word associated with the preceding verb, whereas the adjective constitutes its own prosodic word. What makes this study particularly relevant is that Wheeldon and Lahiri conducted two versions of their experiment: one in which speakers had plenty of time to prepare the response, and another in which preparation time was substantially restricted. In the fully prepared response experiment, reaction times patterned in accordance with the Sternberg findings: RTs were greater for three-word utterances than two-word utterances. However, in the restricted preparation experiment, reaction times were not affected by utterance length. Instead, reaction times increased with the complexity of the initial prosodic word (i.e., the number of syllables in the word): the two-word utterances took longer to initiate than the three-word utterances, because the first prosodic word contained an additional syllable, the cliticized determiner. The absence of the prosodic word effect in the unprepared design suggests that higher-level phonological phrase structure requires more planning time to be fully assembled, and shows that prosodic structure need not be completely built prior to utterance initiation.

Regarding effects of utterance preparation on the segmental level of the prosodic hierarchy, it has been shown that articulatory posturing for the initial gesture(s) of a word occurs well in advance of acoustic response onset in delayed-cue naming tasks. For example, Kawamoto et al. (2008) showed that the extent of articulatory preparation increases with the amount of time between the stimulus and response cue in delayed naming. Even explicit instructions not to initiate articulation prior to the cue

did not eliminate this effect. Hence the articulation of response-initial gestures can be substantially influenced by preparation, and this reinforces the notion that temporal differences in planning can manifest in articulatory variation.
The effect of utterance preparation also emerges in comparisons between choice-RT and simple-RT paradigms. In choice-RT paradigms, the response action is not known until the imperative "go" stimulus occurs, typically because the imperative stimulus also informs the subject of what response action they will perform. Hence the response cannot be prepared prior to the go-cue. In simple-RT paradigms the subject is informed of what action they will perform prior to the go-cue, as was the case in the Sternberg et al. (1978, 1988) experiments. Klapp (1995, 2003) demonstrated that the effect of the number of units on response latency is only present in simple-RT paradigms, not in choice-RT paradigms. This pattern held true for a variety of response types: button presses, alphabet letters, words, and pseudowords. Utterance preparation is related to the choice-/simple-RT distinction, since the basic difference between the two conditions is the amount of time that a response is planned prior to its execution.

1.3 Phonological representations of prominence and the rhythm rule

Of primary concern here is the phonological representation of prosodic patterns associated with the rhythm rule (also: "stress shift"), which is driven by stress clash. Clash-related phenomena of this sort are interesting to investigate because they derive from on-line building of prosodic structure: clash does not generally arise from lexical memory, since most multi-word phrases are not lexically stored. Hence the phonetic manifestations of clash can serve as an index for the influence of preparation on prosodic structure building and on-line implementation of prosodic alternations. The rhythm rule pattern involves the early location of prominence in words where a secondary stress precedes a primary stress, such as "Cornell", "Japanese", and "Minnesota". When these words are produced phrase-finally or in isolation, their most prominent syllables are the ones with primary stress, as expected. However, when they are followed in a phrase by a word with primary stress on the initial syllable, the location of the most prominent syllable appears to "shift" earlier, to the preceding syllable that had secondary stress. Similar patterns have been observed in a number of languages, including Polish (Hayes and Puppel, 1985), Italian, Greek, Catalan (Nespor and Vogel, 1986), Biblical Hebrew (Churchyard, 1999), Bedouin Hijazi Arabic (Al-Mozainy et al., 1985), and Afghan Persian (Bing, 1980).

There are two main approaches to the phonological representation of prominence (Shattuck Hufnagel et al., 1994; Gussenhoven, 2011) and within these, several alternative accounts of how accentual variation arises. One approach, which Gussenhoven (2011) refers to as the "infinite stress view" is based on the idea that accentual differences between words are the same type of phenomenon as accentual differences within words. This conception of prominence is unitary, in that no clear distinction is drawn between the contributions of word-stress and intonational pitch accent. In this view prominence values are associated with each syllable, and rules specify changes to those values - this was the approach employed by Chomsky and Halle (1968). The idea that all prominence is similar favors the use of a single representational formalism for within-word and across-word prominence. One way to express this is with metrical grid marks (Liberman and Prince, 1977; Selkirk, 1984; Nespor and Vogel, 1986), shown in Figure 1a, where the heights of grid marks express their relative prominence.

An alternative representational approach - the "pitch accent view" (Gussenhoven, 2011) - is based on the idea that intonational pitch accents are phonologically autonomous from word stress (Bolinger, 1958; Vanderslice and Ladefoged, 1972; Horne, 1990; Gussenhoven, 1991; Shattuck Hufnagel et al., 1994). Bolinger (1958) proposed that there are two pitch accents in a phrase: a "themic accent" occurring early in the phrase (a pre-nuclear accent), and a "rhemic accent" occurring late in the phrase, which can be equated with the main, or nuclear accent. In the pitch accent view, intonational pitch accents can be associated with syllables having unreduced vowels and can thereby imbue them with additional prominence. Pitch accents thus coexist with primary and secondary metrical stress levels, as shown in Figure 1c. The choice of which pitch accent to associate to a syllable is an independent issue. In English, there are a number of options (H*, H*L, L*H, etc.), only one is shown here.

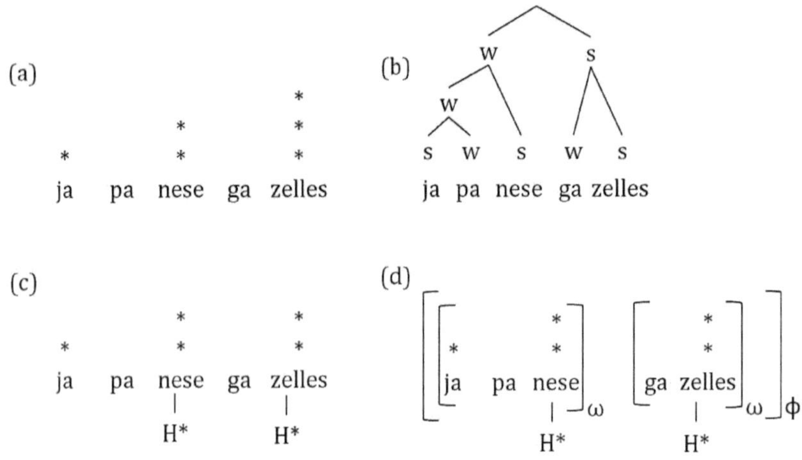

Figure 1: Phonological representations of prominence. (a) metrical grid; (b) metrical tree; (c) metrical grid with pitch accent tier; (d) bracketed grid with pitch accent tier.

A different approach is to use hierarchical metrical tree structures (Liberman, 1975; Liberman and Prince, 1977), which through strong or weak labeling of binary branching nodes can represent both relative prominence and grouping relations, shown in Figure 1b. Both metrical trees and grids are examples of the infinite stress view because they employ a common representational mechanism for within-word and across-word prominence: both frameworks conflate pitch accent and metrical stress in representing prominence.

There are a variety of hybrid approaches to representing metrical and prosodic structure, and a full review is not possible here. The reader should note that some authors use upper-level tiers in a grid to represent positions to which pre-nuclear pitch accents and nuclear pitch accents are associated (Beckman and Edwards, 1994), with the assumption that these upper-level marks do not contribute prominence in the same way as the lower-level marks. It is furthermore common to incorporate labels into a tree structure or brackets into a grid (Hayes, 1995; Nespor and Vogel, 1986), in order to represent the locations of prosodic word ω and phonological phrase boundaries ϕ, as shown in Figure 1d.

Many phonological treatments of the rhythm rule are based upon notions of stress clash and subsequent repair. Adjacent prominent syllables create a clash, for which some form of reparation is desirable. In metrical grids based on a unitary conception of prominence, the repair involves a transfer of a grid mark to a preceding syllable (Liberman and Prince, 1977), as shown in Figure 2a. In metrical trees, the shift has been conceptualized as the exchange of a strong and weak node (Kiparsky, 1979), shown in Figure 2b. There is also a more inclusive construal which allows for non-adjacent primary stressed syllables to clash when no secondary stress intervenes between them, as in "Minnesota apartments" (clash) vs. "Minnesota abbreviations" (no-clash).

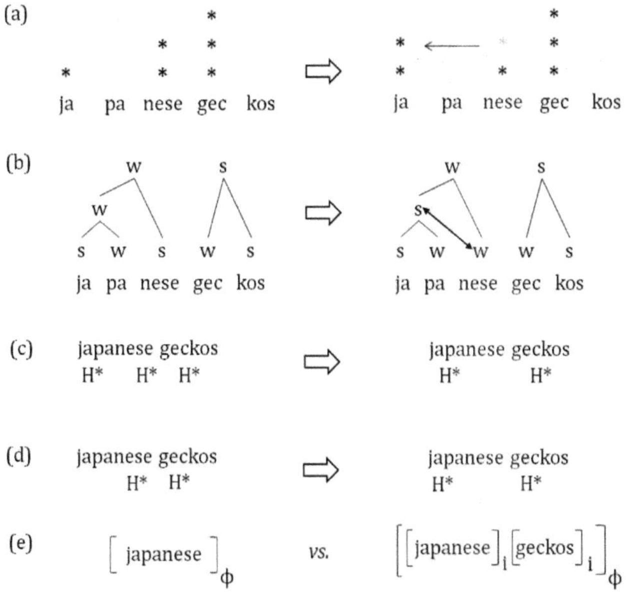

Figure 2: Phonological representations of the rhythm rule. (a) prominence-transfer in a metrical grid; (b) strong-weak label transfer in a metrical tree; (c) pitch accent deletion; (d) early pitch accent; (e) boundary insertion.

In pitch-accent views, the repair can be analyzed as a deletion of an accent or early occurrence of an accent. Gussenhoven (1991, 2011) provides an accent deletion account, shown in Figure 2c. In this analysis both the primary and secondary stressed syllables have pitch accents, and a "rhythm-induced accent deletion" rule deletes medial accents in the phonological phrase. Note that this rule can apply to any phrase-medial accent, regardless of whether there is a clash induced by adjacency to a following accent. Bolinger (1965) presents an early accent account, in which a prominence occurs early due to a desire to have a prenuclear pitch accent early on in the phrase. This account can also be construed to involve a movement of the pitch accent, analogous to the movement of metrical stress.

Early pitch accent and accent deletion analyses are not based on a repair of metrical rhythm. The early location or deletion of pitch accent does not serve to avoid metrical stress clashes between grid marks. However, these patterns can be conceptualized as a repair of the "rhythm of pitch accent", which Bolinger (1965) distinguished from metrical rhythm. Importantly, the pitch accent approaches do not strongly differentiate between clashing and non-clashing stress contexts: they predict that the contribution of pitch-accent to prominence in "Japanese geckos" will be the same as that of "Japanese gazelles" and "Japanese tyrannosaurus".

Beckman and Edwards (1994) describe several accounts of rhythm rule prominence patterns, one that is consistent with deletion, one consistent with early accent, and a third based on prosodic boundaries. In one account, they suggest that the first accent in a word with two prenuclear accents is perceived as stronger because there is an utterance-initial rise in pitch to the first accent. This is consistent in a perceptual sense with deletion of a medial accent, but does not necessarily involve a phonological deletion per se. In the second account, they suggest that a pitch accent is associated with the first accentable syllable in the phrase due to an impetus to have pre-nuclear accent occur as early as possible before the nuclear accent. This account is concordant with the early accent account of Bolinger (1965, 1985).

Phrase boundary structure is crucial in all of the pitch accent accounts. Both deletion of pitch accent and early location of pitch accent require an absence of preceding material in the phrase. Medial deletion only applies in non-phrase-initial words, and early accent should occur in the first word in a phrase. Hence if a word is not phrase-initial, then no pitch accent on a secondary stressed syllable is expected under either account. A third proposal of Beckman and Edwards (1994) is that apparent early prominence occurs when the nuclear accent associated with a phrase-final boundary is no longer present, as shown in Figure 2e. This account differs somewhat from the preceding ones in that it depends on the presence or absence of a nuclear accent in the word with variable accent. The accounts depicted in Figure 2a-e are similar in that they implicate phonological structure or the presence of stress or pitch accent. However, they differ in two regards. First, the unitary prominence accounts (2a,b) describe repairs that serve metrical (stress-based) rhythm. In contrast the pitch accent accounts describe repairs that result in greater separation of pitch-accents (2c, d), or in the case of (2e), patterns of accentuation arising from the organization of prosodic boundaries. Second, the repairs in the unitary prominence accounts are conditioned by specific clash configurations (primary stresses adjacent or separated by one syllable); in contrast, the pitch accent views hold that clash of primary stresses is not responsible for the early occurrence of prominence. In addition to accounts based solely upon metrical stress or intonational pitch accents, there have been a number of integrated accounts which rely upon patterns in both word-level and phrasal/intonational domains. Some possibilities along these lines are discussed by Shattuck Hufnagel et al. (1994). For example, it could be the case that the deletion or movement of a pitch accent is dependent upon a deletion or movement of stress in the metrical grid. Another possibility implies the opposite direction of causation: changes in locations of pitch accents trigger changes in within-word metrical patterns.

1.4 Phonetic studies of the rhythm rule

A key question in phonetic investigations of the rhythm rule is what the phonetic correlates of prominence are. In the unitary view of prominence, variables such as duration, intensity, and F0 are all correlates of prominence; there is no dissociation of F0 with other variables, because prominence is a monolithic phenomenon. In contrast, a number of researchers have argued for drawing a distinction between direct correlates of word stress, pitch accents, and prosodic boundaries. In these views, the correlates of stress are generally considered to be increased duration, vowel quality, and intensity, whereas F0 patterns arise most directly from pitch accents and tones associated with prosodic boundaries. This distinction is accepted by a number of researchers (Beckman and Edwards, 1994; Gussenhoven, 1991; Shattuck Hufnagel et al., 1994). Beckman and Edwards (1994) point out that many studies of stress have conflated pitch accent and prosodic boundary structure with metrical stress. For example, they attribute the association of F0 with stress to a misunderstanding of experimental research in Fry (1958), which showed F0 as the primary cue for distinguishing stress pairs such as per.MIT and PER.mit. The F0 patterns were due to association of nuclear pitch accent when these words are produced or heard phrase-finally.

A complicating factor in phonetic analyses of prominence is that pitch accents, phrasal accents, and prosodic boundaries have effects on duration independent of metrical stress. For example, prosodic boundaries are known to be associated with longer durations of segments and articulatory gestures (Klatt, 1975; Nakatani et al., 1981; Beckman and Edwards, 1994; Byrd and Saltzman, 1998, 2003; Byrd, 2000). The extent to which this additional duration is a "direct" consequence of the boundary, or an indirect consequence of the presence of a nuclear pitch accent, phrasal accent, or boundary tone, is not entirely clear. The opposite direction of interaction - stress influencing F0 independently of intonation - has not been as strongly supported in the literature, although it should not be ruled out given that the presence of stress on a syllable is typically considered a precondition for associating pitch accent.

Due to the above factors, durational patterns cannot be directly attributed either to metrical structure or intonational structure. This results in an unavoidable multiplicity of hypotheses when the potential structural source(s) of experimental effects are unknown. More specifically, if the occurrence of intonational accents, phrasal structure, and metrical stress patterns can be experimentally controlled independently, then effects on duration or F0 would be clearly interpretable. However in the more general condition where accentual patterns, phrasal structure, and metrical structure are unknown, durational effects can be interpreted as consequences of either one or several of these factors. To determine whether durational patterns are solely attributable to just one factor is only possible when independent characterizations of pitch accentuation, phrasal structure, and stress are available. Moreover, if we allow for these factors to be represented gradiently, the difficulties are exacerbated.

It is worth mentioning here that another possible repair in the rhythm

rule context is an elongation of the first stressed syllable in the clashing pair. Liberman (1975) suggested this as a means of promoting rhythmic spacing of stresses. By lengthening this syllable, its peak would be further away from the subsequent stress on the following word. It is also possible to interpret this repair as a consequence of insertion of an additional silent beat between words (Selkirk, 1984). Durational lengthening is an interesting possibility in light of the results of the current study, and notably it runs contrary to what prior investigations have found: shortening of the first primary stressed syllable in a clashing pair.
Limited conclusions can be drawn from phonetic studies of the rhythm rule due to two types of confounds detailed below. The available evidence suggests that metrical stress clash results in a decrease in prominence of the primary stressed syllable (σ_p) in a bipedal word, as opposed to a transfer of prominence to a preceding syllable with secondary stress (σ_s). Hence in a clashing context, σ_p in words like "Cornell", "Japanese", and "Minnesota" experiences a decrease in duration and F0, while prominence on σ_s remains relatively unchanged. For reasons described above, the decrease in prominence may have several explanations: (1) decrease in the metrical stress level of the word, (2) deletion or early placement of a pitch accent, possibly with an indirect influence on duration, (3) change in prosodic boundary structure, or (4) some combination of the preceding. In the following, we will refer to a bipedal word in a rhythm rule context as the "target word".

Table 1: Phonetic studies of stress clash: σ_s = syllable with secondary stress, σ_p = syllable with primary stress, studies are abbreviated as follows: CE86=Cooper and Eady (1986), H90=Horne (1990), GW95=Grabe and Warren (1995), VBH95=Vogel et al. (1995).

	σ_s	σ_p-σ_s	σ_p/σ_s	σ_p
duration		↓GW95		↓GW95, VBH95, H90
F0 peak				↓CE86, H90
F0 average		↓GW95		↓VBH95
F0 range		↓GW95		↓GW95
Intensity	(↓GW95)		↓GW95	↓GW95

Table 1 summarizes previous research on the effects of stress clash, distinguishing between effects on phonetic variables associated with the primary and secondary stressed syllables in the first word of the clashing pair. The clashing and non-clashing contexts contrasted in these studies differ in important ways.

Grabe and Warren (1995) used sentence pairs in which the location of a phrasal boundary was manipulated, e.g., the sentence "when my father watches TV soaps, they are his favorite" contains a clash between "TV" and "soaps", but the sentence "when my father watches TV, soaps are his favorite" contains no such clash due to an intervening phrasal boundary. Horne (1990) contrasted isolation productions of words such as "Dundee" to productions in a clashing context, such as "Dundee tartan". Vogel et al. (1995) contrasted clashing/non-clashing contexts by varying the location of stress in the second word in the clashing pair, e.g. "Japanese clients" (clash) vs. "Japanese canoes" (no-clash). These word pairs were produced as subject NPs in a sentence and were preceded by one of three contexts: no preceding word form, a preceding determiner, or a preceding NP modifier, e.g. "Jack's Japanese clients". Cooper and Eady (1986) elicited similarly clashing and non-clashing word pairs in isolation and in carrier sentences. Note that these studies used read-text response elicitation paradigms, which can be classified as prepared speech.

All of the studies found evidence that clash decreased prominence in σ_p. Grabe and Warren (1995); Vogel et al. (1995); Horne (1990) observed decreased duration in σ_p, while Cooper and Eady (1986) did not measure duration in this syllable. Note that Vogel et al. (1995) measured rhyme durations, rather than syllable durations. All of the studies also observed a decrease of F0 in σ_p, albeit using different measures (peak, average, or range). Grabe and Warren (1995) furthermore observed a decrease in intensity in σ_p.

However, Grabe and Warren (1995) and Horne (1990) conflated nuclear pitch accent, boundary structure, and stress, and hence their results cannot be construed as evidence for metrical clash-induced reduction of prominence. Grabe and Warren (1995) compared clash-context productions with phrase-final productions; the latter context is expected to have nuclear pitch accent on σ_p. Hence differences in F0, intensity, and duration observed in the comparison could be due to nuclear pitch accent,

the presence of a phrase boundary, and/or metrical stress alternation. Assuming that isolation productions are also phrase-final, the same confound applies to Horne (1990). In contrast, Vogel et al. (1995) and Cooper and Eady (1986) did not confound these factors; the phrasal structures they compared should be identical in the local vicinity of σ_p.
The only evidence for a metrical clash-induced increase of prominence in σ_s, which would be due to transfer of stress, was reported by Grabe and Warren (1995). They found an increase in intensity as measured by the amplitude integral over the syllable, and they furthermore observed changes in the relative durations, pitch range, and average pitch between σ_s and σ_p. These relative changes, in conjunction with a lack of absolute changes in duration/F0 in σ_s, suggests that early prominence could result from perceived changes in relative prominence, rather than a movement or augmentation of prominence. A problematic factor here is that early pitch accent could have occurred on σ_p and obscured changes otherwise attributable to metrical clash. An early prenuclear accent of this sort would occur in both metrically clashing and non-clashing contexts, and hence may interfere with observation of effects related to metrical stress. In Vogel et al. (1995), where preceding context was systematically varied, it may have been possible to resolve this confound by looking for an interaction effect between clash and context, but the authors did not report this analysis. A corpus study conducted by Shattuck Hufnagel et al. (1994) attempted to distinguish changes in pitch accent from changes in metrical stress; the study found evidence that early placement of pitch accent occurs without corresponding durational changes associated with metrical clash. The study furthermore observed the occurrence of doubly pitch-accented words, with accents on both the secondary and primary stressed syllables of a word. These findings argue strongly for a dissociation of metrical stress and pitch accent with regard to the rhythm rule context. Shattuck Hufnagel et al. (1994) also found evidence for avoidance of clash between pitch accents, which was independent of metrical stress clash: pitch accents exhibited a tendency for placement earlier in a word when placement on the primary stress would result in adjacent pitch accents. However, the dataset available to the study was not large enough to draw conclusions about the effects of metrical stress clash independent of pitch accent.

In sum, the evidence available from phonetic studies of metrical stress clash is rather limited. Only one study, Vogel et al. (1995), has demonstrated (without apparent intonational or structural confounds) that metrical stress clash results in decrease of duration in σ_p, and two studies, Vogel et al. (1995) and Cooper and Eady (1986), have found evidence for decrease of F0. As for whether there is a transfer of stress to σ_s, it is not clear that any of the studies offer interpretable evidence either way: the designs in Grabe and Warren (1995); Horne (1990) and Cooper and Eady (1986) all potentially suffer from obscuring effects of early pitch accent because their target words were phrase-initial; Vogel et al. (1995) did not present the relevant interaction analysis that could resolve the issue.

1.5 Hypotheses

Prominence reduction in stress clash is a good candidate for testing the effects of preparation on prosodic planning, because the reduction does not arise from lexical memory, but rather, must arise from on-line changes in planning prosodic structure. Since previous studies have shown that preparation time is required for prosodic word structure to have an influence on reaction time to initiate an utterance (Wheeldon and Lahiri, 1997), it is possible that a prosodic alternation such as clash-induced reduction of prominence may likewise depend on preparation. However, because there are several factors that influence prominence - i.e., metrical stress within words, intonational pitch accent, and prosodic boundary structure - related predictions can be generated from a multiplicity of hypotheses. Further complicating the issue, the phonological representations discussed above may involve a number of intermediate representational stages, whose characteristics may influence phonetic observables in unprepared speech. To some extent these hypotheses cannot be differentiated with the data and analyses presented here, but the results do confirm predictions of incremental and dynamical planning models that utterances can be initiated before prosodic alternations have occurred.

Because we are interested in the effect of planning time (preparation) on prosodic alternations, and because there is some evidence from previous phonetic studies that metrical stress clash reduces prominence in the rhythm rule context, our primary interest relates to the interaction of preparation and clash. In other words, the primary hypotheses involve interaction effects: how does preparation affect the phonological and phonetic consequences of clash in the rhythm rule context? To address this question, the experimental design elicited productions of target words in the middle of formulaic three-word noun phrases with or without metrical clash, such as "eleven Japanese geckos" (clashing) or "eleven Japanese gazelles" (non-clashing); furthermore, there were two experimentally controlled preparation conditions, one which encouraged preparation and another that restricted preparation (section 2 details the methodology).

The hypotheses and predictions presented below will remain neutral with regard to conceptualization of phonological representations; hence "reduction" may refer to a categorical deletion of a representational object such as a tone or a grid mark, which accords with conventional phonological representations of structure and the incremental model of Levelt (1989); or alternatively, "reduction" may refer to a gradient diminution of the influence of units on production, which accords with dynamical models of speech planning in which phonological units are associated with activation variables.

Due to the preliminary status of the experimental analysis, pitch accent analyses have not been conducted. Hence the hypotheses must be equivocal regarding whether durational effects are due to metrical or pitch-accentual clash. The clash context potentially induces both varieties of clash: there is an adjacency between a potential pre-nuclear pitch accent on σ_p and the nuclear pitch accent on the primary stress of the following word; there is also an adjacency between the primary metrical stresses of the target word and the following word. Since the target words were embedded in three-word noun phrases, their phrase-mediality should discourage early accent placement. However, if prosodic structure is not fully formed, as might occur in unprepared speech, then each content word may constitute a separate phonological or intonational phrase; this would allow for early pitch accent placement. Such early accent placement would be a confounding factor, particularly for hypothesis 2, which regards changes in σ_s. Without a reliable intonational analysis, it cannot be determined whether an early accent occurred. Nonetheless, measurements of segmental duration and vowel intensity can still offer revealing effects related to clash and preparation.

Future analyses of intonation (e.g. in the ToBI framework, Beckman et al., 2005) will offer further insight into the experimentally observed patterns.

Hypothesis 0 (null hypothesis)
Preparation will have no effect on the phonetic manifestations of prominence. This should be the case if prosodic structure, including potential alternations in stress/pitch accent, is fully built prior to production of an utterance.

Prediction
Clash-induced decreases of duration will be the same in prepared and unprepared speech.

Hypothesis 1
Clash-induced reduction of prominence in σ_p will be heightened in prepared speech compared to unprepared speech, because preparation allows for prosodic structure to be more fully built, resulting in a greater likelihood/magnitude of reduction of stress/pitch accent.

Prediction
The clash-induced decrease in duration of σ_p will be relatively larger in prepared speech compared to unprepared speech.

Hypothesis 2
Clash-induced increase of prominence in σ_s (the secondary stressed syllable in the target word) will be heightened in prepared speech, due to movement of metrical stress and/or early location of pitch accent. These effects should occur in addition to those described by Hypothesis 1.

Prediction
In addition to predictions from Hypothesis 1, there will be a clash-induced increase in duration in σ_s, and this increase will be relatively larger in prepared speech compared to unprepared speech.

The above hypotheses reflect only a subset of possible hypotheses that could be derived from the phonological interpretations of the rhythm rule discussed in section 1.3. They have been selected to represent the most plausible and distinct accounts of the phenomenon. It should be emphasized that hypotheses 1 and 2 predict an interaction between the effect of clash and preparation: the effects of clash will be greater in prepared speech than in unprepared speech. The remainder of this paper presents the experimental method used to test these hypotheses (section 2), reports the results of the experiment (section 3), and discusses interpretations of the findings (section 4).

2 Methodology

This section describes the experimental design, stimuli, tasks, and data analysis methods. Previous studies of the rhythm rule have typically elicited a variety of lexical items from speakers, treating the identity of the response word as a random factor or source of noise that is averaged out in the analysis. In contrast, this study focused on just a single word: "Japanese", which is known to exhibit reduction of prominence in a clashing context. Although the focus on a single word sacrifices some generalizability, it has the advantage that many repetitions of the same word can be obtained; this results in an increase in statistical power and hence enables smaller effects to be detected.

2.1 Experimental design

Five native speakers of American English with normal speech and hearing participated in the experiment (4 females, 1 male). Each subject participated in one 1h session, during which they produced a total of 360 utterances. Each session was divided into 10 blocks of 36 trials. Utterances were recorded with a head-mounted microphone and preamplifier, with a sampling rate of 22050 Hz. Matlab was used for stimuli presentation and audio recording.

On each trial, three visual stimuli of rectangular shape (each approximately 40% of screen dimensions) were displayed simultaneously on a screen with a black background. Each stimulus belonged to one of three classes: a numeral, a flag (representing a nationality), or an animal. The stimuli were positioned in a triangular arrangement, with the numeral centered on the screen in the upper row and in the bottom row, the nationality and animal positioned on the left and right, respectively. There was always exactly one stimulus from each class. Furthermore, each stimulus class consisted of only a small set of images. The numeral set contained images of the numerals twenty, eleven, and seventeen. The nationalities set contained images of the national flags of Mexico, Jamaica, and Japan. The animals set contained images of a gecko, a buffalo, a gazelle, and a piranha. The images were obtained from a Google image search. For the animals, images with minimally salient backgrounds were selected. All combinations of numerals, nationalities, and animals (3 x 3 x 4) were displayed in random order in each block. Subjects responded to the visual stimuli by producing a formulaic phrase that combined the numeral, nationality, and animal into a noun phrase, e.g. "twenty Japanese geckos" or "seventeen Mexican gazelles".

Prior to the experiment, subjects were shown the flags and animals and asked to identify them. Some subjects did not recognize the Jamaican flag and were informed that it referred to the nationality "Jamaican". Several subjects also did not recognize the image of the piranha as such, and were informed of its referent. No subjects reported that any of the nationalities or animals were unfamiliar to them. Subjects were subsequently shown all of the pictures in random order and asked to name them, until they were able to name all of the pictures with 100% accuracy twice in a row. Although there is both within- and across-subject variation in familiarity with these words, the repeated presentation of the stimuli before and during the experiment is likely to minimize the effects of prior differences in familiarity.

The independent variable of preparation was controlled by manipulating the task instructions. Subjects were told before the experiment that there were two different tasks: a quick response task, and a prepared response task. For the quick response task, they were told to respond with the correct phrase as soon as they could, right after the images appeared on the screen. For the prepared response task, they were told to rehearse the response exactly once, without producing any sound or moving their mouths, and then to say it out loud. At the start of each block, they were told which instruction to follow. The immediate (relatively unprepared) and rehearsed (relatively prepared) response tasks alternated

between blocks. The independent variable of clash corresponded to the presence/absence of word-initial stress on the animal noun. Hence the clash condition corresponds to utterances with "gecko" or "buffalo" and the no-clash condition to utterances with "gazelle" or "piranha".
To encourage subjects to conform to the task instructions, feedback was given when they initiated the response too early or too late. Furthermore, to promote consistency in speech rate within and across subjects, feedback was given when the duration of the response was abnormally short or long. After each trial, the responses were analyzed to estimate when the onset and offset occurred. Based on pilot work, it was determined that responses initiated before 400ms or after 1100ms in the quick response task were abnormally early/late. For the prepared response task, these limits were 1200ms and 2500ms. If the response fell outside of these limits, the subject was notified after the trial. Pilot work also showed that the range of response duration is within 900-1500ms. If the response duration fell outside of this range, subjects were informed that their response was too quick or too slow.

2.2 Data analysis

The analysis presented in section 3 is based on the results of all five participants. It focuses on segmental durations and vowel intensities in the word "Japanese". This word is typically transcribed phonetically as [dʒæpəniz]. The intensity measurements were taken separately over the vowels in the initial and final syllables of "Japanese". Intensity was measured by analysis of the vocalic energy envelope (Tilsen and Johnson, 2008), which is a 10Hz low-pass filter of the magnitude of a passband-filtered speech waveform (5th order Butterworth, 400-2400Hz). The vocalic energy amplitude envelope captures slow fluctuations in signal energy that arise primarily from vocalic resonance during voiced speech. Amplitude envelopes were normalized across the production within each trial. Two types of intensity measurements were obtained from each vowel: a peak value and an average value. These values and their ratios between the first and last vowels in "Japanese" served as dependent variables in the regression analyses presented below.
To measure segmental durations, the acoustic waveform from trials with productions of "Japanese" was low-pass filtered to allow for the approx-

imation of syllable and word boundaries, which were then checked for accuracy by visual and auditory inspection and corrected where necessary. In order to automatically locate segmental boundaries within the word "Japanese", a custom forced alignment algorithm was implemented in Matlab. For each subject, the segments in the word were hand-labeled for two trials in each clash and preparation condition. From these, an acoustic template was created for each segment by averaging Mel frequency-scaled cepstral coefficient vectors. These vectors were then cross-correlated with cepstral coefficient matrices (13 cepstral coefficients, 20ms frames, 5ms steps, 80-5000Hz) computed from the acoustic waveform of "Japanese" from all trials. Segmental boundaries were estimated as crossing-points in the cross-correlation functions of segments expected to be adjacent. Subsequently all trials were auditorily and visually inspected for segmentation accuracy with waveforms and spectrograms; in a few instances the segmentations were corrected manually, but more than 99% of them were deemed accurate without correction.

Some trials were excluded from the analysis, for various reasons. The first ten trials of the first block in each session were not analyzed. Responses that occurred early or late (see section 2.1) were excluded (2.2%), as were responses that were abnormally fast or slow, i.e., shorter than 900ms (1.8%) or longer than 1500ms (5.9%). During auditory-visual inspection, responses identified as containing incorrect or disfluent productions were excluded. Most of these involved a hesitation prior to the final word in the utterance or a production of an incorrect (unelicited) word. As one might expect, errors occurred predominantly in the unprepared condition, although they did not occur frequently enough to discern any word-specific biases. With the remaining data, trials were excluded in which a segmental duration was more than 2.2 standard deviations from the mean, calculated within subjects.

Segmental durations were log transformed and analyzed using mixed-effects linear regression. The word boundary-adjacent segments of "Japanese" were excluded from this analysis because the forced alignment estimation of the word-initial and word-final boundaries was strongly influenced by the preceding/following context, due to coarticulation with segments from flanking words. The random factors in the model were SUBJECT and BLOCK nested within SUBJECT. BLOCK effects were treated as random nested effects because they generally reflect subject-specific changes in attention and practice. The fixed effects of primary interest are preparation (PREP, manipulated by task instruction) and CLASH (the presence of initial stress on the following word). Specifically, it is the magnitude and direction of the CLASH x PREP interaction that is of relevance to testing the hypotheses. Additional fixed effects included in the model were the identity of the preceding numeral and the number of syllables in the word following "Japanese". An initial regression with all interactions showed that only the CLASH x PREP interaction term significantly improved the model fit, and hence all other interaction terms were excluded from subsequent regressions. To display the effects graphically in Figure 3, durations were z-score normalized within subjects and pooled by condition.

3 Results

The main result of the experiment is a significant CLASH x PREP interaction effect observed on durations associated with segments in the primary stressed syllable in "Japanese". CLASH decreased these segmental durations in prepared speech but not in unprepared speech, which supports hypothesis 1. Unexpectedly, CLASH actually increased the durations of the same segments in unprepared speech. CLASH x PREP interaction effects were not observed in intensity measures. Section 3.1 reports the main effects of the fixed factors, section 3.2 reports the CLASH x PREP interaction effects.

3.1 Main regression effects

PREP had a significant main effect (χ^2=9.65, p<0.001) on the duration of [i], such that [i] was longer in prepared speech. No similar effects were observed on other segments. There were no significant effects of PREP on peak or average intensity measures or their ratios. One possible explanation for the restriction of the effect to [i] duration is that the relatively long duration of [i] (due to its status as the nucleus of the primary stress) endows it with the greatest susceptibility to subtle changes in speech rate associated with preparation. Consistent with this is the finding that the duration of the entire word was likewise increased by PREP (χ^2=6.46, p<0.01). CLASH had no significant main effect on segmental durations. Regarding the vowel [i] of the primary stressed syllable, CLASH had a quite marginal effect to increase average intensity (χ^2=2.14, p=0.14). Regarding the vowel [ae] in the secondary stressed syllable, CLASH had no effect on average intensity (χ^2=0.01, p=0.92). Similar patterns held for peak intensities, but not the ratios of intensities. Although CLASH had very little effect on segmental durations overall, we see below in section 3.2 that the interaction between CLASH and PREP is responsible for this.

The identity of the numeral had significant main effects on [ae] and [n] durations, as well a marginal effect on [p]. This effect was to increase segmental durations after the numeral "eleven". This finding is not directly relevant to the hypotheses, but including the identity of the preceding word in the regression model facilitates analysis of the effects of interest. The number of syllables in the animal noun following "Japanese" had a strong effect on the duration of [i] (χ^2=33.5, p<0.001), but not on other segments. The trisyllabic animal words were associated with decreased duration of [i]. A reasonable interpretation of this effect can be derived from the assumption that speakers exert some global control on the duration of the entire phrase. When the final word is longer (i.e., trisyllabic as opposed to disyllabic), speakers shorten the medial word in order to approximate a target phrase duration. If [i] is assumed to have a relatively adjustable duration because of its status as nucleus of a syllable with primary stress, then it would be expected to show this effect most strongly. In contrast, the regressions did not show any main (or interaction) effects on the duration of schwa, perhaps because this segment is typically the shortest and the statistical power provided by the experiment was not sufficient to detect durational variation.

3.2 CLASH x PREP interaction effects

The results support hypothesis 1, which predicted that clash would cause a greater durational reduction in the primary stress syllable in prepared speech compared to unprepared speech. This is evidenced by the presence of a significant CLASH x PREP interaction effect on the duration of [n], which constitutes the onset of the primary stressed syllable (χ^2=6.90,

p=0.01). The effect on [i] alone was not significant (χ^2=1.18, p=0.28), but it was significant on the combined duration of the onset and vowel [ni] (χ^2=5.51, p=0.02). Figure 3 shows the mean z-score for each segment for the four combinations of CLASH and PREP, along with 95% confidence intervals. It can be seen that the duration of [n] is significantly lower in a prepared speech clashing context than in a prepared speech non-clashing context. The absolute magnitude of this effect for individual speakers is on average approximately 15ms. However, a larger, opposite effect was unexpectedly observed in unprepared speech: [n] duration was lengthened by CLASH, where the average effect size across speakers was around 35ms. The same pattern holds marginally in [i]. The source of this pattern is further discussed in section 4.

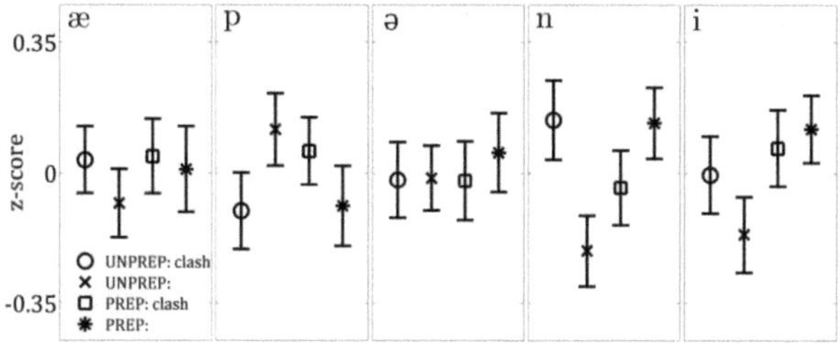

Figure 3: Mean normalized segment durations for combinations of preparation and clash.

The results also provide relatively weak support for hypothesis 2. This hypothesis is derived from transfer-based phonological analyses of the rhythm rule, which predict that CLASH would result in heightened prominence in the secondary stressed syllable. There was indeed a marginal CLASH x PREP interaction effect on the duration of [p] (χ^2=3.30, p=0.07), which resulted in a greater increase in duration in prepared speech than unprepared speech. The segment [p] is arguably affiliated with the secondary stressed syllable by ambisyllabicity, and hence this supports the hypothesis, but the effect was not present in [ae] alone, nor in the combination of the two segments, [aep] (χ^2=1.20, p=0.27). However, as was the case for segments in the primary stressed syllable, the direction of the effect was reversed in unprepared speech, resulting in shorter [p] in the

clashing context (see Figure 1). Why this would occur is somewhat mysterious. On that point, there was no CLASH x PREP interaction effect on the duration of the entire word (χ^2=1.03, p=0.31). Given the presence of such effects on the secondary stressed syllable, this implies that there is some mechanism responsible for complementarity in the durations of the primary and secondary stressed syllables.
No CLASH x PREP interaction effects were observed on any intensity measures, including relative measures that examined the ratios between the values from the primary and secondary stressed syllables. This contradicts findings from one of the previous phonetic studies discussed in section 1.4, which found clash to decrease intensity in the primary stressed syllable. Indeed, the overall pattern reveals an interesting dissociation between duration and intensity: CLASH interacted with PREP to have an effect on duration, but not intensity.

4 Discussion

The main finding, consistent with hypothesis 1, is that a prominence-reducing effect of clash was present in prepared speech only. This supports models of speech planning and production that allow for utterances to be produced before prosodic alternations have occurred, i.e., before structure is fully built. The results did not strongly indicate that a transfer of prominence occurs in prepared speech, as predicted by hypothesis 2. In what follows the results are discussed in detail along with various issues arising in their interpretation. Clash was associated with decreased duration of the primary stressed syllable in prepared speech, and unexpectedly, with increased duration of this syllable in unprepared speech. The pattern in prepared speech was predicted by hypothesis 1. It supports the idea that prosodic alternations require additional planning time to manifest; when insufficient planning time is available, such alternations are less likely to occur. Previous research has shown that prosodic structure - specifically, prosodic words - may not be fully built when an utterance is initiated (Wheeldon and Lahiri, 1997); the current findings extend this phenomenon to prosodic alternations, of which prominence-reduction in the rhythm rule context is an example. This alternation is often the parade example of prosodic alternations, but other sorts of prosodic alternations and prosodically-conditioned segmental alternations may also demonstrate similar behavior (for examples, see Jun, 2005; Ito and Mester, 2007).

The main finding of a preparation-clash interaction effect on segmental durations in the primary stressed syllable of the target was most strongly observed in [n], the onset of the syllable. The decrease was also significant when [n] and [i] were taken as a unit, but not in [i] alone. The coda [z] is expected to pattern similarly, but this cannot be resolved with the current experimental design. The duration of [z] interacts strongly with the onset segment of the following word, which in turn interacts with the stress of the word-initial syllable. Hence it cannot be known if durational patterns in the coda [z] result from stress-modulated coarticulatory influences or more global prosodic effects.

Both incremental and dynamical planning models (cf. section 1.1) predict that preparation can have an effect on the realization of prosodic structure, but the predictions arguably differ regarding the nature of the variation. Incremental models of the sort developed by Levelt (1989) and Levelt et al. (1999) assume a prosody generator that takes as input categorical phonological representations and outputs phonetic parameters for variables such as F0, intensity, and duration. Without further mechanisms, this sort of model predicts a relatively bimodal distribution in phonetic observables associated with a given alternation: the representations that serve as input to the parameter generator are either sufficiently or insufficiently well-specified for the generator to compute an alternation, and hence one would expect some degree of bimodality in the output parameters. If planning time could be varied with high temporal resolution, then a linear increase in planning time should result in a relatively non-linear effect on parameters. In contrast, the dynamical models exhibit gradience in the representations themselves; this could allow for a somewhat more linear relation between planning-time and phonetic realization (albeit with external limits on variation for extremely short or long periods of planning). It is likely, however, that stochastic influences on the time-course of planning render this prediction difficult to test experimentally.

Interestingly, the unprepared speech pattern is not exactly what was anticipated: it was predicted that clash-induced reduction of prominence would be more extensive in prepared than unprepared speech, or would occur only in prepared speech. The unexpected clash-induced increase of primary stressed syllable duration in unprepared speech does not necessarily speak against the hypothesis that prosodic alternations are more likely to apply in prepared speech than unprepared speech; instead it suggests that there is an additional planning mechanism involved, which dominates in relatively unprepared utterances. One possible explanation is that time-pressure in the unprepared condition put greater demands on perceptual or working memory processes, which could include recognizing visual stimuli, mapping from recognized pictured to lexical items, maintaining working memory of items, or accessing motor plans associated with those items. These heightened demands could have resulted in delays in how quickly motor plans associated with an upcoming word can be used for production. In support of this is the observation that, although errors in production were not very common, they occurred more frequently in unprepared than prepared speech, and more frequently between the target word and phrase-final word than elsewhere. Extending the duration of the final syllable of the target could be a strategy for buying additional time to access working memory, or an automatic consequence of heightened demands on processing or working memory. For this explanation to make sense, the presence of initial stress on the final word (clash) would have to increase the time required for planning or accessing working memory; it is not clear why this would be the case - if anything, initial stress would be expected to facilitate lexical access (Schiller, 2006), although it is not known if there is any experimental evidence of stress-related facilitation specific to reaction-time in a production task. Another possible account (a quite speculative one) of the unprepared speech durational patterns can be derived from dynamical models of production. Stress, like phrasal boundaries, may be implemented by a production-slowing mechanism (Byrd and Saltzman, 2003) or alternatively, by mutually inhibitory stress planning systems which heighten activation of associated gestural planning systems, thereby extending the duration of those gestures (Tilsen, 2011a,b). In the latter case, nearby stresses in unprepared speech may overlap and imbue gestures with additional duration. In prepared speech the stress planning systems would have more time to mutually inhibit one another and hence this "stress overlap effect" would be diminished.

The manipulation of preparation was a key aspect of the experimental design. It should be clarified that utterances produced in the "prepared" and "unprepared" conditions are both prepared to some extent - the difference is a matter of relative preparation. In order to control preparation, subjects were instructed to subvocally rehearse the utterance one time before producing it. One possible objection is that referring to the controlled variable as "preparation" misses the true source of the effect: the subvocal rehearsal performed by speakers in the prepared condition. It is conceivable that the source of the effect is not due to preparation time, but rather to the performance of a subvocal rehearsal prior to utterance initiation. However, it is quite sensible to equate the rehearsal itself with "preparation" or planning. Indeed, it is not clear exactly what preparation would be if not some form of unvocalized rehearsal of an utterance. Whether the concepts of rehearsal and preparation can be operationally distinguished in an experimental paradigm remains an open question.

The results provided quite weak and ambiguous support for hypothesis 2, although in the absence of intonational analysis they cannot be interpreted as conclusive. Derived from transfer-based phonological analyses of the rhythm rule, hypothesis 2 predicted that in a clashing context, the secondary stressed syllable would exhibit an increase in prominence due to a transfer of prominence from the primary stress. The duration of [p] was marginally increased by clash in prepared speech, but [ae] duration was unaffected. The segment [p] could be viewed as associated with the secondary stressed syllable, via ambisyllabicity, although it is more typically viewed as the onset of the unstressed medial syllable in "Japanese". As with the primary stress onset [n], the pattern with [p] was reversed in unprepared speech: clash shortened [p]. In other words, [p] and [ni] exhibit opposing patterns of durational variation across conditions, revealing a somewhat striking complementarity between segmental durations in the final syllable and preceding syllable. One possible explanation for this is that speakers exert global control on individual word durations, and hence durational effects on the primary stress are compensated for with opposing effects earlier in the word.

It is likely that analysis of pitch and phrasal boundary accents may shed further light on the source of experimental effects. Treatments of pitch accent clash from Bolinger (1965) and Shattuck Hufnagel et al. (1994)

predict that clash should decrease F0 in the primary stress of the phrase-medial target word. An alternative possibility is that clash is repaired by augmentation of a prosodic boundary between the target word and the phrase-final world, which is partly consistent with the silent beat analysis of Selkirk (1984). An augmented boundary would result in the production of an augmented pitch accent on the primary stressed syllable of the target word. However, this would also predict that clash should have lengthened duration of this syllable, at least in the prepared responses, which was not the case. Hence the idea that clash augmented the word-final boundary is not very convincing.
Finally, a dissociation between effects on duration and intensity was observed: while duration was differently affected by the interaction of clash and preparation, only a marginal main effect of clash was observed on intensity, which resulted in an increase of intensity in the vowel in the secondary stressed syllable. It should be noted that the task design is not particularly well-suited for investigating more global prosodic parameters such as F0 and intensity. Subjects produced many repetitions of similar phrases during the experiment, and they did so in a communicative context that lacked a listener. Primary functions of F0 and intensity in English include the signaling of turn-taking, informational structure, and pragmatic context. Both the repetitive nature of the task and the absence of a listener may have led subjects to under-utilize these variables. It may be the case that F0 and intensity are not manipulated extensively enough to reveal differential effects of clash between preparation conditions.

5 Conclusion

The main finding of this experiment is that the effect of clash on segmental duration differs depending upon the extent to which an utterance has been prepared. Previous studies have almost exclusively examined prepared utterances, and have found some evidence for clash-induced reduction of the primary stress in the rhythm rule context. The present study suggests that this prominence reduction does not occur in relatively unprepared speech. The theoretical implication of this result is that prosodic structure can be incompletely built upon the initiation of an utterance, and prosodic alternations are less likely to occur in speech that is less extensively prepared. This is consistent with current models of speech planning and production, but is not obvious from static phonological representations of prosodic structure.

Another finding is that durational effects of clash were not observed on the preceding secondary stressed syllable, in either prepared or unprepared responses. This is consistent with previous phonetic studies which have generally failed to observe evidence for a "transfer" of prominence in the rhythm rule context, and it supports prominence-reduction based analyses of the prosodic alternation. However, it is possible that analysis of pitch accentual patterns may reveal a transfer of pitch accent in this context, albeit without corresponding durational changes.

An important contribution of this study is the development of an experimental paradigm suitable for investigating the effects of planning time on prosodic structure building and prosodic alternations. Preparation was manipulated by task instruction and stimuli were presented visually to elicit formulaic three-word noun phrases. These methodological devices provide a relatively simple framework for conducting studies of prosodic planning. Moreover, future studies which aim to understand the effects of prosodic structure on speech should take into account the extent to which speakers prepare their utterances, since preparation can have potentially significant effects on phonetic patterns. Experimental manipulation of preparation can provide a potentially rich source of data to inform models of speech planning and production.

6 Acknowledgements

This research was supported by NIH/NIDCD grants #R01-DC006435, #R01-DC003172-14, and #R01-DC008780-04. I would like to thank Louis Goldstein, Dani Byrd, and Rachel Walker for advice in the design and analysis of this experiment. Thanks to Ed Holsinger and Ben Parrell for lively discussions of linear mixed effects regression, which aided the analyses of these data.

References

Al-Mozainy, H. Q., Bley-Vroman, R., and McCarthy, J. J. (1985). Stress shift and metrical structure. *Linguistic Inquiry*, 16(1):135–144.

Beckman, M. and Edwards, J. (1994). Articulatory evidence for differentiating stress categories. In Keating, P. A., editor, *Papers in Laboratory Phonology III: Phonological Structure and Phonetic Form*, pages 1–33. Cambridge University Press, Cambridge U.K.

Beckman, M. E., Hirschberg, J., and Shattuck-Hufnagel, S. (2005). The original ToBI system and the evolution of the ToBI framework. In Jun, S. A., editor, *Prosodic Typology: The Phonology of Intonation and Phrasing*, pages 9–54. Oxford University Press, Oxford.

Bing, J. M. (1980). Linguistic rhythm and grammatical structure in Afghan Persian. *Linguistic Inquiry*, 11(3):437–463.

Bolinger, D. (1958). A theory of pitch accent in English. *Word*, 14(2-3):119–149.

Bolinger, D. (1965). Pitch accent and sentence rhythm. In Abe, I. and Kanekiyo, T., editors, *Accent, Morpheme, Order*, pages 139–180. Hokuo, Tokyo.

Bolinger, D. (1985). Two views of accent. *Journal of Linguistics*, 21(1):79–123.

Browman, C. P. and Goldstein, L. (1992). Articulatory phonology: An overview. *Phonetica*, 49(3-4):155–180.

Byrd, D. (2000). Articulatory vowel lengthening and coordination at phrasal junctures. *Phonetica*, 57(1):3–16.

Byrd, D. and Saltzman, E. (1998). Intragestural dynamics of multiple prosodic boundaries. *Journal of Phonetics*, 26:173–199.

Byrd, D. and Saltzman, E. L. (2003). The elastic phrase: Modeling the dynamics of boundary-adjacent lengthening. *Journal of Phonetics*, 31(2):149 – 180.

Chomsky, N. and Halle, M. (1968). *The Sound Pattern of English*. Harper & Row, New York.

Churchyard, H. (1999). *Topics in Tiberian Biblical Hebrew metrical phonology and prosodics*. PhD thesis, Department of Linguistics, University of Texas, Austin.

Cooper, W. E. and Eady, S. J. (1986). Metrical phonology in speech production. *Journal of Memory and Language*, 25(3):369–384.

Fry, D. B. (1958). Experiments in the perception of stress. *Language and Speech*, 1:126–152.

Grabe, E. and Warren, P. (1995). Stress Shift: Do speakers do it or listeners hear it? In Connell, B., editor, *Laboratory Phonology IV. Phonology and Phonetic Evidence*, pages 95–110. Oxford University Press, Oxford.

Gussenhoven, C. (1991). The English rhythm rule as an accent deletion rule. *Phonology*, 8(1):1–35.

Gussenhoven, C. (2011). Sentential prominence in English. In van Oostendorp, M., Ewen, C. J., Hume, E., and Rice, K., editors, *The Blackwell Companion to Phonology*, pages 2780–2806. Wiley-Blackwell, Malden M.A. & Oxford.

Hayes, B. (1995). *Metrical Stress Theory: Principles and Case Studies*. University of Chicago Press, Chicago.

Hayes, B. and Puppel, S. (1985). On the rhythm rule in Polish. In van der Hulst, H. and Smith, N., editors, *Advances in Nonlinear Phonology*, pages 59–81. Foris Publications, Dordrecht.

Horne, M. (1990). Empirical evidence for a deletion formulation of the rhythm rule in English. *Linguistics*, 28 (5):959–982.

Ito, J. and Mester, A. (2007). Prosodic adjunction in Japanese compounds. In *Proceedings of Formal Approaches to Japanese Linguistics 4*, pages 97–112.

Jun, S. A. (2005). *Prosodic Typology: The Phonology of Intonation and Phrasing*. Oxford University Press, Oxford.

Kawamoto, A. H., Liu, Q., Mura, K., and Sanchez, A. (2008). Articulatory preparation in the delayed naming task. *Journal of Memory and Language*, 58(2):347–365.

Kiparsky, P. (1979). Metrical structure assignment is cyclic. *Linguistic Inquiry*, 10(3):421–441.

Klapp, S. T. (1995). Motor response programming during simple choice reaction time: The role of practice. *Journal of Experimental Psychology: Human Perception and Performance*, 21(5):1015.

Klapp, S. T. (2003). Reaction time analysis of two types of motor preparation for speech articulation: Action as a sequence of chunks. *Journal of Motor Behavior*, 35(2):135–150.

Klatt, D. H. (1975). Vowel lengthening is syntactically determined in a connected discourse. *Journal of Phonetics*, 3(3):129–140.

Levelt, W. J. M. (1989). *Speaking: From Intention to Articulation*. MIT Press, Cambridge M.A.

Levelt, W. J. M., Roelofs, A., and Meyer, A. (1999). A theory of lexical access in speech production. *Behavioural and Brain Sciences*, 22:1–75.

Liberman, M. (1975). *The Intonation System of English.* PhD thesis, MIT, Boston.

Liberman, M. and Prince, A. (1977). On stress and linguistic rhythm. *Linguistic Inquiry*, 8(2):249–336.

Nakatani, L. H., O'Connor, K. D., and Aston, C. H. (1981). Prosodic aspects of American English speech rhythm. *Phonetica*, 38(1-3):84–105.

Nespor, M. and Vogel, I. (1986). *Prosodic Phonology.* Foris Publications, Dordrecht.

Saltzman, E. L. and Munhall, K. G. (1989). A dynamical approach to gestural patterning in speech production. *Ecological Psychology*, 1(4):333–382.

Saltzman, E. L., Nam, H., Krivokapic, J., and Goldstein, L. (2008). A task-dynamic toolkit for modeling the effects of prosodic structure on articulation. In Barbosa, P. A., Madureira, S., and Reis, C., editors, *Proceedings of the 4th Conference on Speech Prosody, Campinas*, pages 175–184.

Schiller, N. O. (2006). Lexical stress encoding in single word production estimated by event-related brain potentials. *Brain Research*, 1112(1):201–212.

Selkirk, E. O. (1984). *Phonology and Syntax: The Relation between Sound and Structure.* MIT Press, Cambridge M.A.

Shattuck Hufnagel, S., Ostendorf, M., and Ross, K. (1994). Stress shift and early pitch accent placement in lexical items in American English. *Journal of Phonetics*, 22:357–388.

Sternberg, S., Knoll, R. L., Monsell, S., and Wright, C. E. (1988). Motor programs and hierarchical organization in the control of rapid speech. *Phonetica*, 45 (2-4):175–197.

Sternberg, S., Monsell, S., Knoll, R. L., and Wright, C. E. (1978). The latency and duration of rapid movement sequences: Comparisons of speech and typewriting. In Stelmach, G. E., editor, *Information Processing in Motor Control and Learning*, pages 117–152. Academic Press, New York.

Tilsen, S. (2009). Multitimescale dynamical interactions between speech rhythm and gesture. *Cognitive Science*, 33:839–879.

Tilsen, S. (2011a). Effects of syllable stress on articulatory planning observed in a stop-signal experiment. *Journal of Phonetics*, 39(4):642–659.

Tilsen, S. (2011b). Metrical regularity facilitates speech planning and production. *Laboratory Phonology*, 2:642–659.

Tilsen, S. and Johnson, K. (2008). Low-frequency Fourier analysis of speech rhythm. *Journal of the Acoustical Society of America*, 124(2):34–39.

Vanderslice, R. and Ladefoged, P. (1972). Binary suprasegmental features and transformational word-accentuation rules. *Language*, 48(4):819–838.

Vogel, I., Bunnell, H., and Hoskins, S. (1995). The phonology and phonetics of the Rhythm Rule. In Connell, B., editor, *Papers in Laboratory Phonology IV. Phonology and Phonetic Evidence*, pages 111–127. Cambridge University Press, Cambridge U.K.

Wheeldon, L. and Lahiri, A. (1997). Prosodic units in speech production. *Journal of Memory and Language*, 37:356–381.

Prosodic planning in speech production

JELENA KRIVOKAPIĆ

Abstract: Theories of language production need to account for how speakers produce prosodic structure. Very few models have addressed the role of prosodic phrasing in speech planning, and little experimental work examining this question has been conducted so far. Four studies designed to investigate the effect of phrase length and prosodic phrasing on speech planning are presented. The first experiment examines the effect of prosodic structural complexity on pause duration using very long phrases (28 syllables). In a second experiment the effect of prosodic structural complexity using phrases of different length (6, 10, 14 syllables) is investigated. Experiment 3 examines the effect of prosodic complexity when the utterances are strings of numbers and Experiment 4 examines local and distant effects of prosodic phrase length on pause duration. The results show that speakers have a large scope of planning and that both local and distant prosodic phrases have an effect on the speech planning process. It is argued that prosodic structure determines the chunk to be planned by speakers. Implications for models of speech production are discussed.

1 Introduction

The goal of this study is to investigate the role of prosodic structure, in particular prosodic phrasing, in speech planning.

A large body of literature has investigated how linguistic structure influences speech planning processes, in particular focusing on syntactic structure, discourse structure, and phrase length. Studies on the effects of syntactic structure on pause duration have found that more complex structure leads to longer pauses, leading investigators to the conclusion that syntactically complex phrases are more demanding on the production system, and that longer pauses indicate the time speakers need to plan the more complex structure (e.g., Cooper and Paccia-Cooper, 1980; Ferreira, 1991; Strangert, 1997).

The effect of prosodic phrasing on pause duration is less well understood. In a set of studies we examine local and distant effects of phrase length and effects of prosodic structure on speech planning, as evident in pause duration. The goal of these studies is to gain an understanding into the nature of prosodic planning and to examine the role of prosodic structure in speech planning (particularly focusing on planning units).

2 Background

2.1 Prosodic structure

In the last couple of decades, the relevance of a hierarchically organized prosodic structure in speech production has become increasingly clear (see Shattuck-Hufnagel and Turk, 1996, for an overview). Prosodic structure refers to the suprasegmental structure of an utterance that encodes prominence and phrasing. Prominence serves to highlight important or new information (e.g., Bolinger, 1972; Halliday, 1967) while phrasing serves to chunk the stream of speech for processing purposes (Cutler et al., 1997; Frazier et al., 2006; Krivokapić, 2007a,b). The focus of this study is on the phrasing aspect of prosody, and particularly on the temporal aspects.

Prosodic structure is hierarchically organized into units, with higher units dominating lower units. In addition to tonal events, prosodic boundaries are characterized by systematic variation in the acoustic and articulatory temporal properties of segments. Research has shown that at boundaries segments increase in duration in the acoustic signal (e.g., Oller, 1973; Klatt, 1975; Shattuck-Hufnagel and Turk, 1998; Wightman et al., 1992). In articulation, it has been found that boundary adjacent gestures become temporally longer and that this lengthening increases cumulatively for larger prosodic boundaries (e.g., Byrd and Saltzman, 1998; Byrd, 2000; Cho, 2005; Edwards et al., 1991).

Depending on the theoretical framework, prosodic units can be largely inferred based on syntactic structure (e.g., Selkirk, 1984; Nespor and Vogel, 1986) or on intonational properties (e.g., Beckmann and Pierrehumbert, 1986; Pierrehumbert, 1980; Jun, 1993, with the latter providing a comparison of the previous two approaches). While there are different proposals in the literature regarding the number and precise definition of categories, in general researchers for English agree on the need for at least one minor and one major category above the word level. In this study we will use the terminology of Beckmann and Pierrehumbert (1986) and refer to these categories as the Intonational Phrase (IP) and the Intermediate Phrase (ip) respectively (for an overview of the various models see Shattuck-Hufnagel and Turk, 1996). The IP is the largest unit, defined as the domain of a coherent intonational contour that has at least a nuclear pitch accent, a phrase accent, and a boundary tone. The IP branches into intermediate phrases, which include at least a pitch accent and a phrase accent. Both IP and ip exhibit final lengthening, but IPs are lengthened more than intermediate phrases. Intermediate phrases branch further into words, and these into syllables. The *Tone and Break Indices* (ToBI) intonation transcription system (Beckman and Elam, 1997), which will be used in this study to examine prosodic structure, is based on this model for intonation and on the work of Price et al. (1991) and Wightman et al. (1992) for the break indices. The distinct prosodic break indices (signaling the perceived boundary strength) in ToBI correspond to the three distinct prosodic categories: word (break index 1), ip (break index 3) and IP (break index 4), and one more break index signaling the within a word boundary, i.e., a clitic boundary (break index 0).[1] A schematic representation of the constituents that are relevant for this study are given in Figure 1.

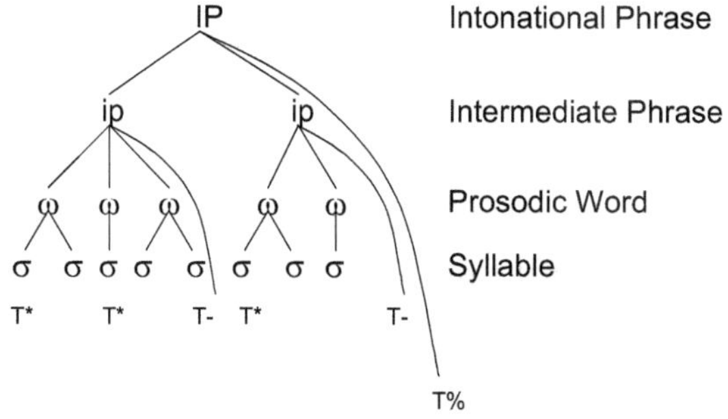

Figure 1: Prosodic constituents (adapted from Beckman, 1989). 'T*' stands for different types of pitch accents, 'T-' for phrase accents and 'T%' for boundary tones. Only the immediately relevant aspects of prosodic structure are shown.

1 Break index 2 signals a mismatch between tonal properties and the perception of the prosodic break.

It is typically assumed that prosodic structure is nonrecursive, as stated in Selkirk's Strict Layer Hypothesis (SLH, see Selkirk, 1984; Nespor and Vogel, 1986). According to this view, a prosodic category always dominates a constituent that is hierarchically immediately lower than itself, thus "in a prosodic tree, any domain at a given level of the hierarchy consists exclusively of domains at the next lower level of hierarchy" (Ladd, 1996, p.238; thus, for example, an ip cannot be dominated by another ip). While this view is generally accepted (but see for opposing views Ladd, 1988, 1996; Itô and Mester, 1992, 2010; Dresher, 1994; Wagner, 2005), there does not exist any experimental support for it, and some experimental evidence argues against this view. For example, acoustic and articulatory studies have found that IP boundaries can systematically be produced with different strength reflecting their depth of the embedding (Ladd, 1988; Byrd and Krivokapić, 2008). Listeners in turn have been found to be sensitive to these distinctions (Byrd and Krivokapić, 2008), and are generally able to distinguish between a larger number of categories than predicted under a nonrecursive view (Ladd, 1996). Based on this kind of evidence, here the view that prosodic recursion is possible is adopted (for a discussion and further arguments against recursion, see Ladd, 1996; Wagner, 2005). For a less strict version of the SLH, see Itô and Mester (1992); Selkirk (1995), where the hypothesis is stated as a set of violable constraints.

2.2 Structural effects in planning

Speech planning involves processes from conceptualization to articulation. It includes, among others, lexical selection, the planning of syntactic structure, prosodic structure, and articulation.
A large body of literature on planning has examined the occurrence and duration of pauses as an indicator of speech planning processes. The most important factors for the present discussion are the structural factors affecting planning (in particular syntactic structure and prosodic structure) and phrase length. These have been found to affect both pause occurrence and pause duration.
A number of studies have investigated the effect of syntactic complexity (syntactic branching) on pause duration and have found that syntactically complex phrases lead to longer pauses compared to syntactically

simpler phrases (e.g., Cooper and Paccia-Cooper, 1980; Grosjean et al., 1979; Ferreira, 1991; Strangert, 1991, 1997; Sanderman and Collier, 1995; Terken and Collier, 1992; Butcher, 1981). Generally, it is assumed that the reason for more complex phrases to be preceded by longer pauses is that the speaker needs more time to plan a syntactically complex utterance, compared to a syntactically simpler phrase, so the time to initiation of the post-boundary phrase increases, allowing planning to occur during this interval (e.g. Ferreira, 1991; Strangert, 1997). Particularly interesting is the study of Ferreira (1991), reporting that pause duration between a subject noun phrase and an object noun phrase (i.e., within a verb phrase) increases with the complexity of the object noun phrase, but only if the subject noun phrase is also complex. She interprets this finding as indicating that when the subject noun phrase is complex, speakers are not able to plan the object noun phrase during the production of the subject, so a pause occurs between the subject and verb phrase, which gives the speaker the time needed for planning the upcoming phrase. In other words, she suggests that planning proceeds in chunks, over structurally defined units. This notion will be particularly relevant in the discussion of the findings presented here (see also Krivokapić, 2007a,b). While these studies have shown that syntactic structure influences pause duration, a large body of research indicates that prosodic structure might be a better predictor of pause duration. A study by Gee and Grosjean (1983) examines the data collected by Grosjean et al. (1979) and finds that pause duration can be better predicted if both syntactic and prosodic structure is used, rather than just syntactic structure. Additionally, Grosjean et al. (1979) examine pause occurrence and show a tendency for speakers to divide phrases into smaller chunks of equal length, even if syntactic structure would lead to a different phrasing, indicating that rhythmical aspects of prosodic structure might be the determining factor of pause occurrence in such cases (see also Krivokapić, 2007a, 154ff on rhythmic effects in prosodic phrasing). Examining the perception of pauses in spontaneous speech Martin (1970) finds that prosodic structure (final lengthening) overrides syntactic structure. Similarly, Ferreira (1993) finds that final lengthening and pause duration are determined by prosodic rather than syntactic structure. These studies lead to the conclusion that prosodic structure might be the critical factor in determining pause duration. The effects of prosodic structure on pause duration are also found in a study by Horne et al. (1995) where it was found that pause duration increases with prosodic boundary strength (see also Choi, 2003).

Phrase length has also been found to have an impact on pause duration. Sternberg et al. (1978) have found that an increase in the number of words in a string of words leads to longer initiation times of the utterance. They suggest that the longer initiation times reflect the time speakers need to retrieve motor programs for the words. In sentences, Zvonik and Cummins (2003) show that the length of prosodic phrases before and after the boundary has an effect on pause duration. Pauses less than 300ms almost exclusively occur with phrases of ten or less syllables before or after the boundary, and the likelihood of a pause being less than 300ms increases when both the prosodic phrase before and after the boundary are less than ten syllables (Zvonik and Cummins, 2003). A study by Ferreira (1991) also finds a length effect, in that she shows that sentence initiation time increases with the number of phonological words in a sentence. Similarly, Watson and Gibson (2004) show that pause occurrence is influenced by phrase length, in that the number of phonological phrases within a preceding and a following syntactic phrase (and thus, the length of the syntactic phrase) is a good indicator of the likelihood of an IP boundary (and therefore of the likelihood of pause occurrence, since IP boundaries are often marked by pauses).

In summary, previous work has provided evidence of the influence of phrase length and even more robust evidence of the influence of syntactic structure on pause duration and speech planning. While some evidence indicates that prosodic structure might play a role in speech planning as well, much less is known about this factor. Furthermore, the process of planning of prosodic structure is also not understood well. We turn to these questions in the remainder of the article.

2.3 Theories of prosodic planning

In contrast to research examining the planning of syntactic structure, and word production models, the planning of larger prosodic phrases has not received much attention in the literature. In what follows we examine two views on prosodic planning, focusing in particular on the question of how incrementaly prosodic structure is planned and on the question of when in the speech production process prosodic structure is built. A non-controversial assumption in models of planning is that speech is produced incrementally, that is, speakers do not plan the whole utterance before speech onset, but instead plan and produce speech simultaneously (e.g., Ferreira, 1996; Ferreira and Swets, 2002; Keating and Shattuck-Hufnagel, 2002; Meyer et al., 2007; Levelt, 1989; Roelofs, 1998; Wheeldon and Lahiri, 1997). Thus speakers plan an utterance in stages (e.g., the stage of planning the conceptual content of a sentence, the stage of its syntactic encoding), and the planning of different fragments of an utterance can proceed in parallel, at different stages. For example, as soon as one fragment is ready, speakers can start articulating, without having entirely planned the rest of the utterance, and the planning of the rest of the utterance proceeds while the speaker is articulating. This allows for efficient and fluent speech production.

It is less agreed upon whether the speech production system is "architecturally incremental" (Ferreira and Swets, 2002), in the sense that incrementality is automatic and a part of the architecture of the language production system. The consequence of such a design of the production system would be that speakers obligatorily start speaking the moment a minimal unit is encoded. Ferreira and Swets (2002) specifically address this question by examining subjects' production when asked to calculate sums of two-digit numbers at their own pace and under time pressure. They show that speakers are able to produce speech in a highly incremental manner, but given the option, they plan further ahead and don't start articulating immediately when encoding is finished for a chunk of the utterance. Ferreira and Swets (2002) argue that the speech production system is not architecturally, but strategically incremental, in the sense that it is the speaker's choice how incrementally they produce speech, and they can choose to plan further than just the smallest unit necessary (Ferreira and Swets, 2002; Wagner et al., 2010). They further show that speakers, even when under time pressure, do plan to some extent up to the end of the sentence (see also Griffin, 2003, for further evidence of a sentential planning scope). The implication of this finding is that speakers are able to plan more than one planning unit at a time, and plan quite large chunks of speech before speech onset.

A second question of interest is how prosodic structure - prosodic phrasing in particular - is planned, and what role in the speech planning process it plays. While the planning of prosodic structure in its entirety is still a largely unexplored field, two approaches have emerged in the literature: a prosody-first approach, developed in Keating and Shattuck-Hufnagel (2002), and a more incremental, prosody-last approach, developed by Levelt (Levelt, 1989; Levelt et al., 1999, see also a related proposal by Ferreira, 1993).

Levelt (1989) is the first model to incorporate prosodic structure into a model of speech production. The approach taken in this model is that speech production is strictly incremental, ideally without any lookahead. Prosodic phrases are created in the Prosody Generator component of the model by scanning the syntactic structure. Thus ip boundaries are placed after a phonological word that is the head of a syntactic constituent (although an adjunct can optionally be included into the ip) and IPs result from the speaker's decision to break at a certain point in an utterance. While the possible locations of the IP boundary are constrained by the syntactic structure, it is the speaker's choice to create a boundary. Whether a speaker does so depends on a number of factors, for example the length of the phrase at that point, the availability of new syntactic material (in the sense that if no further material is available for processing, the speaker is forced to pause), speech rate, prominence of a word, and the speaker's desire to be intelligible. Crucially, in this model prosodic boundaries are determined by looking at just one word at the time, thus with very little lookahead. While Levelt (1989) points out that speakers can occasionally have a larger lookahead (for example in very carefully produced speech) generally the assumption is that there is no lookahead.

Another view is presented in Keating and Shattuck-Hufnagel (2002). They argue that a body of evidence suggests that speakers have a large lookahead in speech production. Regarding phrasing they note that it is influenced, among other things, by the length of not just the preceding but also of the following prosodic phrase (see e.g., Gee and Grosjean, 1983; Watson and Gibson, 2004). This indicates a larger lookahead than the one suggested by Levelt (1989, see Keating and Shattuck-Hufnagel, 2002 for further evidence for a larger lookahead, such as speech errors, stress clash, resyllabification and assimilation patterns). It is also known that speakers use information about prosodic structure during phonetic encoding (e.g., temporal properties of gestures will depend on whether

a syllable is stressed or not). This kind of evidence suggests, Keating and Shattuck-Hufnagel argue, that prosodic structure is an essential part of the process of phonological and phonetic encoding, and that it therefore needs to be available early on. Keating and Shattuck-Hufnagel (2002) suggest a "prosody-first" approach where prior to phonological encoding a rough outline of the prosodic structure (a "skeletal default prosody", Keating and Shattuck-Hufnagel, 2002, p.139) is built based on syntactic information. This representation contains the prosodic phrasing, the marking of the relative prominence of individual constituents, pitch accent marking, and possibly some tonal marking of boundaries. The representation is then restructured in the course of the encoding process based on word form and non-syntactic information. With prosodic structure being available early, prosodic information can inform the encoding process. Keating and Shattuck-Hufnagel's (2002) model necessarily has a large lookahead, as it requires that prosodic structure is built before individual segments can be encoded. The model does not hinge on the exact size of the syntactic chunk available for further planning, it is only important that "the increments ... [are] large enough to account for the facts of phonological and phonetic segmental sensitivity to prosodic structure" (Keating and Shattuck-Hufnagel, 2002, p.139).
In a series of four experiments, we investigate how prosodic phrasing and phrase length affect pause duration. The goal is 1) to examine the role prosodic structure plays in speech planning, and 2) to examine how far ahead speakers plan their utterances and in that way contribute to the discussion of incrementality and to the question whether prosodic structure is build in a "prosody-first" (Keating and Shattuck-Hufnagel, 2002) or a "prosody last" (Levelt, 1989) manner.
Foreshadowing the conclusions of this study, an outline of our view of the role of prosodic structure in speech planning follows: We will assume Keating and Shattuck-Hufnagel (2002)'s "prosody-first" approach, for which we will present additional evidence. Thus based largely on the syntactic structure, speakers build the prosodic structure, as suggested in their model. It will be argued in Experiment 1 that prosodic structure has a critical role in speech planning, namely that it determines the chunk of speech to be phonologically and phonetically encoded at a time. This means that speech planning proceeds over prosodic units (Krivokapić, 2007b). It will be suggested that either the ip or the IP - any

sufficiently large prosodic phrase - can serve as a planning unit. Which prosodic phrase is selected depends on the cognitive load of the upcoming phrase, with hierarchically lower units being selected for cognitively more demanding material. The following four experiments present arguments for this role of prosodic structure and examine how cognitive load affects which prosodic phrase in the hierarchy does in the end serve as the planning unit.

3 Experimental evidence

We examine the effect of prosodic phrasing and how it interacts with phrase length in four experiments. The first experiment (see Krivokapić, 2007b, Experiment 2) examines the effect of prosodic structural complexity (the number of prosodic phrases in an utterance) on pause duration using long phrases (28 syllables before and after the pause). To examine possible interactions of prosodic complexity and phrase length, the second experiment examines the effect of prosodic complexity on pause duration using phrases of different length (6, 10, 14 syllables before and after the pause). The effect of prosodic complexity on pause duration using strings of numbers is investigated in Experiment 3 and Experiment 4 examines the effect of phrase length of phrases immediately after and further away from a boundary. Given that the goal of this article is to examine speech planning, in reporting the results we focus on post-boundary effects.

The four studies are conducted using the synchronous speech paradigm introduced by Cummins (Cummins, 2002, 2003, 2004; Zvonik and Cummins, 2002). In this paradigm, two subjects (one dyad) are seated facing each other and they read sentences simultaneously, at the prompt of the experimenter. Synchronous speech has been shown to reduce inter-speaker variability in pause placement and pause duration without introducing artificial properties into a subject's speech. For example, Cummins (2004) compares the ratio of boundary duration to phrase length in subjects' synchronous and solo productions and finds that the ratios are similar for the two speech styles, but that the variability is reduced in synchronous speech. He finds similar results for the subjects' ratios of phrase length of two phrases. Zvonik and Cummins (2003) further find that both in solo and in synchronous speech speakers had the longest pause following the longest phrase, again indicating that while reducing variability, synchronous speech does not change fundamental properties of speech timing. Given these properties of synchronous speech, and given the large variability speakers exhibit in both duration and placement of pauses (e.g., Goldman Eisler, 1968; Butcher, 1981), this experimental paradigm provides a good way to examine pause duration, as it will minimize individual variation and facilitate comparisons across speakers.

It is worth noting that the experimental design used here - as is the case with the majority of laboratory speech studies - involves certain processes not typical of spontaneous speech, such as reading, repetition, and, in this case, simultaneous speaking with another speaker. Results of such laboratory experiments might not represent the most typical behavior in spontaneous speech processing, however, such studies have a long history of informing us usefully as to properties of the speech production system (see also Ferreira, 1991, 2007, for a discussion of the merits and concerns of laboratory speech).

3.1 Experiment 1

3.1.1 Goal

The first experiment examines the effect of prosodic complexity on pause duration in very long phrases (for a detailed description of the study see Krivokapić, 2007b, Experiment 2). Prosodic complexity is taken to mean, similar to syntactic complexity, the number of prosodic phrases in an utterance. Thus if for example a post-boundary phrase branches into two Intonational Phrases it is prosodically more complex than a nonbranching post-boundary phrase that consists of only one IP (see Figure 2).

non-branching # non-branching

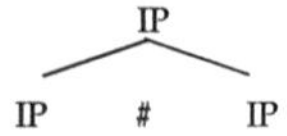

The water pool was surrounded by a large number of tall growing and long living sugarpines from New Brunswick; # all the children were often enchantedly looking at the symmetrically shaped and beautifully smelling cones.

non-branching # branching

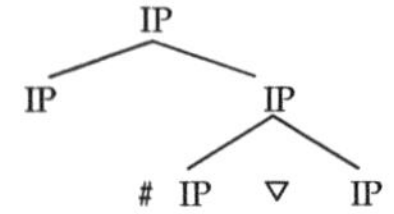

The stylish woman was continuously and excitedly talking about a lovely orange-red carpet; # accompanying her very energetic story ▽ were various examples of fabulous new carpets.

branching # non-branching

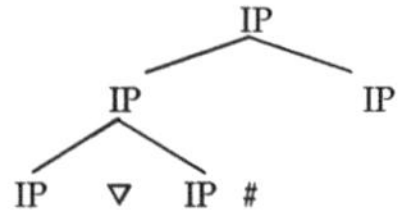

Standing almost invisibly in the furthest corner ▽ was a very tall woman holding a yellowish sack; # all the other people were attentively listening to the rather vehement discussion about peppers.

branching # branching

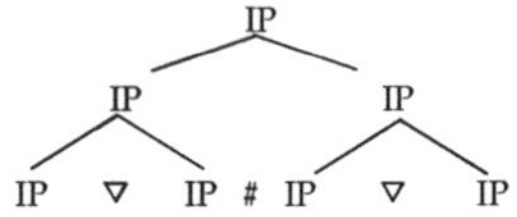

Looking at the funny shaped and oddly colored furniture ▽ Johnny wondered about the strange taste of the tenant; # admiring the beautiful and comfortable chairs ▽ Ann thought of her own pale and uncomfortable sofa.

Figure 2: Structural conditions for Experiments 1, 2, and 3 and sample experiment stimuli for Experiment 1. "Branching" indicates a complex, and "non-branching" a simple structure. The measured pause is indicated with "#", and the branching is indicated with the triangle. These symbols were not present in the sentences the subjects read.

3.1.2 Design and materials

The independent variables in the experiment were: a) complexity of the pre-boundary phrase (whether the pre-boundary phrase was branching into two prosodic phrases or not) and b) complexity of the post-boundary phrase (whether the post-boundary phrase was branching into two prosodic phrases or not). These factors were crossed, yielding four conditions (branching # branching, branching # non-branching, non-branching # branching, non-branching # non-branching, shown in Figure 2). The pause duration between the pre- and post-boundary phrase was the dependent variable. The whole pre-boundary phrase was always 28 syllables, with branching targeted at the 14th syllable, and the same was true for the post-boundary phrase. The targeted prosodic structure was elicited by varying the syntactic structure and the length of syntactic constituents.

There were three utterances for each condition, for a total of twelve utterances. An example for each of the conditions is given in Figure 2. The stimuli for this experiment were combined with stimuli for another experiment (see Krivokapić, 2007b, for randomization procedures). Each item was read three times by each subject, yielding 36 items per subject.

3.1.3 Subjects, recording, and analyses

Data from sixteen speakers (eight dyads) were collected. One dyad was unable to complete the experiment. The results of the remaining seven dyads are reported here. For each dyad, the two subjects were seated facing each other. Before the recording, they familiarized themselves with the stimuli. Once familiar with them, the subjects were asked to read the utterances aloud, at the prompt of the experimenter, together with their co-speaker, as if reading a story to someone. In cases of errors, they were asked to read the utterances again.

Subjects were recorded on a DAT recorder, using two Shure head mounted unidirectional microphones and recordings were made onto the left and right channels of a stereo file.

In order to verify that speakers produced the intended branching and nonbranching structures, the sentences were prosodically analyzed using the Tone and Break Indices labeling system (ToBI Beckman and Elam, 1997). Overall, the branching structures were produced as two IPs, the non-branching ones as one IP. IPs were identified by final lengthening and the presence of a phrase accent and a boundary tone. Only the tokens where both subjects of a dyad produced the targeted structure were

included in the analysis. In all stimuli, the pre-boundary phrase ended in a voiced segment followed by a voiceless stop, and the post-boundary phrase started with a vowel. The duration of the pause was measured from the end of periodic voicing (i.e., the beginning of the voiceless stop closure) to the beginning of periodic voicing for the vowel of the post-boundary phrase. At the end of the pause, occasionally there was a glottal pulse preceding the regular periodic voicing for the vowel, which was taken to be evidence for glotalization of the phrase initial vowel (see Redi and Shattuck-Hufnagel, 2001). In these cases, the pause was taken to end at the onset of the glottal pulse. In all other cases, the pause was taken to start with the end of periodic voicing and to end with the onset of periodic voicing. The threshold for silent intervals to be counted as pauses was 200ms. This threshold was set since all silent intervals included a voiceless stops and shorter intervals could not with certainty be assumed to be pauses. All silent intervals were longer than 200ms.
The duration of the pause was averaged between the two speakers of each dyad. A two-factor ANOVA was performed on these data for each dyad separately testing the effect of the pre-boundary prosodic complexity (with the two levels branching and nonbranching) and the post-boundary prosodic complexity factor (with the two levels branching and non-branching) and their interaction. If the results of the individual dyads patterned in the same manner, the dyads were pooled. To pool the data across the dyads, *z*-scores were calculated over all tokens of each dyad separately. Note that a *z*-score above 0 represents pause durations longer than the dyads' average duration, and a *z*-score below 0 durations shorter than the average duration. Significance for all tests was set at $p<0.05$. In this, as in the other experiments, in reporting the results we focus on the post-boundary effects.

3.1.4 Results

For the pooled data, post-boundary complex phrases lead to significantly ($F(1,185)=23.076, p<.001$) shorter preceding pauses than post-boundary simple phrases, as shown in Figure 3. The same pattern obtained for each dyad separately, though the effect reached significance only for two dyads. The general view of pause duration as it relates to upcoming phrases is that it reflects effects of speech planning processes, in that longer pauses occur in conjunction with longer planning time for the upcoming phrase (e.g., Cooper and Paccia-Cooper, 1980; Ferreira, 1991; Griffin, 2003; Smith and Wheeldon, 1999).

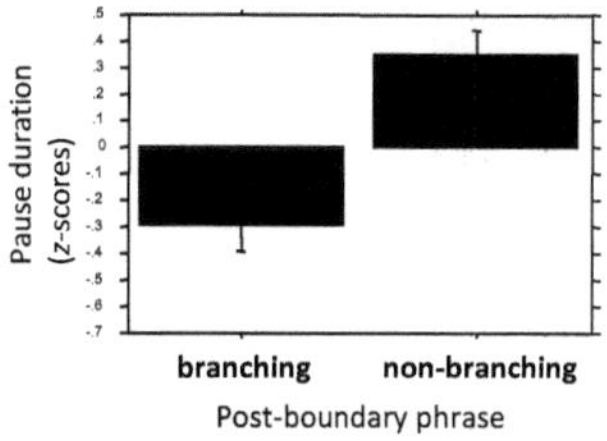

Figure 3: Experiment 1: Effect of post-boundary branching on pause duration (*z*-scores and standard errors) for all dyads pooled. *Z*-scores above 0 represent durations longer than the dyads' average pause duration, and *z*-scores below 0 durations shorter than the average duration.

Based on this, the prediction for this study was that more complex prosodic phrases would lead to longer preceding pauses. Such a result would also correspond to previous studies examining the effect of syntactic structure on pause duration (e.g., Cooper and Paccia-Cooper, 1980; Ferreira, 1991; Strangert, 1997). However, contrary to this prediction, the results showed that shorter pauses precede branching phrases, i.e., more complex prosodic structure leads to shorter preceding pauses. To account for these surprising findings, following Ferreira's (1991) suggestion that speech encoding proceeds over structurally defined units, it was suggested in Krivokapić (2007b) that in the case of the post-boundary branching structure, speakers may be planning only up to the branching node (i.e., planning the first post-boundary IP) before starting to speak the post-boundary phrase. The second post-boundary IP is then planned during the production of the first IP. In the case of the nonbranching post-boundary phrase, speakers plan the complete upcoming phrase. Thus speakers were, in all instances, planning the first upcoming IP, but in the case of branching structures, the first post-boundary IP was 14 syllables long, while in the case of non-branching structures, the first IP was 28 syllables long. The pause duration, on this assumption, reflects the time it takes for the speakers to plan the upcoming prosodic phrase. The implication of this interpretation is that prosodic structure participates in determining the size of the chunk to be phonologically/phonetically encoded at a time. In other words, phonological/phonetic encoding proceeds over prosodic units. Depending on the size of the unit, the pause will be shorter or longer. Note that the suggestion is not that speakers encode the complete upcoming phrase before they start articulating. Rather, following Keating and Shattuck-Hufnagel (2002), the suggestion is that speakers encode the prosodic structure to a certain extent, and continue with the planning process as they are articulating.

Another point to note is that the result of the experiment implies that speakers have a large scope of planning, as they were aware, at the pause, of a branching structure 14 syllables away. This provides some evidence against the view (in Levelt, 1989; Levelt et al., 1999) that speakers produce speech with very little lookahead.

3.2 Experiment 2

3.2.1 Goals

To further examine the scope of planning and the idea that planning proceeds over prosodic units, a second experiment was conducted (as reported in Krivokapić, 2007a). While the first experiment examined the effect of prosodic structural complexity on pause duration using very long phrases (28 syllables), Experiment 2 examined the effect of prosodic structural complexity on pause duration using phrases of different length. The goal is to examine whether a decrease in cognitive load (such as a decrease in phrase length) will affect how prosodic structure affects the planning process.

3.2.2 Design and materials

This study had a 3-factor design, examining the effects of pre-boundary complexity (with the levels branching and non-branching), post-boundary complexity (with the post-boundary phrase being branching or non-branching) and surrounding phrase length, with the levels short (six syllables before and six syllables after the boundary), medium (ten syllables before and ten syllables after the boundary) and long (14 syllables before and 14 syllables after the boundary). The factors were crossed, for a total of 12 conditions (2 pre-boundary x 2 post-boundary x 3 length; Note that the prosodic structures of the stimuli were the same as is Experiment 1, shown in Figure 2). In the complex phrases, branching was targeted at the middle of the phrases (i.e., at the third, fifth and seventh syllable for the short, medium and long sentences respectively). An example utterance (for the short branching # branching condition), is "Although mad, she rang Chap. # Abe picked up, but called him", with branching targeted at the third syllable before and after the boundary (at the comma), and the examined pause being between "Chap" and "Abe". In all utterances, each pre-boundary phrase ended in "Chap" and each post-boundary phrase started with "Abe". There was one utterance per condition. To avoid memorization of the utterances, there were also twelve filler items, matching the experimental items in prosodic structure and length but with different lexical content. The utterances were randomized in blocks of 24 (12 test plus 12 filler utterances). Seven dyads were recorded. In total, 984 test utterances were recorded for analysis (12 utterances x 12 repetitions x 6 dyads, and for one dyad 12 utterances x 10 repetitions). Note that while this study had only one utterance per condition, a follow-up study was conducted, with 4 utterances per condition, varying in syntactic structure and segments surrounding the pause. Only results which were replicated in the verification study are presented here.

3.2.3 Subjects, recording, and analyses

Data from 14 speakers (7 dyads) were collected. The synchronous speech paradigm, described earlier, was used in this study as well. The recording procedure and the pause duration measurements were the same as in Experiment 1. Prosodic labeling (described in Experiment 1) verified that the branching structures were produced as two IPs, the nonbranching ones as one IP. A three-factor ANOVA was performed on the data of each dyad separately, testing the effect of the three factors (pre-boundary complexity, post-boundary complexity, phrase length) and their interactions. If the results of the individual dyads patterned in the same manner, the dyads were pooled, as described in Experiment 1. Significance for all tests was set at $p<0.05$.

3.2.4 Results

For phrase length, the predicted outcome was that with longer phrases, pause duration would increase. Length effects have been reported in the literature and it is assumed that more length will lead to longer pauses as speakers will need more time to process the upcoming phrase. For the pooled dyads, the results showed that phrase length had the expected effect (Figure 4): An increase in the number of syllables led to an increase in pause duration ($F(2,918) = 52.671$, $p<.0001$). Fisher's PLSD shows a significant difference between all 3 levels of length, such that surrounding longer phrases lead to longer pauses (long compared to medium $p=.0011$, long compared to short $p<.0001$, medium compared to short $p<.0001$). The results indicate that more phonological length (syllables) in an upcoming phrase requires longer planning times, which leads to longer pauses.

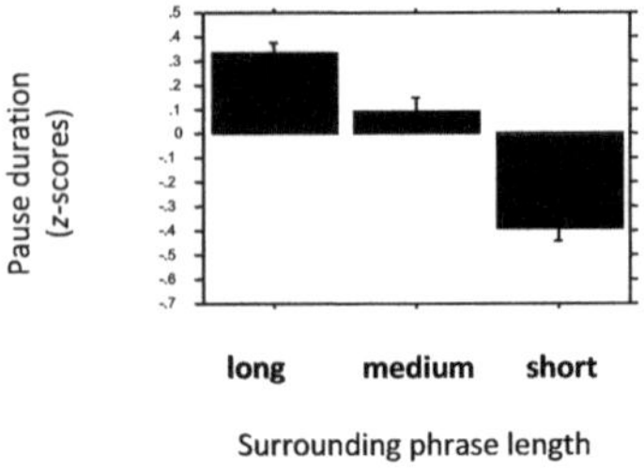

Figure 4: Experiment 2: Effect of length on pause duration (z-scores and standard errors) for all dyads pooled. Z-scores above 0 represent durations longer than the dyads' average pause duration, and z-scores below 0 durations shorter than the average duration.

For post-boundary complexity, there are two possible outcomes, based on previous work: The first possible outcome, based on the results in Experiment 1, is that prosodically complex (branching) structures will induce shorter pauses than non-branching phrases. The second possibility, in line with findings of studies examining the effect of syntactic structure on pause duration, is that phrasal complexity could lead to longer pauses. The reason to expect this latter effect is that the phrases examined in this study were considerably shorter than the ones in Experiment 1 (Krivokapić, 2007b) in which pre-boundary and post-boundary phrases were each 28 syllables. The phrases in Experiment 2 are 6, 10 and 14 syllables. In this case prosodic structure might not be chunking the upcoming phrase into smaller units for encoding, as the upcoming phrase might "as is" be short enough for the processing system to manage in one chunk. The two predictions could combine, in that for shorter phrases, prosodic complexity may increase pause duration, while for longer phrases complexity may decrease pause duration. In other words, as the length of the phrase increases and the load of the upcoming phrase increases as well, prosodic structure may chunk the upcoming phrase, causing pause duration to become shorter for branching/complex than for non-branching/simple phrases. On this scenario, in the long branching condition pauses would be shorter than in the long non-branching condition, while in the short branching condition pauses would be longer than in the short non-branching condition.

For all dyads pooled, the results show that complex phrases induced longer pauses ($F(1,918)=4.805$, $p=.0286$), as shown in Figure 5. Individual dyads patterned in the same manner, and the effect reached significance for one dyad.

Figure 5: Experiment 2. Effect of post-boundary branching on pause duration (z-scores and standard errors) for all dyads pooled. Z-scores above 0 represent durations longer than the dyads' average pause duration, and z-scores below 0 durations shorter than the average duration.

This indicates that, like in previous, syntactic studies, structural complexity increased pause duration as more structure for the same length needs to be planned. These findings differ however from the findings in Experiment 1 (Krivokapić, 2007b), where more complex structure led to shorter pauses. Both findings can be accounted for by assuming that prosodic structure participates in determining the size of the chunk to be planned. Depending on the size of a potential chunk, speakers might plan only up to the branching node rather than the whole post-boundary phrase, or, for smaller utterances, they might plan the whole post-boundary phrase. In other words, depending on the size of the chunk (and probably other factors) a hierarchically higher or lower IP (presumably ip as well) might be the chunk to be planned (Krivokapić, 2007a). Note that this interpretation assumes prosodic recursion, but we suggest that the crucial point is that a hierarchically higher or lower category can determine the chunk to be encoded, while the exact type of the category is not important, as any prosodic category above the word level could potentially be the chunk to be planned.[2]

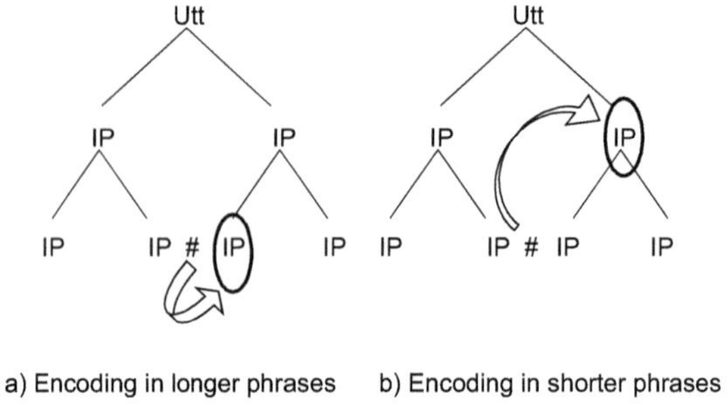

Figure 6: Prosodic chunking. The arrow points to the prosodic chunk that is planned during the pause (marked with #).

2 In addition to the size of the potential chunk, other factors are likely to influence whether a hierarchically higher or lower prosodic phrase will be the chunk to be planned by the speaker. A likely factor is individual differences. Swets et al. (2007) for example showed that individual differences influence prosodic phrasing in silent reading. Readers with a low working memory had a greater tendency to break up larger chunks of text into smaller chunks than readers with a high working memory. These findings could be due to a difference in planning scope. Petrone et al. (2011) show that working memory span affects the scope of planning, as evidenced in phrase initial F0, again indicating an effect of individual differences. Simultaneous cognitive demands on the speaker could also have an impact such that the chunks to be planned at a time become smaller.

Thus when phrases are shorter (as in Experiment 2) speakers plan the whole post-boundary phrase and do not chunk it into smaller planning units. In this case then, the prosodically more complex phrases lead to longer planning time as there is more structure to be planned. On this analysis, prosodic structure interacts with phrase length in heterogeneous ways. For very long phrases, speakers use hierarchically lower phrases to determine the planning chunk, but when the phrases are shorter, hierarchically higher phrases determine the chunk to be planned (Figure 6).

3.3 Experiment 3

3.3.1 Goals

This study examines how pause duration is affected by prosodic structure in strings of numbers. The goal is to examine the scope of planning in a string that is more difficult to plan due to the near absence of semantic meaning and syntactic structure.

3.3.2 Design and materials

Four strings were constructed to measure the effect of prosodic structure on pause duration.[3] As in Experiment 1, the independent variables were a) the complexity of the pre-boundary phrase (whether the pre-boundary phrase was branching into two prosodic phrases or not) and b) the complexity of the post-boundary phrase (whether the post-boundary phrase was branching into two prosodic phrases or not). As in the first study, the branching and non-branching strings consisted of 28 syllables, and the branching was targeted at the 14th syllable. One number string was constructed for each condition. Subjects saw each number string both as a number (as in 1a) and spelled out, as shown in (1b). It was assumed that reading the numbers just by themselves would be too difficult, therefore the subjects were asked to look at the numbers (as in 1a) first, but to read aloud the numbers written as words (as in 1b). In order to induce the prosodic branching, the branching number strings were visually grouped, and when spelled out, they were connected with

3 I would like to thank Jean-Roger Vergnaud for suggesting this experiment.

"and". Thus for example the 'branching # non-branching' condition was as given in (1a/1b). In (1a) the first line is the pre-boundary branching condition, and the second line is the post-boundary nonbranching condition. The branching occurs before "772 308" in the string in (1a), and in the spelled version in (1b) before "and". To avoid additional branching, the complete pre-boundary line, and the complete post-boundary condition on the second line (not as represented below, where the pre- and post-boundary condition didn't fit on one line each). The measured pause was, as in the previous experiments, between the pre- and the post-boundary condition. In the example below, the pause was between the number "eight" of the pre-boundary phrase and the number "one" of the post-boundary phrase. All pre-boundary phrases ended in a voiceless stop, and all post-boundary phrases started with a vowel. Each utterance was repeated three times and the data were randomized in blocks of four utterances, for a total of 12 utterances per subject.

(1a) Branching # non-branching utterance presented as numbers

952 469 772 308
177 977 797

(1b) Branching # non-branching utterance presented as words

nine hundred fifty two thousand four hundred sixty nine *and*
seven hundred seventy two thousand three hundred eight

one hundred seventy seven million nine hundred seventy seven
thousand seven hundred ninety seven

3.3.3 Subjects, recording, and analyses

Data for 14 subjects (seven dyads) were collected. The synchronous speech paradigm was used in this study as well. The recording procedure, the pause duration measurements, the data pooling process, and the statistical analysis were the same as in Experiment 1.
As in the previous experiments, a prosodic analysis (the ToBI labeling system, see Beckman and Elam, 1997) was used to verify that subjects produced the targeted prosodic structure. The analysis showed that

all utterances were produced with the anticipated prosody (branching structures were produced as two IPs, the non-branching ones as one IP), but, in addition, all utterances had IPs branching into intermediate phrases. The nonbranching utterances were thus produced as branching structures as well.

3.3.4 Results

The results showed that there were no effects of prosodic complexity. This leads to the question whether number strings are planned differently than other utterances, such that prosodic structure does not have an effect on planning. We suggest that the difference between strings of numbers and regular utterances is not as surprising as it might seem at first: A string of unrelated numbers not connected conceptually, and with an impoverished syntactic structure, is cognitively more demanding than a coherent sentence. In this case then, speakers might be producing speech more incrementally, i.e., they might use smaller chunks for planning. If we assume that prosodic constituents are not qualitatively different for purposes of planning, any prosodic constituent could be used to chunk speech into planning units. In the case of cognitively demanding tasks, as numbers most likely are, speakers might choose to plan an ip, and not an IP. Since all utterances in Experiment 3 were produced with ip-branching, if subjects planned ip rather than IP phrases, the lack of effect can be accounted for.

3.4 Experiment 4

3.4.1 Goals

It is known that boundary strength is affected by properties of phrases immediately adjacent to the boundary (e.g., by phonological length, syntactic structure, and, as has been established in the previous studies, by prosodic structure). What is not well understood is the influence that phrases further away from the boundary have on pause duration. The goal of the last study is to examine local and distant effects of prosodic phrase length on boundary strength (see Krivokapić, 2010, for further details of the experiment). The larger goal is to examine incrementality in speech production, as it relates to prosodic planning.

In a study examining word planning effects, Griffin (2003) found that in a two word sequence, when a short word precedes a long word, speech onset occurs later than when the first word is also long. Griffin (2003) interprets these findings as indicating that in the short-long sequence the first word is not immediately articulated when planned, but buffered while the second word is being sufficiently prepared (enough to avoid disfluency). In the long-long sequence, the first word is immediately articulated, as there will be enough time for the preparation of the second word during the production of the first (cf. also Ferreira, 1991).
A second line of research finds that distant prosodic boundaries affect boundary strength in both production and perception (e.g., Wagner, 2005; Schafer, 1997; Carlson et al., 2001; Clifton et al., 2002; Jun, 2003). A study by Frazier et al. (2004) has found that the naturalness in prosodic boundary production (as judged by listeners) depends not just on the strength of a specific boundary but also on the strength of surrounding boundaries. Studies by Schafer (1997); Carlson et al. (2001); Clifton et al. (2002); Jun (2003) have shown that listeners' interpretation of boundary strength depends on the boundary strength of surrounding boundaries, indicating that global prosodic structure guides listeners' interpretation. Given such distant effects, and the fact that speakers may plan more than one structural unit at a time, the question arises whether more than one prosodic phrase might be planned as well - at least to some degree - before speech onset. Experiment 4 examines the effect of the length of the first and the second post-boundary IP on pause duration.

3.4.2 Design and materials

The study was a two factor design: a) post-boundary length (short or long) of the first IP following a target pause and b) post-boundary length (short or long) of the second, more distant IP following the pause. The factors were crossed, yielding four conditions. The dependent variable was the pause before the first post-boundary phrase (see Table 1). Note that it was not possible to systematically vary phrase length while keeping overall post-boundary length constant. In order to control for the overall length of the post-boundary phrase, the duration of the second phrase varied, depending on whether the first phrase was two or four syllables, as seen in Table 1. To eliminate pre-boundary effects, the pre-boundary sentence was always the same ("Bob was buying books for Sam"), and was seven syllables long. There were six utterances for each of the four conditions and twelve repetitions of each utterance, for a total of 288 utterances per subject. An example for each of the conditions is given in Table 1.

Table 1: Experimental conditions with one example utterance. The comma separates the two post-boundary IPs (as verified in the ToBI transcription). The pre-boundary phrase was always "Bob was buying books for Sam". # indicates the measured pause.

Post-boundary phrase (IP_1, IP_2)
Short first phrase, short second phrase (2 + 10 syllables) # Zack sang, claiming that this would help him choose the books.
Short first phrase, long second phrase (2 + 16 syllables) # Zack sang, claiming that this would help him choose the best children's book in the store.
Long first phrase, short second phrase (4 + 8 syllables) # Zack sang loudly, claiming that this would be helpful.
Long first phrase, long second phrase (4 + 14 syllables) # Zack sang loudly, claiming that this would help him choose the best book in the store.

3.4.3 Subjects, recording, and analyses

Data from 14 subjects (seven dyads) were collected. The synchronous speech paradigm was used in this experiment as well. The recording procedure and prosodic analysis were the same as described in Experiment 1. Pause duration was measured from the end of voicing for the nasal stop closure of the pre-boundary phrase (pause onset) to the beginning of voicing or frication for the phrase-initial segment (pause end), depending on what the first post-boundary segment was (the post-boundary phrase started with one of the following: [z, m, ɹ, s, l, n]). The duration of the pause was averaged between the two speakers of each dyad.

A two-factor ANOVA was performed on these data for each dyad separately testing the effect of the two factors: 1) length of the first post-boundary IP (with the two levels: short and long) and 2) length of the second post-boundary IP (with the two levels: short and long) and their interaction. If the results of the individual dyads patterned in the same manner, the dyads were pooled, as described in Experiment 1. Significance for all tests was set at $p<0.05$.

3.4.4 Results and discussion

For the pooled data, the results show that both the first and the second post-boundary phrase had an effect, such that longer phrases lead to longer pause duration (first post-boundary IP: $F(1,2009)= 9.043$, $p=.0027$; second post-boundary IP: $F(1,2009)= 10.521$, $p=.0012$), shown in Figure 7. Thus both the local and the more distant phrase had an effect on pause duration. The same pattern obtained for the individual dyads, though the effects did not reach significance.

Figure 7: Effects of length of the first and second post-boundary IP on the duration of the pause (z-scores and standard errors) for all dyads pooled. Z-scores above 0 represent durations longer than the dyads' average pause duration, and z-scores below 0 durations shorter than the average duration.

The results indicate that speakers plan quite far ahead, since at speech onset they have planned, at least to some extent, the two post-boundary IPs. Note that we cannot say that in this case speakers select the hierarchically higher IP (rather than the hierarchically lower IP) and are thus planning the whole post-boundary phrase, as we suggested for the results in Experiment 2. If that were the case we would not expect to see the effects of the individual post-boundary phrases. Thus, the experiment provides further evidence that prosodic phrases determine the chunk to be planned by the speaker.

4 Discussion

The preceding studies examined the influence of phrase length and prosodic structure on pause duration in a variety of contexts. Phrase length was found to have an effect such that longer phrases lead to longer pauses. For prosodic structure it was found that depending on the length of the post-boundary phrase, prosodic structure impacts pause duration differently. For longer phrases, a complex structure leads to shorter pauses (Experiment 1), while for shorter phrases, a more complex structure leads to longer pauses (Experiment 2). No effect of IP branching was found in Experiment 3. Experiment 4 found both local and global effects of prosodic structure on pause duration.

The results of the experiments show that speakers have a fairly large lookahead in speech planning. At the time of the post-boundary phrase initiation, speakers were aware of the prosodic branching occurring at the third, fifth, seventh, and even 14th syllable after the boundary, and Experiment 4 provided evidence that speakers plan not only the first but also the second post-boundary phrase before speech onset. Note that the experimental paradigm used in these studies reduces the amount of planning needed for the sentences, in that reading and repetition most likely ease the planning load (see also Ferreira, 1991, 2007). Thus speakers in these experiments likely have a larger lookahead than speakers usually do. But importantly, the results show that speakers are capable of a large lookahead.

This large lookahead provides further evidence that speech production is not, in Ferreira and Swets (2002)' terminology, architecturally incremental. Speakers do not start speaking as soon as a minimal production unit is ready. Rather, speakers plan a large chunk–to a certain degree at least–before they start articulating.

This large lookahead is compatible with Keating and Shattuck-Hufnagel's (2002) "prosody-first", but not with Levelt's (1989) "prosody-last" approach. Thus we will assume Keating and Shattuck-Hufnagel's (2002) model, in which speakers, based largely on the syntactic structure, build a rough prosodic structure before phonological encoding. We suggest that prosodic structure then chunks the upcoming material into phrases that will be planned (phonologically and phonetically encoded) by the speaker before speech onset. The phonological length of the prosodic phrase (in number of syllables, or some other indicator of length), will then determine the time it will take the speaker to encode the upcoming phrase. The time needed will be reflected in the duration of the pause preceding the phrase. Any prosodic category (ip or IP) can be the chunk to be planned, and which category is selected will depend on the cognitive load of the upcoming material. For very long utterances a hierarchically lower category might be selected, thus chunking the utterance into smaller planning units, as was seen in Experiment 1. For shorter utterances a hierarchically higher category might be selected, since the utterance is already short enough for planning purposes, as in Experiment 2. In line with this suggestion, there was no effect of prosodic structure when the utterances were strings of numbers (Experiment 3). It was argued that these semantically and syntactically impoverished strings are cognitively demanding and that for that reason a hierarchically lower phrase (an ip) is selected for encoding. Since all utterances were branching into ip-s, there was no effect of prosodic branching. Also, as mentioned before, speakers under different circumstances might have a smaller scope of planning than the participants in these studies. Consequently, speakers might typically use hierarchically lower prosodic categories to determine the chunk to be processed (for example a lower IP, or an intermediate phrase).

5 Conclusion

The preceding studies have shown that phrase length has an effect on speech planning times (as instantiated in pause duration) both locally and globally, such that longer phrases lead to longer planning time. Speakers have been found to be able to plan their production at least two Intonation Phrases ahead, supporting the idea from Ferreira and Swets (2002) that speech production is not architecturally (strongly) incremental and supporting a prosody-first approach (as in Keating and Shattuck-Hufnagel, 2002). Prosodic complexity was found to have an effect on speech planning time, such that for longer phrases, prosodically complex structures lead to shorter pauses, while for shorter phrases, a complex structure leads to longer pauses. It was argued that prosodic phrasing serves to chunk the upcoming material into planning units, and that prosodic constituents of any category can serve this purpose. Whether a hierarchically higher or lower prosodic phrase is selected as a planning unit will depend on the length and difficulty of the upcoming material. The phonological length (in syllables) of that phrase will determine how long the time to encode it will be.

6 Acknowledgements

I am grateful to Sun-Ah Jun, Sungbok Lee, Jean-Roger Vergnaud, Stefanie Shattuck- Hufnagel, Jessica Hsieh, Kathy Cooke, Tine Mooshammer, and especially to Dani Byrd for their generous help with this study. I would like to thank two anonymous reviewers and Pascal Perrier, who provided very thoughtful and insightful reviews of the first draft of the manuscript. I would also like to thank the organizers of the Summer school "Cognitive and physical models of speech production, speech perception and the production-perception interaction" and the audience there for their feedback. I gratefully acknowledge the support of the NIH (Grant No. DC03172 to Dani Byrd) and the USC and Yale Phonetics Laboratory.

References

Beckman, M. E. (1989). Notes on intonation. In *Course reader of Ling 694B (Intonation), winter 1989, Department of Linguistics, Ohio State University.*

Beckman, M. E. and Elam, G. A. (1997). Guidelines for ToBI labelling. Version 3.0, unpublished ms. *Available online at: http://www.ling.ohio-state.edu/ tobi/ame_tobi/labelling_guide_v3.pdf.*

Beckmann, M. E. and Pierrehumbert, J. B. (1986). Intonational structure in Japanese and English. *Phonology Yearbook*, 3:255–309.

Bolinger, D. (1972). Accent is predictable (if you're a mind reader). *Language*, 48:633–644.

Butcher, A. (1981). Aspects of the speech pause: Phonetic correlates and communicative functions. *Arbeitsberichte des Instituts für Phonetik der Universität Kiel*, 15.

Byrd, D. (2000). Articulatory vowel lengthening and coordination at phrasal junctures. *Phonetica*, 57:3–16.

Byrd, D. and Krivokapić, J. (2008). Prosodic variation: Understanding scope, categoricity, and recursion in speech production and perception. *Journal of the Acoustical Society of America*, 123:3423.

Byrd, D. and Saltzman, E. (1998). Intragestural dynamics of multiple phrasal boundaries. *Journal of Phonetics*, 26:173–199.

Carlson, K., Clifton, C., and Frazier, L. (2001). Prosodic boundaries in adjunct attachment. *Journal of Memory and Language*, 45:58–81.

Cho, T. (2005). Prosodic strengthening and featural enhancement: Evidence from acoustic and articulatory realizations of /a, i/ in English. *Journal of the Acoustical Society of America*, 117:3867–3878.

Choi, E. (2003). Pause length and speech rate as durational cues for prosody. *Journal of the Acoustical Society of America*, 114:2395.

Clifton, C., Carlson, K., and Frazier, L. (2002). Informative prosodic boundaries. *Language and Speech*, 45:87–114.

Cooper, W. E. and Paccia-Cooper, J. (1980). *Syntax and Speech.* Harvard University Press, Cambridge MA.

Cummins, F. (2002). On synchronous speech. *Acoustic Research Letter Online*, 3:7–11.

Cummins, F. (2003). Practice and performance in speech produced synchronously. *Journal of Phonetics*, pages 139–148.

Cummins, F. (2004). Synchronization among speakers reduces macroscopic temporal variability. In *26th Annual Meeting of the Cognitive Science Society*, pages 304–309.

Cutler, A., Dahan, D., and Donselaar, W. (1997). Prosody in the comprehension of spoken language: A literature review. *Language and Speech*, 40:141–201.

Dresher, E. B. (1994). The prosodic basis of the tiberian hebrew system of accents. *Language*, 70:1–52.

Edwards, J., Beckman, M. E., and Fletcher, J. (1991). The articulatory kinematics of final lengthening. *Journal of the Acoustical Society of America*, 89:369–382.

Ferreira, F. (1991). Effects of length and syntactic complexity on initiation times for prepared utterances. *Journal of Memory and Language*, 30:210–233.

Ferreira, F. (1993). Creation of prosody during sentence production. *Psychological Review*, 100:233–253.

Ferreira, F. (2007). Prosody and performance in language production. *Language and Cognitive Processes*, 22:1151–1177.

Ferreira, F. and Swets, B. (2002). How incremental is language production? Evidence from the production of utterances requiring the computation of arithmetic sums. *Journal of Memory and Language*, 46:57–84.

Ferreira, V. (1996). Is it better to give than to donate? Syntactic flexibility in language production. *Journal of Memory and Language*, 35:724–755.

Frazier, L., Carlson, K., and Clifton, C. (2006). Prosodic phrasing is central to language comprehension. *Trends in Cognitive Sciences*, 10:244–249.

Frazier, L., Clifton, C., and Carlson, K. (2004). Dont break, or do: Prosodic boundary preferences. *Lingua*, 114:3–27.

Gee, J. P. and Grosjean, F. (1983). Performance structures: A psycholinguistic and linguistic appraisal. *Cognitive Psychology*, 15:411–458.

Goldman Eisler, F. (1968). *Psycholinguistics. Experiments in Spontaneous Speech.* Academic Press, London, New York.

Griffin, Z. (2003). A reversed word length effect in coordinating the preparation and articulation of words in speaking. *Psychonomic Bulletin and Review*, 10:603–609.

Grosjean, F., Grosjean, L., and Lane, H. (1979). The patterns of silence: Performance structures in sentence production. *Cognitive Psychology*, 11:51–58.

Halliday, M. A. K. (1967). *Intonation and Grammar in British English.* Mouton de Gryuter.

Horne, M., Strangert, E., and Heldner, M. (1995). Prosodic boundary strength in Swedish: Final lengthening and silent interval duration. In *Proceedings of the XIIIth International Congress of Phonetic Sciences, Stockholm*, pages 170–173.

Itô, J. and Mester, A. (1992). Weak layering and word binarity. Technical report, Linguistic Research Center, LRC-92-09, University of California, Santa Cruz.

Itô, J. and Mester, A. (2010). *Phonological Domains: Universals and Derivations.*, chapter The extended prosodic word, pages 135–194. Mouton de Gruyter.

Jun, S. A. (1993). *The phonetics and phonology of Korean prosody.* PhD thesis, PhD dissertation, The Ohio State University, Columbus, Ohio.

Jun, S. A. (2003). Prosodic phrasing and attachment preferences. *Journal of Psycholinguistic Research*, 32:219–249.

Keating, P. and Shattuck-Hufnagel, S. (2002). A prosodic view of word form encoding for speech production. *UCLA Working Papers in Phonetics*, 101:112–156.

Klatt, D. (1975). Vowel lengthening is syntactically determined in connected discourse. *Journal of Phonetics*, 3:129–140.

Krivokapić, J. (2007a). *The planning, production, and perception of prosodic structure.* PhD thesis, PhD dissertation, University of Southern California.

Krivokapić, J. (2007b). Prosodic planning: Effects of phrasal length and complexity on pause duration. *Journal of Phonetics*, 35:162–179.

Krivokapić, J. (2010). Speech planning and phrase length. In *Proceedings of the 5th Conference on Speech Prosody, Chicago, paper number 100311.*

Ladd, D. R. (1988). Declination "reset" and the hierarchical organization of utterances. *Journal of the Acoustical Society of America*, 84:530–544.

Ladd, D. R. (1996). *Intonational Phonology.* Cambridge University Press.

Levelt, W. J. M. (1989). *Speaking. From Intention to Articulation.* MIT Press, Cambridge MA.

Levelt, W. J. M., Roelofs, A., and Meyer, A. S. (1999). A theory of lexical access in speech production. *Brain and Behavioral Sciences*, 22:1–38.

Martin, J. (1970). On judging pauses in spontaneous speech. *Journal of Verbal Learning and Verbal Behavior*, 9:75–78.

Meyer, A. S., Belkeb, E., Häckera, C., and Mortensen, L. (2007). Use of word length information in utterance planning. *Journal of Memory and Language*, 57:210–231.

Nespor, M. and Vogel, I. (1986). *Prosodic Phonology.* Foris Publications, Dordrecht, Riverton.

Oller, K. D. (1973). The effect of position in utterance on speech segment duration in English. *Journal of the Acoustical Society of America*, 54:1235–1247.

Petrone, C., Fuchs, S., and Krivokapić, J. (2011). Consequences of working memory differences and phrasal length on pause duration and fundamental frequency. In *Proceedings of the 9th International Seminar on Speech Production, Montréal, Canada*, pages 393–400.

Pierrehumbert, J. B. (1980). *The phonology and phonetics of English intonation.* PhD thesis, MIT, Cambridge, Massachusetts.

Price, P. J., Ostendorf, M., Shattuck-Hufnagel, S., and Fong, C. (1991). The use of prosody in syntactic disambiguation. *Journal of the Acoustical Society of America*, 90:2956–2970.

Redi, L. and Shattuck-Hufnagel, S. (2001). Variation in realization of glottalization in normal speakers. *Journal of Phonetics*, 29:407–429.

Roelofs, A. (1998). Rightward incrementality in encoding simple phrasal forms in speech production: Verb–participle combinations. *Journal of Experimental Psychology: Learning, Memory, and Cognition*, 24:904–921.

Sanderman, A. and Collier, R. (1995). Prosodic phrasing at the sentence level. In Bell-Berti, F. and Lawrence, R., editors, *Producing Speech: Contemporary Issues. For Katherine Safford Harris*, pages 321–332. American Institute of Physics, New York.

Schafer, A. J. (1997). *Prosodic parsing: The role of prosody in sentence comprehension.* PhD thesis, PhD dissertation, University of Massachusetts, Amherst, Massachusetts.

Selkirk, E. (1984). *Phonology and Syntax: The Relation Between Sound and Structure.* MIT Press, Cambridge MA.

Selkirk, E. (1995). *Papers in Optimality Theory.*, chapter The prosodic structure of function words, pages 439–470. GLSA Publications.

Shattuck-Hufnagel, S. and Turk, A. (1996). A prosody tutorial for investigators of auditory sentence processing. *Journal of Psycholinguistic Research*, 25:193–247.

Shattuck-Hufnagel, S. and Turk, A. (1998). The domain of phrase-final lengthening in English. In *Proceedings of the 16th International Congress on Acoustics and 135th Meeting Acoustical Society of America*, pages 1235–1236.

Smith, M. and Wheeldon, L. (1999). High level processing scope in spoken sentence production. *Cognition*, 73:205–246.

Sternberg, S.and Monsell, S., Knoll, R. L., and Wright, C. E. (1978). The latency and duration of rapid movement sequences: Comparisons of speech and typewriting. In Stelmach, G., editor, *Information Processing in Motor Control and Learning*, pages 117–152. Academic Press, New York.

Strangert, E. (1991). Pausing in texts read aloud. In *Proceedings of the XIIth International Congress of Phonetic Sciences, Université de Provence, Aix-en-Provence, France*, volume 4, pages 238–241.

Strangert, E. (1997). Relating prosody to syntax: Boundary signaling in Swedish. In Kokkinakis, G., Fakotakis, N., and Dermatas, E., editors, *Proceedings of the 5th European Conference on Speech Communication and Technology*, pages 239–242.

Swets, B., Desmet, T., Hambrick, D. Z., and Ferreira, F. (2007). The role of working memory in syntactic ambiguity resolution: A psychometric approach. *Journal of Experiment Psychology: General*, 136:64–81.

Terken, J. and Collier, R. (1992). Syntactic influences on prosody. In Vatikiotis-Bateson, E., Sagisaka, Y., and Tohkura, Y., editors, *Speech Perception, Production and Linguistic Structure*, pages 427–438. IOS Press, Amsterdam, Washington, Oxford, Tokyo, Osaka, Kyoto.

Wagner, M. (2005). *Prosody and recursion.* PhD thesis, PhD dissertation, Massachusetts Institute of Techonology.

Wagner, V., Jescheniak, J. D., and Schriefers, H. (2010). On the flexibility of grammatical advance planning during sentence production: Effects of cognitive load on multiple lexical access. *Journal of Experimental Psychology: Learning, Memory, and Cognition*, 36:423–440.

Watson, D. and Gibson, E. (2004). The relationship between intonational phrasing and syntactic structure in language production. *Language and Cognitive Processes*, 19:713–755.

Wheeldon, L. and Lahiri, A. (1997). Prosodic units in speech production. *Journal of Memory and Language*, 37:356–381.

Wightman, C. W., Stefanie, S. H., Ostendorf, M., and Price, P. J. (1992). Segmental durations in the vicinity of prosodic phrase boundaries. *Journal of the Acoustical Society of America*, 91:1707–1717.

Zvonik, E. and Cummins, F. (2002). Pause duration and variability in read texts. In *Proceedings ICSLP02, Seventh International Conference on Spoken Language Processing*.

Zvonik, E. and Cummins, F. (2003). The effect of surrounding phrase lengths on pause duration. In *Proceedings of Eurospeech, Geneva, Switzerland*, pages 777–780.

Gesture planning integrating knowledge of the motor plant's dynamics: A literature review from motor control and speech motor control

PASCAL PERRIER

Abstract: In order to study how dynamical properties of the motor plant are accounted for in movement planning, an optimal motor planning hypothesis was proposed in the late eighties. It suggested that forward and inverse internal models of the dynamics of the motor plant are learned in the brain, and that these models are used to compute and minimize a cost along the movement sequence. In this paper, the original form of this optimal motor planning hypothesis is described in detail in order to introduce the main issues that have since been investigated in relation to this hypothesis. A selected number of experimental studies carried out in the context of arm and speech movements are presented and analyzed. It is shown that while models of the motor plant's dynamics seem to be used in arm movement planning, no evidence currently exists in support of this hypothesis for speech movement. In general for both arm and speech movements, recent findings suggest that representations of the motor plant's dynamics in the brain could be spatially local or dedicated to a specific task. This raises the question of whether these representations are based on models or on motor memory. These findings are discussed more specifically in the context of speech motor control. Updates of the original hypothesis are given and some alternative hypotheses are briefly introduced.

1 Introduction

Speech communication is based on the transmission of acoustic signals from speakers to listeners. Hence, speech is acoustics. However, to generate the acoustic signals, the speakers move their jaw, their tongue, their lips, and their vocal folds. Listeners also use facial movements when perceiving speech in a face-to-face interaction with a speaker. Hence, speech is undoubtedly movements. Because of the bimodal nature of speech, the literature is full of debates related to the deep nature of the speech goals: are they primarily in the acoustics (e.g., Stevens, 1972) or in the articulatory domain (Browman and Goldstein, 1990)? From a cognitive perspective, one can argue whether speech movements are determined by the necessity to produce specific desired goals in the acoustics or whether speech movements are the goals of speech production, which are made perceivable to listeners via the acoustic signal. However, from a purely physical perspective, speech movements precede the acoustic signal. Speech movements are the causal factors that determine the time variation in vocal tract geometry and, consequently, the spectro-temporal characteristics of the acoustic speech signal. In that sense, speech movements are the basis of oral linguistic communication. To communicate with speech humans have to know how to generate the appropriate gestures in their vocal tract, independently of whether these gestures are the ultimate goals of the task or just the obligatory means of achieving the ultimate goals in the acoustics. This is why the focus of this paper is on the way humans plan sequences of gestures in their vocal tract to communicate with speech; we have already addressed in other papers the issue of the nature of the speech goals (Savariaux et al., 1995, 1999; Perrier, 2005; Brunner et al., 2009, 2011; Grimme et al., 2011). From a physical perspective, these movements are a result of the actions of muscle forces on mechanical structures, namely the articulators of the vocal tract. The characteristics of movements, their spatial paths, their velocities and their accelerations, depend strongly on the intrinsic mechanical properties of the articulators and on the mechanical interactions that the articulators have with each other and with external mechanical structures, such as the palate, the teeth or the pharyngeal walls. Some of the articulators are rigid bodies (jaw and hyoid bone), and some of them are made of soft tissue (tongue, lips, velum, pharyngeal walls). Mechanical interactions among speech articulators or between articulators and external structures induce time-varying frictions or damping with a range of magnitudes, which in some cases can be considered equivalent to obstacles on the movement paths. Stiffnesses of the articulators vary in time as functions of the activation of the muscles that act on them or that are part of them (in the case of soft tissues). All these complex mechanical phenomena, which initiate or influence movement properties, constitute the *dynamical properties* of the speech motor plant. The resulting observable movement properties, i.e. spatial paths, velocities and accelerations, without consideration of any forces that are involved in the generation of the movement, are its kinematic properties. Kinematic properties can relatively easily be recorded with video systems, ultrasound systems, dynamical MRI or motion capture systems such as the Optotrack or Electromagnetic Articulometers. The dynamics of a mechanism, in contrast, correspond to the causes of its motion. The system's dynamics are the underlying mechanical processes that enable and constrain movements and determine their kinematic properties (see Figure 1 for a summary). Dynamical properties are not easy to measure directly during speech production. Investigating and analyzing them using easily available measures usually necessitates the use of models based on theoretical assumptions concerning the mechanical characteristics of the articulators of the vocal tract.

Some dynamical properties of the motor plant, such as muscle force intensity and direction and the stiffness of joints or tissues, can, to a certain extent, be controlled[1] by the Central Nervous System (CNS). Let us call these properties *controllable properties*. Other dynamical properties, such as friction, damping or weight, are intrinsic to the motor plant in its environment (henceforth called the *physical motor plant*) and they cannot be voluntarily modified. Let us call these properties *intrinsic properties*. By specifying controllable properties of a dynamical system, a controller can influence the kinematic properties of a movement. However, the actual influence strongly depends on the intrinsic properties of the system. Let us consider the simple theoretical case of a controller that is designed to control the duration of the first free oscillation of an undamped mass-spring system, starting from an initial stretched length different from its rest length. For an undamped mass-spring system it is well known that under these conditions the free oscillation duration (i.e. the period) is directly linked to the square root of the mass-normalized spring stiffness (i.e. the stiffness divided by the mass).

1 Muscle forces result both from descending inputs from the Central Nervous System to the brainstem or the spinal cord and from afferent inputs from the muscles (see Schmidt, 1988). Muscle force directions are strongly dependent on anatomy. Stiffness of a muscle is the result of combined influences of passive tissue properties and muscle activations (McMahon, 1984).

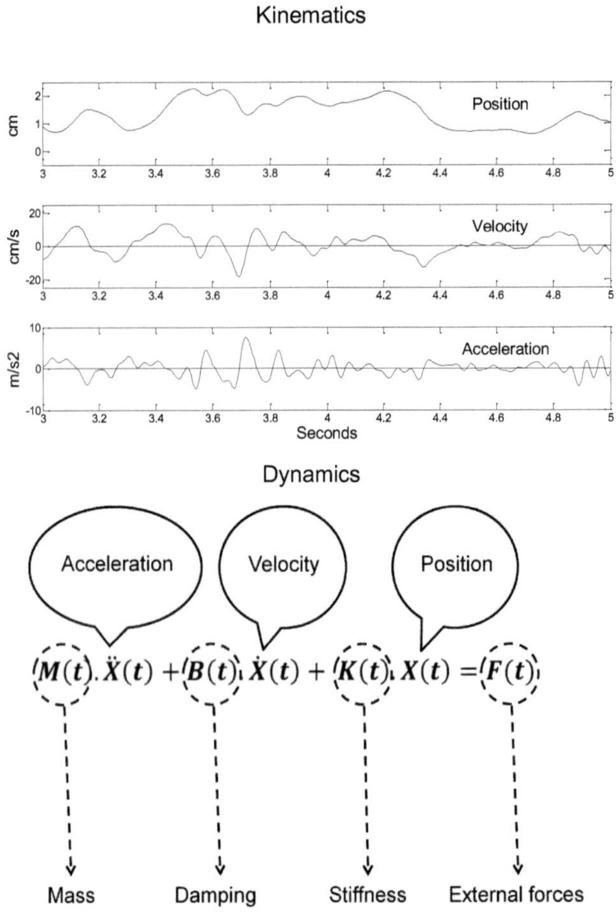

Figure 1: An illustration of differences and relations between kinematic properties (top panel) and dynamical properties (bottom panel) of movements.

Hence, if the controller knows the value of the mass that will be moved, it can control the oscillation duration of the movement by specifying the stiffness of the spring. However, if the mass-spring system is damped (due, for example, to external frictions), the duration of the first oscillation (i.e. the pseudo-period) is determined by both the mass-normalized stiffness and the mass-normalized damping factor. This damping factor is intrinsic to the system and cannot be controlled. Consequently, an accurate control of the first oscillation duration via the specification of the spring's stiffness is only possible if the mass and the damping factor are perfectly known, i.e. if the controller has a perfect knowledge of the intrinsic properties of the system.

This example illustrates the crucial issue that motor control studies in general, and speech motor control studies in particular, investigate with regard to the integration of the dynamical properties of the motor plant in motor control strategies. To what extent and in which forms are these dynamical properties taken into account in movement planning and movement execution? Is the motor control system able to learn the dynamical behavior of the motor plant and to predict the influences of the dynamical properties on movements? Does the motor control system know enough about the dynamical behavior to compensate for the impact on movement of intrinsic properties by tuning the controllable properties? Is it possible for the controller to precisely guide the motor plant along a specified spatial trajectory with a specified timing? If the motor control system does not know the dynamical behavior in its whole complexity, what minimal knowledge is required to ensure the achievement of the motor goals? If knowledge of the motor plant's dynamics is incomplete, how can feedback compensate for this deficiency, and ensure acceptable movement accuracy and stability?

All these issues are crucial. In order to address them in motor control studies, the concept of a *dynamical internal model* has been proposed, which provides hypotheses about the way the CNS integrates knowledge of the motor plant's dynamics in gesture planning. Internal models are extensively used in the literature to investigate issues in motor control in general and in speech motor control in particular. Internal models are mathematical models of the relations between the inputs and the outputs of a system. In the literature, they differ from one another in the extent to which they model the physical mechanisms underlying the relations between inputs and outputs, and in the way they account for the relations between inputs and outputs (static, time-varying, etc). Classic examples of internal models are models of the relations between the joint angles in the arm and the finger position in the space, models of the relations between joint torques and joint angles in the arm, of the relations between muscle activations in the vocal tract and spectral peaks of the acoustic speech signal, or models of the relations between articulatory positions in the vocal tract and spectral peaks in the acoustics. In this paper, the focus is on how the CNS integrates knowledge of the dynamics of the motor plant in gesture planning in general, and in speech gesture planning in particular. The general concept of dynamical internal models will be presented first and it will be shown how it helps in formalizing and then clarifying the problem. To do this, we will first refer to the original proposals that were made at the end of the eighties. Since then, many changes have been made to these original proposals, because of a number of experimental studies that have challenged them. The following section is devoted to the presentation of some important published experimental studies of this kind that have investigated whether the CNS uses knowledge of the dynamical behavior of the motor plant to control it, and if it does, with what level of complexity and accuracy. More recent publications have been taken into account in this section. In the last section, the existence and the nature of dynamical internal models will be discussed in the specific context of speech motor control. As far as speech production in particular is concerned, the work carried out with the DIVA model (Guenther et al., 1998; Tourville and Guenther, 2011) incorporating experimental data and functional brain imaging studies provided strong support for the existence of internal models linking articulatory positions in the vocal tract and spectral characteristics of the speech signal. It also found evidence for the cortical localization of this internal model (Guenther et al., 2006).

2 Dynamical internal models

2.1 Basic principles

2.1.1 Internal models: Representations of the motor plant stored in the brain

To our knowledge, the internal model principle was originally proposed by Francis and Wonham (1976) in the field of robust control theory. The underlying idea was that a controller needs to use a model of how the system to be controlled reacts to perturbation and to change in control parameters to ensure robust control. This principle was introduced in the field of human motor control theory by Kawato et al. (1987) in order to explain how skilled human movements can be produced rapidly in spite of the intrinsic limitations of the biological feedback system:

"*There are substantial delays in the feedback loop; for example the transcortical loop requires 40-60ms (Evarts, 1981). Further, experimental results indicate that the contribution of the supraspinal loop to load compensation is insubstantial (Evarts, 1981). Feedback delays and small gains both limit controllable speeds of motions [if they are controlled using these feedback signals, Author's Note]. Consequently, in learning a movement, we first must execute the movement very slowly, because otherwise the control system becomes unstable.*" (Kawato et al., 1987, p.17).

Kawato et al. (1987) proposed that, in order to overcome these limitations and to precisely control rapid movements, the CNS would learn and use different kinds of generalized representations of the relations between motor commands, forces and the properties of movements. These learned models are stored in the brain and they are called internal models. Internal models can be of two kinds depending on their inputs and outputs: they are forward or inverse models.

2.1.2 Forward models: Causal representations of the motor plant from commands to sensory signals

Kawato et al. (1987) suggested that, in the first stage of the learning process of a skilled motor task (such as pointing, reaching, grasping, or speaking), movements would be executed slowly. Slow movements would be required in order for the CNS to adjust and correct the sequence of motor commands on the basis of the biological feedback, which provides information on the actual position of the motor plant, as compared to *desired trajectories*, which are the motor goals specified by the CNS. This way of controlling movement is called *feedback control* (Figure 2). To speed up the execution of the movement, according to Kawato et al. (1987), it would be necessary for the CNS not to have to rely only on the slow biological feedback. An efficient way to do so would be to learn an internal model that tells the CNS how the motor plant behaves in response to motor commands. Kawato et al. (1987) suggested that the CNS would use the first stage of the motor learning process, during which various slow movements are executed using a feedback control, to learn the relationships between the motor commands and the sensory signals that motor commands induce (described in terms of position, velocity, acceleration, forces or torques). These relationships would be stored in the brain in the form of an internal model, a so-called forward model, which mimics the motor plant and describes the relationships between motor commands and sensory signals (Figure 2).

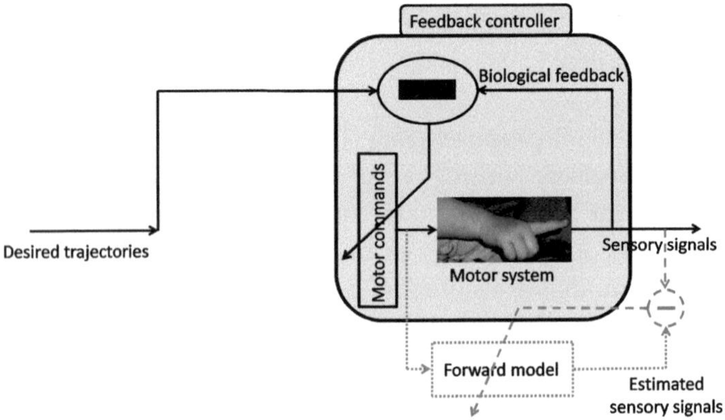

Figure 2: First stage of the motor learning process according to Kawato et al. (1987). The CNS specifies the motor goals in the form of desired trajectories and it adjusts the sequence of motor commands accordingly using the information that the biological feedback sends back about the state of the motor plant. Due to noticeable feedback delays, this adjustment cannot be done quickly. In parallel the CNS learns an internal model of the relation between motor commands and sensory signals, a so-called *forward model*. For more details about the symbols used in this representation, see the Appendix.

The core hypothesis of the internal model framework for motor control suggests that thanks to this *forward model*, the CNS can predict the sensory signals that the real motor plant would generate in response to the motor commands. This prediction can be used by the CNS to evaluate the consequences of the motor commands without having to wait for the biological feedback to send back this information. Hence, the predicted sensory signals can be considered as *internal feedback.* With a *forward model,* the estimation of the sensory signals from the motor commands can be done prior to the execution of movement, since it relies on an internal simulation of the movement. These internal feedback loops are much faster than biological feedback loops arising from the true physical motor plant. Thanks to the *forward model,* the Central Nervous System can control and execute fast movements using a *feedback control* strategy based on the fast internal feedback loops (Figure 3) (see also Miall and Wolpert, 1996, for more details).

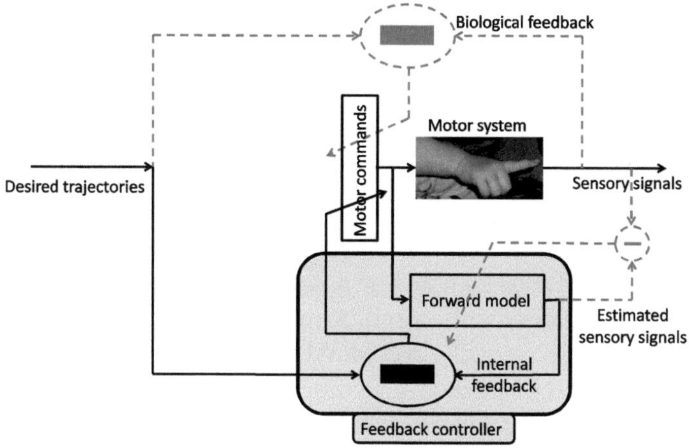

Figure 3: Second stage of the motor learning process according to Kawato et al. (1987). In order to control fast movements, the CNS uses the forward model and its internal feedback to adjust the commands in such a way that the motor plant moves along the specified desired trajectories. The CNS can still use the biological feedback (see Figure 2) if the forward model is not accurate enough or if external perturbations are applied to the motor plant. The forward model is continuously adapted, if necessary, on the basis of the comparison between the estimated and the actual sensory signals.

Obviously, the accuracy of the control depends on the quality of the *forward model.* If the *forward model* simulates the true motor plant precisely, the internal feedback will be very close to the real sensory signals, and the control will be accurate. If the *forward model* simulates the motor plant poorly, the control will be worse. In this case, if the movement actually produced is too far from the desired trajectory, the biological feedback can be used to correct movement, but only if it is made slowly because of the time delay involved.

2.1.3 Inverse models: Inverse mappings in the motor system that compute motor commands directly from motor goals

According to Kawato et al. (1987), after successfully achieving a very large number of various motor tasks, the CNS also learns how to infer the sequence of motor commands directly from the specification of a desired trajectory, and no longer requires corrective feedback. This relationship between the output of the motor plant, namely the trajectory of the end-effector, and the input of the motor plant, namely the sequence of motor commands, is stored in a second internal model, called the *inverse model*. An accurate learning of an *inverse model* requires a large number of motor tasks. The actual achievement of all these motor tasks with the physical motor plant would take a long time. Hence, Kawato et al. (1987) suggested (see also Miall and Wolpert, 1996) that the learning of the *inverse model* could be done more quickly and more efficiently by simulating these tasks with the *forward model*. Thus, the large number of required movements could be simulated internally and rapidly, instead of being physically and slowly generated (Figure 4). In this scheme, if the *forward model* is inaccurate, the *inverse model* that develops will obviously also be inaccurate, and the inferred sequence of motor commands not particularly appropriate to the actual achievement of the desired trajectory. Once the *inverse model* has been learned, the sequence of motor commands can be directly determined from the specification of the desired trajectory; sequences of motor commands are the outputs of the *inverse model*, while the desired trajectory is the input to this model. This kind of control is called *feedforward control*, as opposed to *feedback control*, since there is no need for the controller to use any information sent back from the motor plant, or from its *forward model*, to the controller (Figure 5). In the absence of unexpected external perturbation, if the *inverse model* has been learned correctly, the *feedforward control* should ensure accurate achievement of the desired trajectory. In the presence of an external perturbation or if the model is inaccurate, the feedback control, based on the biological feedback, is required to correct the sequence of motor commands initially computed by the *inverse model*.

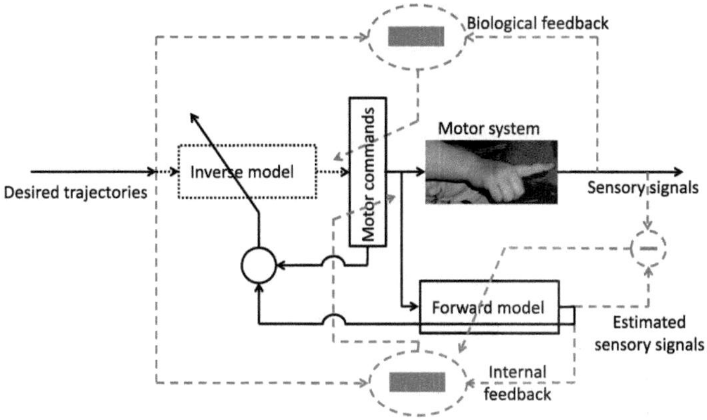

Figure 4: Third stage of the motor learning process according to Kawato et al. (1987). The CNS learns an internal model, called the inverse model, which allows inference of the sequence of motor commands from desired trajectories. This is made possible by an extensive set of movements simulated with the forward model. Biological feedback can also be used, but due to its long delay the learning would be less efficient.

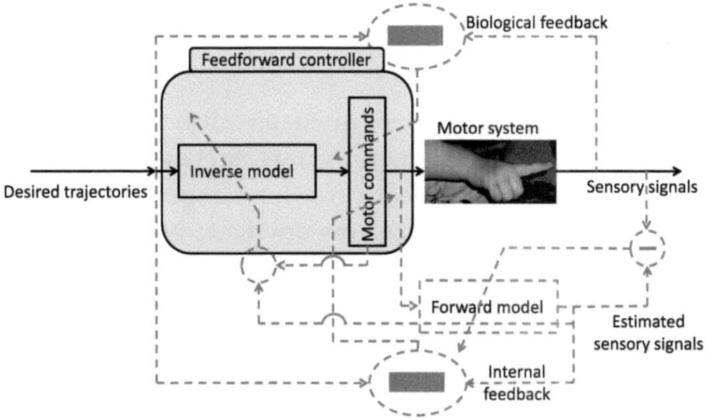

Figure 5: Last stage of the motor learning process according to Kawato et al. (1987). The inverse model has been learned and it is used to infer directly the sequence of motor commands from the desired trajectories. This is the so-called feedforward control. The CNS can still use the biological feedback if the forward and inverse models are not accurate, or if an external perturbation is applied to the motor plant.

2.1.4 The "feedforward control and desired trajectories" scheme: The need for very accurate dynamical internal models

According to Kawato et al. (1987), by successively learning a *forward* and an *inverse internal model*, the CNS can, in the absence of any perturbation, accurately and rapidly guide the motor plant along desired trajectories using a *feedforward control*. This scheme provides a very strong and powerful theoretical model for investigating and understanding skilled human motor control. However, for this motor control scheme to be efficient, three strong key-hypotheses should be fulfilled:

- The CNS specifies extensively the *desired trajectories* that are the goals of the movements.
- The *forward model* is an appropriate simulator of the dynamical motor plant; if this were not the case, an inappropriate *inverse model* would be learned.
- The *inverse model* accounts perfectly for all the dynamical properties of the system; if it did not, the computed sequence of motor commands would not be appropriate to the achievement of the desired trajectory.

The last two hypotheses seem to be quite unrealistic for most of the motor plants in humans. Human motor plants can have very complex dynamical properties and this is clearly true for the speech apparatus, since the majority of the speech articulators are made of soft tissues, where elasticity and damping can vary significantly with strain and muscle activation (McMahon, 1984; Gerard et al., 2005; Nazari et al., 2011b). Hence, it seems difficult to believe that the *forward* and *inverse internal models* can capture these dynamical properties in their whole complexity. In addition, more generally, learning the dynamical *inverse model* requires access to errors at the level of the motor commands, and, according to Wolpert et al. (1998, p.338) (see also Kawato, 1999), these errors are not directly available to the CNS. For all these reasons, it does not seem reasonable to assume that the CNS can achieve a perfect description of the motor plant in its entirety, either in its causal forward form or in its inverse form. Consequently, the theoretical model proposed in Kawato et al. (1987), based on the specification of desired trajectories and on the learning of a *feedforward controller*, does not seem to be realistic. In this respect, Kawato et al. (1990) have proposed interesting modifications based on the concepts of *trajectory formation and optimal motor planning*.

2.2 Trajectory formation and optimal motor planning

Kawato et al. (1990) modified the original hypothesis of the existence of motor goals in the form of fully specified desired trajectories. They suggested that motor goals could instead be specified by a limited number of discrete key-points in the task space. The task of the controller would be to ensure that the motor plant actually reaches the different key-points in the right serial order and with the appropriate timing, from the starting position all the way to the final position. Kawato et al. (1990) called these key-points *via-points*. For a given sequence of via-points there is an infinity of possible trajectories for the motor plant (see Figure 6).

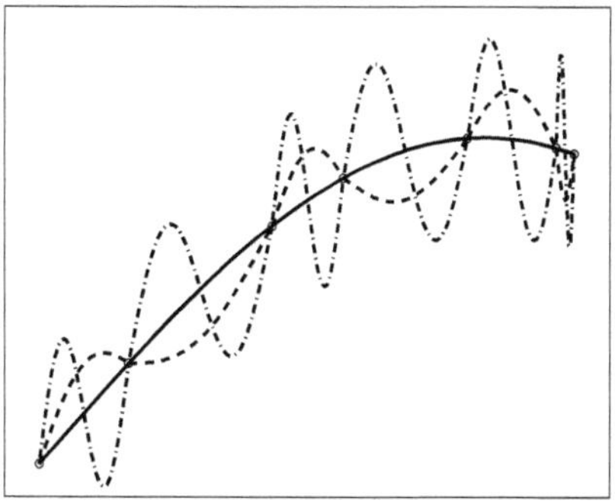

Figure 6: Via-points (circles) and examples of possible trajectories joining these via-points. The bold solid line corresponds to the trajectory with maximal smoothness.

The emergence of a particular trajectory from the specification of the *via-points* is called *trajectory formation*. Kawato et al. (1990) proposed that trajectory formation is based on an optimization process that minimizes a certain cost for the motor plant along the whole trajectory in order to have maximum smoothness for the trajectory ("*maximum smoothness*" principle). For multi-joint arm movements, according to Kawato et al.

(1990), two costs are suited to the achievement of the maximal trajectory's smoothness: the integral of the square of the jerk (the jerk is the derivative of the acceleration) as proposed by Hogan (1984) in his *minimum jerk model*, or the integral of the square of the derivative of the torques at the arm joints as proposed by Uno et al. (1989) in their *minimum torque-change model*. The minimum jerk model optimizes trajectory smoothness by acting directly on kinematic characteristics of the movement: position, velocity, acceleration and jerk. It does not require an explicit formulation of the dynamical characteristics of the motor plant. The minimum torque-change model acts at the level of the muscle force generation mechanism and requires, to be effective, a detailed knowledge of the torque distribution at the joints and of the way these torques influence movements. Thus, the minimum torque-change model requires a detailed representation of the dynamics of the motor plant. The optimization process determines both the optimal trajectory joining the intended via-points and the sequence of motor commands enabling the motor plant to follow this trajectory. It is an *optimal motor planning* of the movement toward the successive intended via-points. According to Kawato et al. (1990), this kind of *optimal motor planning* uses a *forward model* of the motor plant in order to compute the cost via the prediction of the trajectory in response to a sequence of motor commands, and to determine how to change this sequence of motor commands in order to minimize the cost. This is summarized in Figure 7. Consequently the internal model should include a description of the sensitivity of the cost to local changes in motor commands. The optimal trajectories are intended trajectories, in the sense that the actual achievement of these trajectories by the motor plant will depend on the accuracy of the *forward model* and on the effectiveness of the optimization process. Once the CNS has found optimal sequences of motor commands and trajectories for a sufficiently large number of via-point sequences, it should be able, according to Kawato et al. (1990), to generalize to new sequences without going through the optimization process. In doing so the CNS learns an *inverse model* that determines the optimal sequence of motor commands and the corresponding intended optimal trajectories directly from the specification of the via-points (see Figure 8). At this stage, the CNS uses a *feedforward control* to generate the appropriate movement. The actual achievement of the motor goals depends on the accuracy of the *internal forward* and *inverse models*. Note that Jordan and Rumelhart (1992) made a similar proposal. Both Kawato et al. (1990) and Jordan and Rumelhart (1992) also showed that such an *optimal motor planning* is useful for determining motor commands from motor goals in motor plants with redundant degrees of freedom. For systems having degrees of freedom in excess, many different sets of motor commands can generate the same positions of the end-effector in the task space.

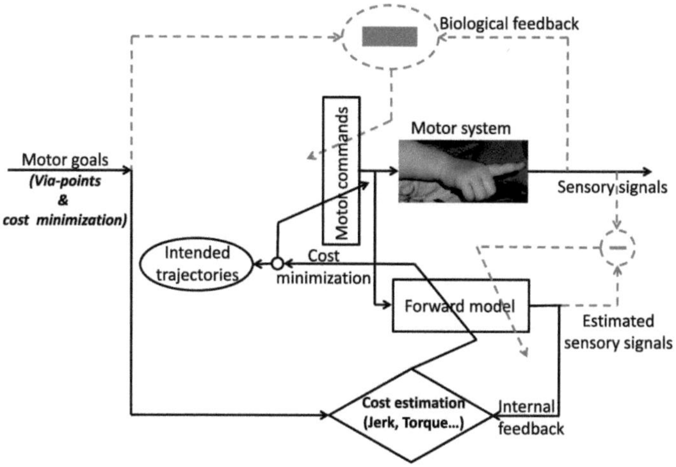

Figure 7: Optimal motor planning using a forward model according to Kawato et al. (1990). The forward model generates an estimation of the outputs of the motor plant, on the basis of which the CNS estimates the cost (jerk or torque). The CNS also uses the forward model to find how to change motor commands with the aim of minimizing the cost. Once the cost has been minimized, the optimal intended trajectory joining the via-points is determined together with the appropriate motor commands.

For example, in a planar pointing task, the end-effector is the forefinger. The same position of the forefinger can be reached for a large number of joint angles at the shoulder, the elbow and the wrist, and for an even larger number of muscle activations at these joints. Hence, the specification of the forefinger position in the task space does not determine the motor commands. Such an excess of degrees of freedom is extremely important and useful in motor control, since it allows the elaboration of motor equivalence strategies, i.e. the selection of various strategies to reach the same goal in the task space. However, determining motor commands from the specification of the forefinger position in the task space only is not possible.

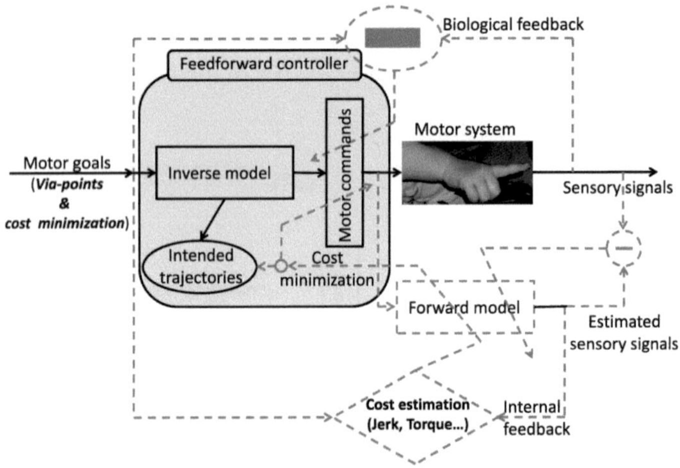

Figure 8: *Feedforward control* after optimal motor planning according to Kawato et al. (1990). After having found optimal trajectories and motor commands for a sufficiently large number of via-point sequences, the CNS generalizes and learns an inverse model; this inverse model determines the motor commands and the intended optimal trajectories directly from the specification of the via-points, according to a *feedforward control scheme.*

This is an inverse problem with many solutions, and for this reason it is called an *ill-posed inverse problem* (see, for example Marroquin et al., 1987, for an interesting explanation of the concept of ill-posed problems). Ill-posed problems can only be solved by taking into account additional constraints. Kawato et al. (1990) and Jordan and Rumelhart (1992) suggested that for a sequence of motor goals, this additional constraint could consist in looking for maximal smoothness for the trajectory connecting these goals, which means using an *optimal motor planning*.

In the context of *optimal motor planning*, some publications have proposed other costs. For walking, Anderson and Pandy (2001) proposed that the CNS would minimize the metabolic energy expenditure used per unit distance traveled. For target-oriented motor tasks, such as eye saccades or pointing tasks, Harris and Wolpert (1998) suggested that the sequence of motor commands could be determined so as to minimize the variance of the end-position across repetitions of the same task (the so-called *minimum of variance model*). Depending on the cost to be minimized during the *trajectory formation* and *optimal motor planning* process, different complexity is required for the *forward* and *inverse internal* models. In the context of the *minimum jerk model*, in which the cost is computed from kinematic variables, there is no need to have a very accurate model of the dynamical properties of the motor plant in interaction with its environment (see Jordan and Rumelhart, 1992). In the context of the minimum variance model, Harris and Wolpert (1998) simulated fairly realistic movement patterns for eye saccades and planar arm movements by using simplified dynamical representations of the motor plant. However, if it is hypothesized that the torque-change is minimized, accurate internal models of the dynamical characteristics of the motor plant are required (Kawato et al., 1990; Wolpert and Kawato, 1998; Kawato, 1999). In their model for walking control, Anderson and Pandy (2001) computed the energy expenditure with a model consisting of 10 segments controlled by 54 muscles and having 23 degrees of freedom! A fairly complex internal model! Hence, the choice of the cost to be minimized in *optimal motor planning* has strong consequences for the level of complexity that is required for the description of the motor plant in the *forward* and *inverse internal models.*

2.3 Summary

In the original papers going back to the late eighties and the beginning of the nineties, two main motor control schemes were proposed to account for the potential existence of dynamical representations of the motor plant in the CNS. Both schemes apply to the control of fast movements, for which a feedback control based on the long-delay and low-gain biological feedback would not be appropriate. Both schemes also suggest that after motor learning and in the absence of unexpected external perturbations, motor control should be based on a *feedforward control* using a *dynamical inverse internal model* of the motor plant. The *inverse internal model* is considered to be learned on the basis of numerous movement simulations using a *forward internal model* of the motor plant. In the first scheme, motor goals are defined as fully specified desired trajectories in the task space. Part of the planning, namely that of the desired trajectories, is done at a high level (it is not clear which), and does not take into account any information about the dynamical properties of the motor plant. Only the choice of the motor commands appropriate for the achievement of the desired trajectories integrates information about these dynamical properties. In this context, controlling the motor plant with accuracy requires both the *forward* and the *inverse internal models* to be extremely accurate and to correspond to complex descriptions of the physical motor plant.

In the second scheme, motor goals are described less extensively with a limited number of *via-points* discretely distributed in the task space, between the starting point and the end point of the movement. Determining the intended continuous trajectory connecting the via-points, the so-called *trajectory formation process*, is part of the motor planning since this trajectory is the output of an optimization process, which minimizes a certain cost. The choice of the appropriate motor commands is the other output of this *optimal motor planning*. The proposed framework for this *optimal motor planning* is based on the learning and the use of a *dynamical forward model* of the motor plant, and its last stage consists of the learning of a *dynamical inverse model* that will be used afterwards in the *feedforward controller*. However, depending on the cost to be minimized in the optimization process, various levels of complexity can be considered for the dynamical representation of the motor plant which is included in the *forward*, and then in the *inverse, model*. In addition, the consequences of potential inaccuracies or simplifications in this dynamical representation are not as strong as in the first motor scheme, based on the specification of desired trajectories. The planned intended trajectories are not the goals of the motor task; their formation is just one step in the motor planning process that aims at achieving the true motor goals, namely the via-points. Hence, a certain amount of difference between the actual trajectory and the intended optimal one can be tolerated, as long as via-points are reached with the required amount of accuracy.

In the second part of this paper, a number of experimental findings will be presented. These have contributed to investigating whether dynamical representations of the motor plant do exist in the brain, and with what level of complexity. They will be interpreted in the context of the *optimal motor planning scheme* that has been described above.

3 Experimental findings

Biological evidence has been found in support of the existence of inverse models in the cerebellum (Wolpert and Kawato, 1998). For example, Gomi et al. (1998) found that, during reflex eye movements, the Purkinje cells that exist in the cerebellum react to inputs related to the position, the velocity and the acceleration of the eyes: their firing rate varies as a function of these inputs. Since it is known that these cells send information to the motor cortex, they could undoubtedly be the basis for the implementation of inverse internal models. However, it is not clear whether the information about position, velocity and acceleration is actually processed and used in a way compatible with the computation of a cost and the learning of a dynamical inverse model of the motor plant. Hence, additional experimental evidence is needed to confirm the internal model and optimal motor control hypotheses.
There are numerous examples of experimental studies of how the CNS integrates the dynamical properties of the motor plant to determine motor commands. In this section we do not claim to be exhaustive by summarizing all these works. Only a few studies that illustrate our own understanding and interpretation of a very rich and controversial literature are presented. This presentation is organized along three main issues:

- Does the CNS learn about the dynamics of the motor plant to ensure gesture accuracy?

- Does the CNS learn about the dynamics of the motor plant to optimize gestures?

- Does the CNS learn generalized dynamical internal models or does it learn simpler and more local information about dynamics in the context of a specific motor task?

In each case, examples from limb motor control studies and from orofacial motor control studies are presented.

3.1 Integrating dynamics to control movement accuracy

3.1.1 Inertial sensitivity is taken into account in trajectory planning

Sabes et al. (1998) studied the role of inertial sensitivity in motor planning during an obstacle avoidance experiment in three dimensions. In this experiment, the subjects were placed in a 3D virtual environment where they could see on a screen two small virtual spheres, representing the starting and end positions of the movement, a virtual cylindrical obstacle located between the two spheres, and a virtual cube displaying the actual position of their hand. The main axis of the cylindrical obstacle was orthogonal to the plane defined by the two spheres and the center of gravity of the cylinder. The position of the center of gravity of the cylinder was the center point of the workspace. The subjects could not directly see their arm and the only visual feedback was given via this 3D virtual environment. The subjects were asked to move their finger from the starting point to the end point going around the obstacle and making sure to avoid hitting it. The experiment was run under three different conditions as regarding the orientation of the main axis of the obstacle in reference to the body. The main axis of the cylinder was either vertical, or horizontal and oriented from the right to the left, or horizontal and oriented in the front-back direction. The movement was essentially done in the plane orthogonal to the main axis and passing through the two spheres. Hence, the different orientations induced different arm postures during the execution of the movement, and thus, different dynamical properties of the arm. Movement directions were specified in such a way that they turned from 0 to 360° around the obstacle. Many trials were considered for all directions in the three orientations of the plane of movement. The task was done for both the right and the left hand.

The authors measured the spatial distribution of the point of the trajectory which was the closest to the obstacle, the so-called "near-point", in relation to the center of gravity of the virtual cylinder obstacle (center point). This near-point is important from a motor control point of view, since it corresponds to the point where collision with the obstacle could easily happen if control is not accurate or if the movement is sensitive to slight changes in dynamical constraints. The authors observed that, for each orientation of the main axis of the obstacle, the near-points clustered for all movement directions in the same location of the workspace and along the same direction from the center point. The main orientation of the cluster changed according to the orientation of the main axis of the obstacle, i.e. according to the posture and the dynamical properties of the arm during movement execution.

According to Sabes et al. (1998), the constancy of the near-point cluster's orientation across movement directions together with its variability with obstacle orientation could be attributed either to perceptual factors, corresponding to anisotropy in the visual perception of the task space, or to factors intrinsically related to the arm posture and the arm dynamics during movement execution. If perceptual factors were the explanation for the patterns of near-point distribution, the same patterns should be observed for the right and the left hand movements. This was not the case. The patterns of distribution observed for the left hand were mirror images of those of the right hand reflected about the midline of the workspace. Hence, the orientations of near-point clusters seem not to have their origins in perceptual factors but in factors intrinsically related to arm posture and arm dynamics, during movement.

Sabes et al. (1998) measured the 3D mobility of the left and right arms at the center point of the task space (i.e. at the location of the center of gravity of the virtual cylindrical obstacle in the experiment). This was done by applying local force perturbations to the arm in all directions and by looking at the amplitude of the arm displacements caused by this perturbation. The arm mobility was characterized in the plane of movement by an ellipse whose minor axis describes the direction in which the arm provides the best resistance to perturbations. The authors found that for both arms, and for the three orientations of the obstacle, the near-point distribution was located in relation to the center point along a direction that matches the direction of the minor axis of the mobility ellipse quite well. This suggests that the point of the trajectory where accuracy and stability is required, namely the near-point, is planned so as to ensure the best possible resistance to factors that could affect the distance between the trajectory and the obstacle. Thus, it seems that intrinsic dynamical properties of the arm are taken into account by the CNS in trajectory planning in order to ensure maximum stability of the movement at the location where stability requirements are the strongest to avoid collision with the obstacle.

3.1.2 Jaw movement: Speech motor control does not seem to integrate the influence of gravity

Shiller et al. (1999) investigated how gravity is taken into account in speech motor control. This question is well justified and important, since every human is able to speak clearly in the upright, supine or inclined position of the body, while, depending on the orientation of the head, weight exerts its influence along different directions relative to the head. Consequently, it is logical to assume that changes in dynamical conditions associated with changes in head orientation are taken into account by the CNS in order to compensate for their consequences and make sure that the perceptually relevant acoustical characteristics are actually produced. Shiller et al.'s (1999) methodological approach consisted in analyzing simulations generated with a 2D biomechanical model of the jaw and hyoid bone complex Laboissière et al. (see 1996) and experimental data. The goal of the simulations was to provide an objective characterization of how jaw movements change with head orientation (upright, supine and prone) within the gravity field, in the absence of any modification of the motor commands. The empirical study consisted in recording acoustic signals and articulatory data (in the mid-sagittal plane) from subjects speaking either in upright, in supine or in prone head orientations, and to observe how movement patterns change with orientation. The comparison of the predictions with the experimental data was the means of assessing to what extent the CNS adjusts the motor commands in order to compensate for the influence of gravity: if data and simulations match, it can be assumed that nothing is done at the level of the CNS to take into account orientation.
Shiller et al. (1999) reported a generally good match between the changes in jaw movements that they observed experimentally and the changes predicted with the model assuming no changes in motor commands. Compared with the upright condition, in the prone orientation the jaw moved closer to the palate, whereas in the supine orientation the jaw moved further away from the palate. Compared with the prone condition, in the supine position the jaw trajectory was located further back in the head. In the acoustics, they observed that the first formant (an indicator of vocal tract aperture) was higher in the upright orientation, and that the second formant (an indicator of the front/back position of

the tongue) was higher in the prone orientation. These results support the hypothesis that the CNS does not adjust the motor commands in order to compensate for the influence of gravity, in spite of the fact that changes in head orientation in the gravity field have a significant impact on movements and acoustics. Shiller et al. (1999) interpreted the absence of compensatory adjustments as evidence that the CNS does not learn about the new dynamical conditions, in spite of the fact that the preservation of the task's goal would have required this learning. Their interpretation was based on the fact that the spectral changes associated with changes in head orientation were systematic and significant. However, the amplitude of the spectral changes was within a range of variation compatible with the correct perception of the vowels. Hence, another explanation is possible for Schiller et al.'s (1999) observation: the CNS did not adjust the motor commands simply because the changes in the articulatory paths due to the change in gravity orientation did not endanger the goal of the task, which is the correct perception of the sounds. In this case, the differences between Sabes et al.'s (1998) observations for arm movements and Shiller et al.'s (1999) observations for speech movements would be due to differences in the impact of the inertial constraints on the achievement of the task, and not to the inability of the CNS to achieve a dynamical learning for speech movements. At this stage, it is not possible to discard one or the other of these two possible explanations. However, Shiller et al.'s observation is important in itself: in speech production the CNS does not seem to take into account the influence of gravity when setting up the motor commands suited for the achievement of the desired motor goals.

3.1.3 Arm movements: The stiffness of the motor plant is controlled to increase stability

Franklin et al. (2007) investigated how the end-point stiffness of the arm varies in planar pointing tasks when the arm has to move under the influence of an external force field. The end-point stiffness of the arm corresponds to the resistance to displacements measured at the hand when the arm is in a stable posture and when external forces are applied to the end point from all possible directions. When there is a high degree of stiffness, the displacement induced by the external force is small.

When there is a lower degree of stiffness, the displacement induced by the same force is large. The representation of stiffness for forces arising from all possible directions in the task plane, 360° degrees around the hand, is an ellipse, the so-called "*stiffness ellipse*". The major axis of the stiffness ellipse represents the direction in which the stiffness (i.e. the resistance to external forces) is the largest, while the minor axis corresponds to the direction in which the stiffness is the smallest. The direction of the major axis is called the orientation of the stiffness ellipse.
During this experiment, the forearm of the subject was coupled to the handle of a robotic manipulandum that constrains the arm to move in the horizontal plane and can apply forces to the arm at anytime and in any direction of the task plane. Subjects were asked to perform a point-to-point reaching task between two small circles located directly in front of the subject and on a line orthogonal to the line joining the two shoulders of the subject. Under perturbed conditions, three divergent force fields were applied to the arm during movement. These force fields were oriented along three directions that were specifically selected because they correspond to directions in which, according to a modeling study, end-point stiffness can be specifically increased by the activation of a specific pair of antagonist muscles. If the subject was moving her/his arm along the straight line joining the circles used as starting point and goal in the reaching task, no perturbing force field was applied. However, if the subject deviated from this straight line, a divergent force field was applied, which was proportional to the amplitude of the deviation. Hence, the duration, the nature and the amplitude of the perturbation were unpredictable. End-point stiffness was measured for the three force field conditions and in the absence of force field. Electromyography (EMG) signals were also recorded from the three muscle pairs that were considered to act specifically on the stiffness in one of the three force fields conditions.
After learning all subjects were able to properly achieve the reaching task in the absence of perturbation and for the three different force field conditions. It was found that after training, under perturbed conditions, the main orientation of the end-point stiffness was close to the orientation of the force field orientation. Hence stiffness was specifically increased in the direction of the force field. In addition, the patterns of EMG activation revealed that the activated muscles were those

of the pair that could increase the stiffness in the direction of the force field: this suggests that the CNS knows enough about the dynamics of the arm in its physical environment to selectively activate the muscles that increase the stiffness in the direction where the perturbation is the strongest. In doing so, the CNS increases the stability of the motor plant.

3.1.4 Jaw movements: Kinematic variability coincides with intrinsic stiffness patterns

From Franklin et al.'s (2007) study, it can be concluded that in limb motor control the CNS is able to adjust stiffness in order to control kinematic variability according to the accuracy requirement of the task. In this context, it is interesting to know whether the CNS is able to do the same in orofacial motor control, and more specifically in speech motor control. Shiller et al.'s (2002) study provides interesting information to deal with this question. Indeed, these authors investigated the relation between stiffness and kinematic variability in jaw movements, in speech and non-speech conditions. Measures of the jaw stiffness were measured during the production of steady-state vowels by applying small perturbing forces to the jaw. These forces were applied in the sagittal plane and in all directions via a computer-controlled robotic device connected to the lower teeth. Four vowels of English corresponding to four different jaw heights were considered. The results of these measures were depicted in the sagittal plane in the form of 4 stiffness ellipses, as described above, each of which is associated with a specific vowel and thus with a specific jaw height. It was found for all vowels that the major axis of the stiffness ellipse is oriented along the jaw protrusion-retraction direction and the minor axis along the jaw raising-lowering direction. Globally the stiffness was higher for high than for low vowels.
Variability of jaw positioning was also measured, in speech and in non-speech conditions. In speech conditions, the subjects were asked to pronounce several repetitions of different consonant-vowel-consonant sequences, in which the vowel was one of the four vowels for which jaw stiffness was to be measured. For each of these sequences, the variability of the jaw position was measured for the inter-consonantal vowel. In non-speech conditions, two kinds of movements were considered, vertical movements between positions similar to the ones of the lowest and

highest vowels used in the speech production experiment, and protrusion movements for a high jaw position similar to that of the highest vowel. For all these jaw movements, the variability of the jaw position was measured at the upper and lower turning point of the jaw trajectory. The results were displayed in the sagittal plane in the form of ellipses, whose major axes represent the directions of maximum variability, and whose minor axes depict the directions of minimum variability. In both speech and non-speech conditions the major axes of the ellipses (i.e. the directions of maximal variability) were along the jaw raising-lowering direction, and the minor axes along the jaw protrusion-retraction directions. Both for speech and non-speech tasks, these ellipses were oriented orthogonally to the stiffness ellipses measured for speech production.

At this stage, two important observations deserve emphasis: (1) the patterns of jaw variability do not depend on the nature of the task, speech versus non-speech, and (2) the patterns of variability are consistent with the stiffness patterns measured in speech production. These observations can be interpreted in two ways: either stiffness patterns have been learned for speech production to match accuracy requirements, and they have been generalized to non-speech movements, or the stiffness patterns have not been learned and are the result of natural and intrinsic properties of the orofacial system. In order to know more about the stiffness patterns linked with intrinsic properties of the orofacial system, Shiller et al. (2002) used a 2D biomechanical model of the jaw and hyoid bone complex (see Laboissière et al., 1996). The stiffness ellipses were computed for different jaw heights, similar to the experimental one, and for different levels of muscle activations. The authors computed these ellipses under these different conditions for various geometries of the jaw. In all cases, the patterns of stiffness ellipses were found to be very close to those measured experimentally in speech production.

In conclusion, Shiller et al.'s (2002) study suggests that in jaw movements involved in speech and non-speech production, contrary to the observations made for arm motor control by Franklin et al. (2007), the CNS does not adjust motor commands in order to control jaw stiffness and to match accuracy requirements imposed by the motor task. On the contrary, it seems that jaw positioning accuracy measured in speech production could be a simple consequence of the intrinsic physical properties of the jaw associated with muscle anatomy, muscle force generation capabilities and the geometry of the jaw.

3.2 How knowledge about dynamics is used to generate a specific trajectory

Shadmehr and Mussa-Ivaldi (1994) asked their subjects to produce reaching movements in the right part of their workspace while grasping the handle of a robotic manipulandum. During the course of the movement no visual feedback was given to the subjects about the position of their hand, so that they could not follow a visible trajectory. The manipulandum constrained the arm to move in the horizontal plane but it did not limit freedom of movement in the plane, except in the case where it applied a force field to the hand varying in direction and amplitude. This force field was a function of the velocity of the subject's shoulder and elbow joints during the movements. Hence, when this field was active, its strength was maximum in the middle of the movement (velocity profiles are essentially bell-shaped) and it was zero at the beginning and end of the movement. In the absence of an external force field, the trajectories of the hand were gently curved. This geometrical characteristic has been shown to be the possible consequence of an optimization process (see Flash and Hogan, 1985; Gomi and Kawato, 1996).

Introducing the force field means modifying the dynamical properties of the motor plant in interaction with its environment. If it is correct to assume that movement trajectory results from an optimization process based on the combination of forward and inverse dynamical models, then movement trajectory should change dramatically when the force field is applied. The authors observed that during the first trials following the onset of the perturbation, the trajectories were indeed very different from the normal path: the hand deviated strongly from the direction of the targeted end point, before quickly returning to it at the end of the movement. This induced the emergence of a strongly curved hook in the very last part of the trajectory. The more the task was repeated under perturbed conditions, the more this hook disappeared, up to the stage where all the subjects were able to compensate for the perturbation and to follow movement paths that were very similar to the

normal ones, i.e. gently curved and without any hook, matching the characteristics of an optimized movement. In addition, once the perturbation had been removed, after-effects were observed, in the sense that the subjects did not immediately return to the trajectories that they had followed before the perturbation had been introduced.
After-effects are interpreted by Shadmehr and Mussa-Ivaldi (1994) as evidence that for all subjects the adaptation to the mechanical perturbation involved the learning of internal models which took into account the new dynamical conditions of the motor plant associated with the introduction of the force field. The fact that trajectories after learning are gently curved is consistent with the hypothesis that the internal models are used in an optimization process.

3.2.1 Jaw movements: Adaptation to a velocity-dependent force field provides evidence that dynamics is taken into consideration in movement planning and/or execution

A similar study was carried out by Tremblay et al. (2003) with the jaw, in speech and non-speech conditions. With a robotic device connected to the lower teeth and controlled by computer, Tremblay et al. (2003) also delivered velocity-dependent mechanical perturbations to the jaw during lowering movements. Perturbing forces were applied in the sagittal plane in the direction of jaw protrusion. Three different conditions were tested: production of the utterance /siat/ slowly and clearly with vocalization; articulation of the same utterance without vocalization (silent speech) and still slowly and clearly; and non-speech jaw movement that matched the amplitude and duration of the two speech conditions. For each condition the task was first performed several times without perturbation; it was then performed several times with perturbation, and finally the perturbation was removed and the task was again repeated several times.
The results were as follows. In the first trials following the introduction of the perturbing force field, a noticeable modification of the trajectory of the jaw was observed for all subjects and for the three conditions: its curvature increased significantly in the front direction. After training, for the two speech conditions (vocalized and silent), an adaptation to the perturbation was observed and the motion path of the jaw be-

came similar to the one produced without the perturbation. This adaptation was not observed in the non-speech condition. In addition, for the two speech conditions, an after-effect was noticed: once the perturbation was removed, a few trials were necessary for the subjects to go back to the jaw trajectories observed before the onset of the perturbing force field. An acoustical analysis of the vocalized speech signals and perception tests on these signals did not reveal any significant differences between the normal, the perturbed and the post-perturbation conditions. It would seem that the adaptation process observed in speech conditions is not guided by some kind of desired trajectory specified in the acoustic or perceptual domain.

The results obtained with speech movements are consistent with Shadmehr and Mussa-Ivaldi (1994). They suggest that the CNS is able to learn about the new dynamics of the jaw under perturbed conditions in order to generate the same trajectories as under normal conditions. Differences observed between speech and non-speech movements can be attributed neither to differences in muscle mechanics and jaw dynamics, nor to differences in the learning capabilities of the CNS, since both tasks used the same articulators in very similar ranges of displacement and duration. According to Tremblay et al. (2003), these differences reflect differences in the specification of the motor goals. In the context of the optimal planning hypothesis, we can suggest another interpretation, namely that optimal planning is not universal for all tasks or that the criteria to be optimized vary across tasks. However, it should be noted that Tremblay et al. (2003) did not in any way suggest that their data would provide evidence that either speech or non-speech movements were optimized.

Overall, the experimental observations of Shadmehr and Mussa-Ivaldi (1994) and Tremblay et al. (2003) that are summarized above suggest that the CNS learns about the dynamics of the motor plant and assimilates this knowledge in order to shape trajectories. These results are consistent with the internal model and optimal planning hypotheses, but they do not provide clear evidence for them. Curved paths have been shown to be potentially explained by anatomical factors and muscle mechanics, for arm movements (Flanagan et al., 1993; Gribble and Ostry, 1996; Gribble et al., 1998) as well as for orofacial movements (see Perrier et al., 2003; Perrier and Fuchs, 2008). In addition, they show that the CNS can integrate changes in dynamics, but only locally, i.e. for the very gestures for which the subjects were trained in the presence of the force field. The results summarized above do not show that the CNS stores a model of the dynamics that could be used for other gestures or in other locations in the space. In the following section, experimental studies related to this question are described.

3.3 Learning: Generalized models, local learning or task specific learning?

Kawato et al.'s (1987, 1990) original papers suggested that a comprehensive model of the dynamics of the motor plant could exist in the brain. Since then, numerous studies have been carried out for arm movements to study the complexity of the knowledge that is actually stored in the brain. The large majority of these studies tend to show that the knowledge is not stored in the form of a generalized model of the dynamics. With a generalized model, we understand a model that was learned for a certain task and in a certain location in the task space, and that could then apply to another task or to another location in the task space. For speech movements, there are not many studies in this domain, but those that have been conducted also tend to reject the hypothesis of a generalized model of the dynamics of the vocal tract articulators. In this section only two studies are presented, one for the arm and one for speech. They have been selected because they illustrate well the debate and the experimental paradigms used in this investigation.

3.3.1 Arm movements: Learned models of dynamics seem to be local

In the study described above, Shadmehr and Mussa-Ivaldi (1994) also investigated the issue of whether or not the CNS learns a generalized model of dynamics. With this aim, they asked their subjects to do reaching movements in the left part of the workspace, after they had learned how to compensate for the influence of the force field in the right part of the workspace (see section 3.2.1). As in the right part of the workspace, they observed after-effects in the left part, since the trajectories after learning were different once the perturbation had been removed. This observation is consistent with the hypothesis that subjects have learned an internal model of the new dynamics that generalizes to the whole workspace, from the right part to the left part, solely on the basis of the training done in the right part. However, the after-effects in the left part of the workspace were different from those in the right part, and the differences were consistent with the changes in joint geometry associated with the displacement of the arm from the right to the left part of the workspace. The authors interpreted this last observation as evidence for the fact that the generalized dynamical internal models had been learned in relation to the arm joints, which are the same in the displacement from the right to the left part, and not in relation to the absolute position of the hand in the space. However, another explanation can be proposed. These findings are also consistent with the "rote learning" hypothesis according to which the CNS would not learn a generalized internal model, but, more simply, a set of sequences of motor commands that allow the subject to compensate for the perturbation in a given task and in a given arm configuration. In the context of Shadmehr and Mussa-Ivaldi's (1994) study, the "rote learning" hypothesis would suggest that subjects have learned how to compensate for the perturbation in a certain angle configuration at arm joints and that they use the same strategy for the same angles at elbow and wrist joints in spite of the change in the angle at the shoulder. Learning would explain after-effects, and the local nature of learning would explain the differences in after-effects between movements made in the right and the left parts of the workspace.

In this context, the study carried out by Conditt et al. (1997) is interesting. The authors used the same experimental setup as Shadmehr and Mussa-Ivaldi (1994) with the same kind of perturbing force field. The differences were in the task required from the subjects. A group of subjects was asked to perform a drawing task. As in the reaching task of Shadmehr and Mussa-Ivaldi (1994), subjects were able after learning to compensate for the perturbation and to reproduce in perturbed conditions the same drawing patterns as in normal conditions. After-effects were also observed. Another group of subjects was asked to perform a reaching task and to draw a circle. During the adaptation phase in the presence of the force field, the subjects executed only the reaching task. However, after learning, both the reaching and the circle drawing tasks were considered. The authors observed a transfer of learning from the

reaching task to the circle drawing task. After learning, based only on the reaching task, subjects were able in the presence of the force field to draw a circle the shape of which was similar to the one they had drawn in the absence of the force field. After-effects were also observed for both tasks. These results tend to rule out the "rote learning hypothesis," and support the hypothesis that an internal model which is not task specific has been learned. However, both tasks were executed in the same location of the workspace, in the same range of positions. Hence, there is still no evidence supporting the hypothesis that a generalized internal model, which would be valid everywhere in the space, had been learned during the adaptation phase.
Mattar and Ostry (2010) investigated this issue, also for arm movements. Again the experimental setup was similar to the one used by Shadmehr and Mussa-Ivaldi (1994). The perturbation consisted in a clockwise force field that pushed the hand toward the right of the trajectory described under normal conditions. The subjects were asked to do reaching movements toward 2 targets located in front of them, along the midline of their body, at two different distances, 15cm and 30cm. Subjects were split into two groups. In the first group, subjects learned how to compensate for the perturbing force when moving toward the closest target (15cm), and transfer of learning was assessed in movements toward the more distant target (30cm). In the second group, the experiment was reversed: the training phase was done with the more distant target (30cm), and transfer of learning was evaluated in movements toward the closer target (15cm). The results showed that transfer of learning did not systematically occur for the first group of subjects. It only occurred when movements toward the 30cm target were achieved at velocities in the range of the velocities observed in the movements toward the 15cm target. In contrast, transfer of learning was systematically observed in the second group, from the movements toward the 30cm target to the movements towards the 15cm target. According to the authors, this result shows that there was no generalization of dynamics learning beyond the range of the dynamical conditions (here, the relations between perturbing force, velocities and positions) that were experienced in the learning phase.

3.3.2 Jaw movements in speech: Dynamics learning seems to be task specific

Generalization of dynamics learning in speech production was studied by Tremblay et al. (2008). These authors used the same experimental setup as in the study of Tremblay et al. (2003), which is described above, consisting of a computer-controlled robot connected to the lower teeth of the subject. Three different experiments were run. In the first experiment, the subjects were trained to adjust motor commands in order to compensate for the deviating force field applied to the jaw for the production of the speech sequence /siæs/ only. After this training, transfer of learning was assessed for the speech sequence /suæs/, which essentially requires the same jaw movements as /siæs/. In the second experiment, a group of subjects was trained to compensate for the force perturbation during the speech sequence /siæs/ (downward jaw movement) only and another group was trained during the speech sequence /sæis/ (upward jaw movement) only. For both groups, transfer of learning was assessed for the speech sequence /siæis/ (downward and upward jaw movement). In the third experiment, a group of subjects was trained to compensate for force perturbation during the speech sequence /siæs/ articulated with vocalization, and the transfer of training was evaluated on the same sequence articulated silently, while the order was reversed for a second group of subjects. It was found in the three experiments that, in general, the subjects were able to properly adjust the motor commands for the learned sequence in order to compensate for the force perturbation (in agreement with Tremblay et al., 2003). However, transfer of learning was not observed in any of the three experiments: the force field perturbed the task chosen to assess transfer of learning in exactly the same way as it had perturbed the other task before learning, and no after-effect was observed after the removal of the perturbation for the task that was not learned. Hence, not only does dynamics learning in speech seem not to be generalized, a result which accords with what has been found in arm movements, but it seems to be task specific, even if the learned task and the test task share the same motor plant and the same location in space.

4 Discussion

In the first part of the paper, it was shown that the concept of a *dynamical internal model* is powerful and useful in order to concretely understand how the CNS can learn about the dynamical properties of the motor plant and how it can use this knowledge in movement planning. In its original form, the hypothesis had strong implications and requirements since it assumed (1) that dynamical internal models are accurate and realistic descriptions of the physical motor plant in its entirety, and (2) that internal models are used either to guide the motor plant along *desired trajectories* specified by the brain as motor goals, or to determine *optimal trajectories* and then guide the motor plant along these trajectories. This last assumption, which corresponds to an *optimal motor planning*, seems to be more realistic since it provides explanations about the principles underlying the emergence of the intended trajectories as consequences of planning principles. Various modeling studies using dynamical internal models and optimal motor planning to control biomechanical models of the arm have simulated movements that have strong similarities with real arm movements recorded in humans (see, for example, Kawato et al., 1990; Gomi and Kawato, 1996; Kawato, 1999). These results undoubtedly support the hypothesis that optimal motor planning based on internal dynamical models is used for arm movement. This model is a potential explanation for the characteristics of human arm movements. However, the results of these simulations do not demonstrate that humans actually control their movements in this way. To confirm this hypothesis, experimental evidence is required and this was the aim of numerous studies in the last decade.

In the second section of the paper, a number of selected experimental studies were described and interpreted. Obviously the proposed selection is not exhaustive, but it is, from our point of view, reasonably representative of the state of the art. This literature review shows that in arm movements the CNS takes dynamical properties of the motor plant into account when planning the motor task: Sabes et al. (1998) showed that inertial constraints are taken into account to avoid collision in obstacle avoidance; Franklin et al. (2007) found evidence for the fact that the CNS adjusts the end-effector stiffness in order to increase stability and gestural accuracy; Shadmehr and Mussa-Ivaldi (1994) found that new dynamical constraints can be learned in order to achieve the same trajectory as before these new constraints were introduced; and Conditt et al. (1997) even showed that this learning can be extended to other kinds of movements produced with the arm in similar positions. However, no or very little evidence has been found for the arm supporting the hypothesis that learning consists in building up full and generalized models of the motor plant's dynamics (Mattar and Ostry, 2010). It does not therefore seem realistic to assume that motor planning of arm movements could rely on accurate and complex models of the dynamics of the motor plant in its entirety. This statement is now widely accepted, in particular by Kawato and colleagues:

Considering the number of objects and environments, and their possible combinations, that can influence the dynamics of the motor system, the controller must be capable of providing appropriate motor commands for a multitude of distinct contexts, such as different tasks and interactions with objects, that are likely to be experienced. Given this multitude of contexts, there are two qualitatively distinct strategies to motor control and learning. The first is to use a single controller that uses all the contextual information in an attempt to produce an appropriate control signal. However, such a controller would demand enormous complexity to allow for all possible scenarios (Wolpert et al., 1998, p.344-345).

This explains why in the last decade the focus of studies investigating the nature of dynamical internal models was shifted from the investigation of their existence in the form of generalized models to the investigation of how multiple localized or specialized models could be learned and used to control different tasks in various contexts. Wolpert and Kawato (1998) proposed a neural architecture based on multiple paired forward-inverse models. In this architecture, for a given motor task, the CNS would first evaluate which one of the different forward models best predicts the dynamical state of the motor plant in interaction with its environment. Once the best forward model has been selected, the corresponding paired forward and inverse models would be used to control the task. Imamizu and Kawato (2009), using functional brain imaging, found evidence for this modular structure of the representation of the motor plant's dynamics in the brain. For example,

they observed that when their subjects were trained to interact with a computer using different kinds of mouses (a normal mouse, a mouse rotated in direction, or a velocity-dependent mouse), different brain regions were activated. Krakauer et al. (2006) studied the influence of the context on the generalization of internal models learned for a given motor task to another motor task. They concluded that generalization depends on the history of prior motor behavior. In parallel, Mattar and Ostry (2010) proposed that simplified generalized models could be built up in the CNS by interpolating between local models learned in the regions of the motor space that have been already reached by the motor plant.
All these studies suggest that for arm movements a representation of the dynamics of the motor plant does exist in the brain, and that this representation is local and/or task specific. However, the issue of whether this representation is used in the context of an optimal motor control is still unsolved. Hence, if these representations are used in the context of an optimal motor planning, it is likely that the optimality is limited to a part of the task space and influenced by the nature of the task. The curvature of the experimental arm trajectories (Flash and Hogan, 1985; Gomi and Kawato, 1996) and the relation between this curvature and movement speed (Viviani and Flash, 1995) are consistent with the assumption that planning is optimal. However, simulations carried out with accurate biomechanical models of the arm have shown that these experimental results are also consistent with the influence of arm dynamics in the context of a non-optimal motor control (Flanagan et al., 1993). Hence these kinematic characteristics are not a convincing demonstration that trajectories actually result from any kind of optimal motor planning. In addition, it has been shown that, in some cases, when complex perturbations are applied to the arm during its movements, simple and non-optimal strategies, using very rough representations of the dynamics of the motor plant, are selected to maintain gesture accuracy. This phenomenon was observed among others by Franklin et al. (2008), who found that the adaptation of arm motor commands to time-varying changes in the environmental dynamics could be attributed "*to a single adaptive process, without explicit calculation of inverse dynamics or impedance*", (p.11172) i.e. to a "simple" increase in the arm stiffness.

In conclusion, for arm movement, there is considerable evidence that dynamics is taken into account in planning to ensure gesture accuracy, but certainly not in the form of generalized and comprehensive internal models, and there is no convincing evidence that motor planning uses these dynamical representations in order to optimize a physical cost.
Our review of the literature suggests that speech motor control and arm motor control are different from the point of view of the integration of dynamical constraints in motor planning. We did not find any evidence supporting the idea that dynamical properties of the speech production system are learned by the CNS:

- Gravity does not seem to be integrated in speech motor planning (Shiller et al., 1999; Buchaillard et al., 2009).
- Jaw variability in speech production seems to be the passive consequence of the intrinsic stiffness of the jaw (Shiller et al., 2002), which is not specifically controlled.
- There is no transfer of learning between motor tasks for the jaw, even if these motor tasks share the same location in the task space (Tremblay et al., 2008).
- The fact that, in speech production, the CNS compensates for the impact of a perturbing force field (Tremblay et al., 2003) applied to the jaw can be explained without any dynamical learning. According to the authors themselves and consistent with Franklin et al.'s (2008) suggestion for arm motor control, a compensation based on a stiffness increase is possible, and this does not require any complex dynamical representation (Tremblay et al., 2008; Nasir and Ostry, 2006).

Thus, contrary to what could be concluded from experimental observations in arm movements, it does not seem necessary for speech motor control to integrate the dynamical properties of the speech motor plant in the form of a model even for the control of movement accuracy.
A first explanation for this difference between arm movement planning and speech movement planning could lie in the fact that the number of experimental studies of dynamical internal models in speech motor control is significantly lower than the number of studies regarding arm

motor control. Hence, this difference could be an illusion due to a lack of knowledge about speech motor control. However, this difference can also be explained by a number of intrinsic differences between speech and arm motor control: (1) the motor goals of speech production are more tolerant to gestural inaccuracy than arm movements, because they are cognitive and not physical in nature; (2) the dynamical properties of the orofacial motor plant are extremely complex (see, for example, Koolstra and van Eijden (2005), for jaw dynamics, Buchaillard et al. (2009), for tongue dynamics, and Nazari et al. (2010), for face dynamics); thus it is likely that speech motor control can only adapt roughly to these properties and can neither learn nor integrate them accurately.

When accuracy is an issue, a global control based on stiffness increase could be used in speech motor control in order not to endanger speech perception (as suggested for lip protrusion by Nazari et al., 2011a), as is done in arm movements. However, other strategies exist that could rely on the use of external mechanical structures (like the palate in high vowels and in alveo-palatal and palatal consonants, see Stone and Vatikiotis-Bateson, 1995) or on the use of saturation effects in the relation between articulation and acoustics (Perkell et al., 2000).

Speech production is certainly optimal in a way, since it has been shown that speakers can adapt to various speaking conditions (fast speaking rate, noise, non-native listeners...) in order to ensure an efficient communication with listeners (Lindblom, 1990). However, we could not find in the speech literature in general and in our own studies in particular any convincing evidence that speech gestures are controlled in order to optimize any physically measurable cost. Nelson (1983) proposed that the bell-shaped velocity profiles observed in jaw movements for speech are consistent with a minimum jerk model. Löfqvist and Gracco (2002) also suggested that the curved paths observed in vowel-consonant-vowel sequences support the minimum jerk model. Tasko and Westbury (2004) and Perrier and Fuchs (2008) found relations between speed and curvature in speech movements that have been shown to be consistent with the minimum jerk model Viviani and Flash (1995). However, we were able to reproduce all these different patterns using a biomechanical model of the tongue that was not controlled optimally in any way (Payan and Perrier, 1997; Perrier et al., 2003; Perrier and Fuchs, 2008). This suggests that these patterns could arise from the intrinsic dynamics of the speech articulators. Hence, for motor control in general, and for speech motor control in particular, it is still unclear whether motor planning aims at optimizing any measurable physical cost (global torque change, minimum of jerk, minimum of variance...). Alternative models of motor control have been elaborated. All these models are controversial, just as optimal motor control models are. However, they offer interesting ways to think further about the way the CNS integrates dynamical constraints and uses this knowledge in gesture planning.

Feldman and colleagues have, for many years, been strong opponents of the idea that motor control is guided by optimality and that it relies on internal models of dynamics (see, for example, Ostry and Feldman, 2003; Feldman, 2009). Their criticisms are based mainly on two points: (1) force, which is by nature the output of a dynamical internal model, cannot be a controlled parameter, since it is the result of combined influences arising from the CNS and from the motor plant itself via different kinds of afference; and (2) feedback can be tuned by the CNS, so learning complex dynamics on the basis of comparisons between desired outputs and feedback signals (see Figures 2 and 3) does not seem to be a realistic hypothesis. Feldman (1986) proposed a motor control model, the so-called model, based on the Equilibrium Point Hypothesis. The model assumes that movement is generated by continuously shifting the mechanical equilibrium point of the motor plant along relatively simple paths between specified target equilibrium positions. This is done by controlling the muscle length above which the muscle starts to generate an active force. According to this model the trajectory of the motor plant is determined by the combined influences of the motor commands and of reflex loops that ensure that the movement reaches the successive locations of the target equilibrium positions. In this context, none of the kinematic properties of the movement would result from any optimal process and there is no need for any explicit representation of the dynamics of the motor plant. In addition the model proposes an interesting way to control stiffness via a co-contraction parameter, C. In the context of the experimental findings listed above, which suggest an important role of stiffness in accuracy and stability control, this model deserves special attention. Proponents of optimal control models based on internal models of dynamics have developed numerous arguments against the model. For example, Wolpert et al. (1998) argued that this model would require unrealistic mechanical and neural feedback gains; Gomi and Kawato (1996) considered that the model would necessitate much too complex time variations of the motor commands; and Hinder and Milner (2003) showed for goal-directed wrist flexion movements that the patterns of variability at the end of the movements were not compatible with the basic hypotheses of the model. Now, our own implementations of the model in the context of speech articulators have provided interesting similarities between simulated movements and experimental data (Perrier et al., 1996, 2003; Buchaillard et al., 2009). However, this speech production modeling work has also shown how difficult it is to properly define a co-contraction parameter for complex and deformable motor plants (tongue, lips, etc.). Work is in progress in our research group (Winkler et al., 2011; Nazari et al., 2011a) to further evaluate the usability of this model in the context of speech motor control.

Recently, Kawato contributed to an article (Ganesh et al., 2010) in which the authors suggested that the search for optimality could be secondary in motor planning. Asking their subjects to achieve motor tasks that are more complex than reaching tasks (i.e. maintaining the wrist within a certain angle amplitude under the influence of vibratory disturbances), they observed that their subjects (1) did not all use the same motor control strategies to compensate for the perturbation, and (2) did not in general adopt any optimal strategy even if they had previously realized the optimal movement. Their investigations of the different strategies used by their subjects led them to assume that, instead of looking for a globally optimal movement, the CNS would instead remember a previously used solution that enabled the task to be achieved in a satisfactory way, and then look for a locally optimal movement around this solution. Thus, Ganesh et al. (2010) suggested that motor memory, and not optimal motor planning, would play the major role in the determination of motor strategies. The search for optimality would come after, in a second stage, and it would be local. This finding is consistent with the conclusion that dynamical internal models, if they exist, are first local. The finding is also compatible with a major criticism made by Friston (2011) of the optimal motor control hypothesis: there is no realistic way of thinking of a process with which the CNS could compute and minimize a global cost such as the jerk or the torque change during a movement. Instead of cost minimization Friston (2011) suggested that motor control strategies could be guided by prior beliefs characterizing expectations of the consequences of movement in the perception domain, based on the principle of active inference. In this context, the CNS would select the motor control strategies that have the highest probability of achieving the goals in the perception domain, according to Bayesian inference principles and using probabilistic forward models linking motor commands and perceptual parameters. This is an interesting alternative to the hypothesis of optimal motor control based on forward and inverse internal models of complex dynamical motor plants for two reasons: (1) it avoids the computation of a valued cost that would require some kind of measurement of physical parameters; and (2) it proposes a functional way to account for the dynamical properties of the motor plant, which globally and statistically relates motor commands and their impact in the perception domain. Taken together this direct link with perception instead of with physical parameters and the absence of any computation of physical costs makes less crucial the question of the accuracy of the dynamical internal models in motor planning. This is particularly interesting in the context of speech motor control, in which movements are not produced with the aim of reaching clearly specified physical goals, but with the cognitive aim of producing a signal that can be perceived and identified by a listener. The probability approach is well adapted to the intrinsic variability of speech signals, in which the same percept can be associated with different physical signals, depending on the context, the speaking style or the speaker.

5 Conclusion

The review of the literature in this article has shown that little experimental support exists in favor of motor sequence planning based on optimal control and learned generalized dynamical internal models in the brain. While evidence was found in support of the integration, at least partial, of some dynamical properties of the motor plant in arm movement planning, no evidence was found in support of this hypothesis in speech production. We cannot discard the possibility that this absence of evidence may be due to the paucity of studies investigating this issue in speech production. However, some specific aspects of speech production as compared to other motor tasks could also explain why dynamical properties of the speech production apparatus do not need to be modeled in the brain. In arm as well as in speech movements, experimental findings have shown that the assumption that generalized internal models of the physical motor plants could exist in the brain is not realistic at all. Recent researches have proposed that internal models of the dynamics would rather be local and sometimes task specific. Current studies are investigating how transfer can operate from internal models learned for a given task and in a given location in the task space to other tasks. Internal models of the dynamics are usually considered in the context of an optimal motor planning in which the predictions provided by the forward model are used to optimize a certain cost in the physical domain, while optimal solutions are stored in the inverse model. A number of kinematic properties of arm and speech movements are consistent with the optimization of costs, such as minimum of effort, minimum of jerk or minimum of torque. However, simulations using non-optimal motor planning have been shown to generate similar kinematic properties. Hence, there is little convincing evidence that arm and speech movement are controlled as to minimize such a cost. The debate is still open. Alternative hypotheses that have been shown to be biologically plausible and do not require cost computation do exist. However, further evaluation of these hypotheses is still required in the context of speech sequence planning. In speech the control of time is crucial, since segmental duration can be associated in speech with meaning. Since motor plant dynamics influences the time behavior of the motor plant, hypotheses about speech motor planning should be evaluated more precisely in relation to time control. Experimental studies investigating this issue could open new doors to the clarification of the role of articulatory dynamics and optimal control in speech production.

References

Anderson, F. and Pandy, M. (2001). Dynamic optimization of human walking. *Journal of Biomechanical Engineering*, 123:381–390.

Browman, C. P. and Goldstein, L. (1990). Gestural specification using dynamically-defined articulatory structures. *Journal of Phonetics*, 18:299–320.

Brunner, J., Fuchs, S., and Perrier, P. (2009). On the relationship between palate shape and articulatory behavior. *Journal of the Acoustical Society of America*, 125(6):3936–3949.

Brunner, J., Hoole, P., and Perrier, P. (2011). Adaptation strategies in perturbed /s/. *Clinical Linguistics & Phonetics*, 25(8):705–724.

Buchaillard, S., Perrier, P., and Payan, Y. (2009). A biomechanical model of cardinal vowel production: Muscle activations and the impact of gravity on tongue positioning. *Journal of the Acoustical Society of America*, 126(4):2033–2051.

Conditt, M., Gandolfo, F., and Mussa-Ivaldi, F. A. (1997). The motor system does not learn the dynamics of the arm by rote memorization of past experience. *Journal of Neurophysiology*, 78:554–560.

Evarts, E. V. (1981). Role of motor cortex in voluntary movements in primates. In Brooks, V. B., editor, *Handbook of Physiology*, chapter sect1, Vol. 11, part 2, pages 1083–1120. American Physiol. Soc., Bethesda.

Feldman, A. G. (1986). Once more on the Equilibrium-Point Hypothesis (model) for motor control. *Journal of Motor Behavior*, 18(1):17–54.

Feldman, A. G. (2009). New insights into action–perception coupling. *Experimental Brain Research*, 194:39–58.

Flanagan, J. R., Ostry, D. J., and Feldman, A. G. (1993). Control of trajectory modifications in in target-directed reaching. *Journal of Motor Behavior*, 25(3):140–152.

Flash, T. and Hogan, N. (1985). The coordination of arm movements: An experimentally confirmed mathematical model. *Journal of Neuroscience*, 5(7):1688–1703.

Francis, B. A. and Wonham, W. M. (1976). The internal model principle of control theory. *Automatica*, 12(5):457–465.

Franklin, D. W., Burdet, E., Tee, K. P., Osu, R., Chew, C. M., Milner, T. E., and Kawato, M. (2008). CNS learns stable, accurate, and efficient movements using a simple algorithm. *Journal of Neuroscience*, 28(44):11165–11173.

Franklin, D. W., Liaw, G., Milner, T. E., Osu, R., Burdet, E., and Kawato, M. (2007). Endpoint stiffness of the arm is directionally tuned to instability in the environment. *Journal of Neuroscience*, 27(29):7705–7716.

Friston, K. (2011). What is optimal about motor control? *Neuron*, 72:488–498.

Ganesh, G., Haruno, M., Kawato, M., and Burdet, E. (2010). Motor memory and local minimization of error and effort, not global optimization, determine motor behavior. *Journal of Neurophysiology*, 104:382–390.

Gerard, J.-M., Ohayon, J., Luboz, V., Perrier, P., and Payan, Y. (2005). Non linear elastic properties of the lingual and facial tissues assessed by indentation technique. Application to the biomechanics of speech production. *Medical Engineering & Physics*, 27(10):884–892.

Gomi, H. and Kawato, M. (1996). Equilibrium-point control hypothesis examined by measured arm stiffness during multijoint movement. *Science*, 272 (5258):117–120.

Gomi, H., Shidara, M., Takemura, A., Inoue, Y., Kawano, K., and Kawato, M. (1998). Temporal firing patterns of Purkinje cells in the cerebellar ventral paraflocculus during ocular following responses in monkeys I. Simple spikes. *Journal of Neurophysiology*, 80:818–831.

Gribble, P. L. and Ostry, D. J. (1996). Origins of the power law relation between movement velocity and curvature: Modeling the effects of muscle mechanics and limb dynamics. *Journal of Neurophysiology*, 76 (5):2853–2860.

Gribble, P. L., Ostry, D. J., Sanguineti, V., and Laboissière, R. (1998). Are complex control signals required for human arm movement? *Journal of Neurophysiology*, 79(3):1409–1424.

Grimme, B., Fuchs, S., Perrier, P., and Schöner, G. (2011). Limb versus speech motor control: A conceptual review. *Motor Control*, 15(1):5–33.

Guenther, F., Ghosh, S., and Tourville, J. A. (2006). Neural modeling and imaging of the cortical interactions underlying syllable production. *Brain and Language*, 96:280–301.

Guenther, F. H., Hampson, M., and Johnson, D. (1998). A theoretical investigation of reference frames for the planning of speech movements. *Psychological Review*, 105:611–633.

Harris, C. M. and Wolpert, D. M. (1998). Signal-dependent noise determines motor planning. *Nature*, 394:780–784.

Hinder, M. and Milner, T. E. (2003). The case for an internal dynamics model versus equilibrium point control in human movement. *Journal of Physiology*, 549(3):953–963.

Hogan, N. (1984). An organizing principle for a class of voluntary movements. *Journal of Neuroscience*, 4(11):2745–2754.

Imamizu, H. and Kawato, M. (2009). Brain mechanisms for predictive control by switching internal models: Implications for higher-order cognitive functions. *Psychological Research*, 73:527–544.

Jordan, M. I. and Rumelhart, D. E. (1992). Forward models: Supervised learning with a Distal Teacher. *Cognitive Science*, 16:316–354.

Kawato, M. (1999). Internal models for motor control and trajectory planning. *Current Opinions in Neurobiology*, 9:718–727.

Kawato, M., Furukawa, K., and Susuki, R. (1987). A hierarchical neural-network model for control and learning of voluntary movement. *Biological Cybernetics*, 57:169–185.

Kawato, M., Maeda, Y., Uno, Y., and Suzuki, R. (1990). Trajectory formation of arm movement by cascade neural network model based on minimum torque-change criterion. *Biological Cybernetics*, 62:275–288.

Koolstra, J. H. and van Eijden, T. M. G. J. (2005). Combined finite-element and rigid-body analysis of human jaw joint dynamics. *Journal of Biomechanics*, 38:2431–2439.

Krakauer, J. W., Mazzoni, P., Ghazizadeh, A., Ravindran, R., and Shadmehr, R. (2006). Generalization of motor learning depends on the history of prior action. *PLoS Biology*, 4(10):1798–1808.

Laboissière, R., Ostry, D. J., and Feldman, A. G. (1996). The control of multi-muscle systems: Human jaw and hyoid movements. *Biological Cybernetics*, 74:373–384.

Löfqvist, A. and Gracco, V. L. (2002). Control of oral closure in lingual stop consonant production. *Journal of the Acoustical Society of America*, 111(6):2811–2827.

Lindblom, B. (1990). Explaining phonetic variation: a sketch of the h & h theory. In Hardcastle, W. and Marchal, A., editors, *Speech Production and Speech Modeling*, pages 403–439. Kluwer, Dordrecht.

Marroquin, J., Mitter, S., and Poggio, T. (1987). Probabilistic solution of iii-posed problems in computational vision. *Journal of the American Statistical Association*, 82, No. 397:76–89.

Mattar, A. A. G. and Ostry, D. J. (2010). Generalization of dynamics learning across changes in movement amplitude. *Journal of Neurophysiology*, 104:426–438.

McMahon, T. A. (1984). *Muscles, Reflexes, and Locomotion*. Princeton University Press, Princeton, New Jersey.

Miall, R. C. and Wolpert, D. M. (1996). Forward models for physiological motor control. *Neural Networks*, 9(8):1265–1279.

Nasir, S. and Ostry, D. J. (2006). Somatosensory precision in speech production. *Current Biology*, 16:1918–1923.

Nazari, M., Perrier, P., Chabanas, M., and Payan, Y. (2011a). A 3D muscle element based on Equilibrium Point Hypothesis (EPH) and its application in a biomechanical face model. In *Proceedings of the 9th International Seminar on Speech Production, Montreal*, pages 144–145.

Nazari, M. A., Perrier, P., Chabanas, M., and Payan, Y. (2010). Simulation of dynamic orofacial movements using a constitutive law varying with muscle activation. *Computer Methods in Biomechanics & Biomedical Engineering*, 13:469–482.

Nazari, M. A., Perrier, P., Chabanas, M., and Payan, Y. (2011b). Shaping by stiffening: A modeling study for lips. *Motor Control*, 15(1):141–168.

Nelson, W. L. (1983). Physical principles for economies of skilled movements. *Biological Cybernetics*, 46:135–147.

Ostry, D. J. and Feldman, A. G. (2003). A critical evaluation of the force control hypothesis in motor control. *Experimental Brain Research*, 153:275–288.

Payan, Y. and Perrier, P. (1997). Synthesis of V-V sequences with a 2D biomechanical tongue model controlled by the Equilibrium Point Hypothesis. *Speech Communication*, 22(2/3):185–205.

Perkell, J. S., Guenther, F. H., Lane, H., Matthies, L. M., Perrier, P., Vick, J., Wilhelms-Tricarico, R., and Zandipour, M. (2000). A theory of speech motor control and supporting data from speakers with normal hearing and with profound hearing loss. *Journal of Phonetics*, 28(3):233–272.

Perrier, P. (2005). Control and representations in speech production. *ZAS Papers in Linguistics*, 40:190–132.

Perrier, P. and Fuchs, S. (2008). Speed-curvature relations in speech production challenge the 1/3 power law. *Journal of Neurophysiology*, 100 (3):1171–1183.

Perrier, P., Ostry, D. J., and Laboissière, R. (1996). The Equilibrium Point Hypothesis and its application to speech motor control. *Journal of Speech and Hearing Research*, 39(2):365–378.

Perrier, P., Payan, Y., Zandipour, M., and Perkell, J. (2003). Influences of tongue biomechanics on speech movements during the production of velar stop consonants: A modeling study. *Journal of the Acoustical Society of America*, 114 (3):1582–1599.

Sabes, P., Jordan, M. I., and Wolpert, D. M. (1998). The role of inertial sensitivity in motor planning. *Journal of Neuroscience*, 18(15):5948–5957.

Savariaux, C., Perrier, P., and Orliaguet, J. P. (1995). Compensation strategies for a lip-tube perturbation of the rounded vowel [u]. *Journal of the Acoustical Society of America*, 98(5):2428–2442.

Savariaux, C., Perrier, P., Orliaguet, J. P., and Schwartz, J. L. (1999). Compensation strategies for the perturbation of french [u] using a lip tube. part ii: Perceptual analysis. *Journal of the Acoustical Society of America*, 106(1):381–393.

Schmidt, R. A. (1988). *Motor Learning and Control*. Champaign, Human Kinetics.

Shadmehr, R. and Mussa-Ivaldi, F. A. (1994). Adaptive representation of dynamics during learning of a motor task. *Journal of Neuroscience*, 14(5):3208–3224.

Shiller, D. M., Laboissière, R., and Ostry, D. J. (2002). Relationship between jaw stiffness and kinematic variability in speech. *Journal of Neurophysiology*, 88:2329–2340.

Shiller, D. M., Ostry, D. J., and Gribble, P. L. (1999). Effects of gravitational load on jaw movements in speech. *Journal of Neuroscience*, 19(20):9073–9080.

Stevens, K. N. (1972). The quantal nature of speech: Evidence from articulatory-acoustic data. In David, J. E. and Denes, P., editors, *Human Communication: A Unified View*, pages 51–66. Mc Graw Hill, New York.

Stone, M. and Vatikiotis-Bateson, E. (1995). Trade-offs in tongue, jaw, and palate contributions to speech production. *Journal of Phonetics*, 23:81–100.

Tasko, S. R. and Westbury, J. R. (2004). Speed–curvature relations for speech-related articulatory movement. *Journal of Phonetics*, 32:65–80.

Tourville, J. T. and Guenther, F. H. (2011). The DIVA model: A neural theory of speech acquisition and production. *Language and Cognitive Processes*, 25(7):952–981.

Tremblay, S., Houle, G., and Ostry, D. J. (2008). Specificity of speech motor learning. *Journal of Neuroscience*, 28(10):2426 –2434.

Tremblay, S., Shiller, D. M., and Ostry, D. J. (2003). Somatosensory basis of speech production. *Nature*, 423:866–869.

Uno, Y., Kawato, M., and Suzuki, R. (1989). Formation and control of optimal trajectory in human multijoint arm movement: Minimum torque-change model. *Biological Cybernetics*, 61:89–101.

Viviani, P. and Flash, T. (1995). Minimum-jerk, two-thirds power law, and isochrony: Converging approaches to movement planning. *Journal of Experimental Psychology: Human Perception and Performance*, 21(1):32–53.

Winkler, R., Ma, L., and Perrier, P. (2011). A model of optimal speech production planning integrating dynamical constraints to achieve appropriate articulatory timing. In *Proceedings of the 9th International Seminar on Speech Production, Montreal*, pages 235–236.

Wolpert, D., Miall, R. C., and Kawato, M. (1998). Internal models in the cerebellum. *Trends in Cognitive Sciences*, 2(9):338–347.

Wolpert, D. M. and Kawato, M. . (1998). Multiple paired forward and inverse models for motor control. *Neural Networks*, 11(7-8):1317–1329.

6 Appendix

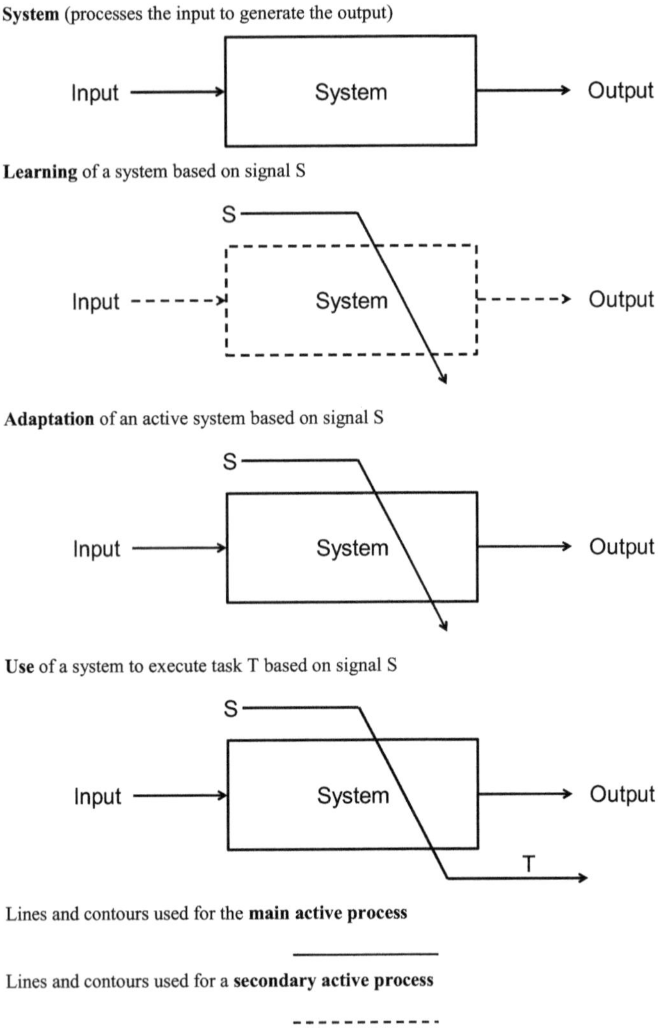

Figure 9: Symbols used in Figures 2, 3, 4, 5, 7, 8.

A survey of methods for the analysis of the temporal evolution of speech articulator trajectories

LEONARDO LANCIA
MARK TIEDE

Abstract: In this chapter we will survey methods for comparison and description of sampled movement data, with focus on techniques able to capture the characteristics of the temporal evolution of the signals under study. Functional data analysis, the cross wavelet transform and cross recurrence analysis will be introduced and applied to the analysis of speech movement data.

1 Introduction

Speech activity can be observed through a variety of transduced signals: these can be acoustic signals, aerodynamic signals, recordings of the movements of the speech articulators, etc. Such signals evolve over time in a generally continuous fashion, describing trajectories that are characteristic of both the linguistic content of the utterances produced and of non linguistic aspects such as the emotional or health state of the speaker, the communicative context, and so forth. In speech production research, it is common practice to focus on particular events present in these signals such as peaks, valleys or discontinuities. As a consequence, speech is often quantified through measures anchored to particular time points or averaged over portions of the signals where no discontinuity is observed. In such an approach, the critical points of analysis must be defined before the analysis takes place, with many evident drawbacks: information concerning the trajectories themselves is lost; the results are strongly dependent on the theoretical assumptions that lead to the choice and the location of the events on the signal; and a large amount of time-consuming manual labeling is generally required. In recent years, new methods have been proposed for characterizing the evolution over time of multivariate time series and which offer viable alternatives for studying the signals recorded in speech production experiments. The purpose of this chapter is to contribute to the diffusion of these methods with a tutorial introduction focused on the analysis of the motion of oral articulators.

1.1 The Labial Coronal Effect

The application of these techniques will be illustrated using the movements of three articulators observed by electromagnetic articulometry (EMA): the jaw (as characterized by the movement of the lower incisors), the tip of the tongue (henceforth TTip) and the lower lip (henceforth LLip). The data were collected using a speeded repetition paradigm to replicate the so-called *labial coronal effect* observed by Rochet-Capellan and Schwartz (2007). In several languages of the world, disyllabic CVCV sequences in which the two consonants are a labial and a coronal are found more often in labial-coronal order than in coronal-labial order. A hypothesis defended by Rochet-Capellan and Schwartz is that this preference is observed because the labial-coronal order (henceforth La-Co order) is inherently more stable than the reverse order (Co-La). To test their hypothesis, Rochet-Capellan and Schwartz had French speakers repeat Co-La or La-Co disyllabic nonsense words (eg. /pata/, /tapa/). Nonsense words were uninterruptedly repeated during trials of 10 seconds. In the first half of each trial, speakers had to gradually increase their speech rate and in the second half the speech rate was gradually decreased. Regardless of the order of the consonants in the intended utterance, at fast speech rates speakers tended to produce the sequences with an underlying La-Co order.

An important observation made by Rochet-Capellan and Schwartz concerns the evolution of the jaw's behavior during a sequence of utterances. At slow speech rate, two upward movements of the jaw are observed per disyllable. This is expected, because in the presence of an oral constriction, the jaw is generally raised (Lindblom, 1983; Keating et al., 1994) However, at fast speech rates, the upward movements tend to be

reduced to one per utterance. In a replication of the Rochet-Capellan & Schwartz study applied to German, Fuchs et al. (2009) emphasize the presence of several instances in which at high speech rates the jaw tends to be frozen, and its vertical displacement is minimal. This behavior was also observed by Rochet-Capellan and Schwartz, who explicitly discarded from the analysis the utterances produced in this way. On the basis of this behavior Fuchs and colleagues were led to emphasize the role of the jaw in the production of the Labial Coronal effect.
Subsequently Lancia and Fuchs (2011) formulated a revised hypothesis in which this effect is promoted by the interaction of the two following constraints operating on different levels: 1) As speech rate increases, it becomes increasingly difficult to produce two jaw oscillations per utterance, due to both biomechanical and cognitive factors. Because the jaw is the most massive articulator, preserving its oscillatory frequency as the double of the oscillatory frequency of the other, less massive articulators during several sequences in which dozens of repetitions are produced becomes untenable. In addition, when the jaw produces two oscillations per utterance, the ratio between the oscillatory frequency of this articulator and the oscillatory frequency of the other two articulators is 2:1. It is known that this kind of coordination pattern is generally harder to maintain than the 1:1 frequency ratio which characterizes the coordination of the articulators when one jaw cycle per syllable is produced (Pouplier, 2007; Goldstein et al., 2007). 2) To produce an audible coronal gesture, the jaw must achieve a high position; at the same time, the constraints on the height of the jaw during the labial constriction seem to be weaker (Lindblom, 1983; Keating et al., 1994; Hertrich and Ackermann, 2000; Koenig et al., 2003; Mooshammer et al., 2007). According to Lancia and Fuchs (2011), the joint effect of these constraints produces a weakening of the jaw cycle which is synchronous with the movement of the LLip. The reduction of this cycle of jaw movement produces a reduction of the vowel following the labial consonant and a reduction of the interval between this consonant and the following coronal. For this reason the two consonants tend to be perceived as grouped as if they were produced with a LC order. However, in order to test this revised hypothesis, three tasks must be performed. First, the evolution from two jaw cycles per utterance to one jaw cycle per utterance has to be quantified. Second, relative coordination among the articulators has

to be determined, together with how this changes as speech rate is increased. Finally, the variability of fast speech rate utterances produced with an underlying La-Co must be compared to those produced with an underlying Co-La order.

1.2 Plan of the chapter

The goal here is not to test the hypotheses described in the preceding section, but rather to explain and illustrate the analysis methods adopted to accomplish the three tasks described above. In the following sections, we will first introduce some basic terms. We will then illustrate how functional data analysis can be used to characterize the evolution of the jaw's behavior as speech rate is increased. In order to relate the behavior of the jaw to the other articulators, we will use the cross-wavelet transform to derive their relative phase relationships and show the evolution of these variables as speech rate increases. We will also introduce recurrence quantification analysis as a method for assessing the variability of motion patterns corresponding to different consonant orders (Co-La or La-Co). In the last section of this chapter we will briefly discuss choices confronting the researcher for the correct application of these methods. In the appendix, the reader is directed to essential literature describing these techniques and to the internet resources providing software and examples.

1.3 Basic terminology

The data studied here have been obtained using electromagnetic articulometry (EMA), in which signals transduced in sensors within an oscillating electromagnetic field are used to track their positions and orientation in three dimensions. By gluing sensors to accessible parts of a speaker's vocal tract anatomy (anterior tongue, jaw, lips) and correcting for head movement using additional reference sensors, the simultaneous and overlapping movements of the speech articulators relative to the hard structure of the palate can be observed using this technique. At time t the position of each of these sensors can be characterized by three spatial coordinates corresponding to its 3D offset from a common origin (typically the speaker's upper incisors). The set of values that constitute the spatial configuration of the ensemble of the articulators is a coordinate vector. When dealing with position data, the values correspond to spatial coordinates, but when dealing with other kinds of data (eg. pressure, flow, etc.) each vector describes the state of the observed signals at a given moment in time and it can therefore be called a **state vector**. A **multivariate time series** is a sequence of state vectors describing the simultaneous evolution of several processes, each one projected onto a different dimension of the state vectors. In the case of speech movements, a given dimension of the state vectors (and, by extension, of the whole time series) corresponds to the evolution over time of the position of one particular articulator over one of the three spatial dimensions. It is often the case that one or more spatial dimensions are dropped from analysis, on the assumption that movement along those dimensions is not relevant for the phenomenon under study. The sequences of values on the different dimensions, when plotted separately, constitute **curves** on a plane which have time on the abscissa and the displacement mapped to the ordinate. Particular shapes determined by the evolution over time of one curve or by the joint evolution of several curves are defined as **spatio-temporal patterns**. It is often the case that we consider a one dimensional signal as the combination of simpler curves which are called **components**. This approach can of course be extended to multidimensional signals. When analyzing a roughly periodic signal (a signal which is repeated in a more or less cyclical fashion over time), it is common to decompose it as the sum of basic oscillations or building-blocks occurring at different frequencies. In Fourier analysis, the components are sinusoidal functions of time multiplied by appropriate constants. Other analysis methods adopt different building-blocks, as shown in the two following sections.

2 Part I: Functional data analysis (FDA)

2.1 Introduction

Rochet-Cappellan and Schwartz observed that when speakers repeat CVCV disyllables at a moderate speech rate their jaw produces two oscillations. The vertical position of the jaw reaches its maximum at consonant closure, and its minimum corresponds to vowel production. At high speech rates however the jaw often makes only one oscillation per utterance. In the first part of this chapter we will analyze the trajectories of the jaw from 20 /pata/ utterances produced in the same trial sequence.

In order to compare the trajectories and to understand how they depend on speech rate, we follow Ramsay and Silverman (1997) and consider each trajectory X as the instance of a smooth function of time.

$$X \approx F(t) \tag{1}$$

Such a function can be approximated by a linear combination of primitive functions of time. The behavior of the primitive (or basis) functions is well known and can be adapted to approximate the behavior of the raw data. This is done by tuning the multiplicative coefficients of the basis functions.

$$X = \sum_{i=1}^{n} c_i f_i(t) \tag{2}$$

with $t = \{1, \ldots, m\}$. In other words, the time series X, of length m, can be described as the sum of n functions f multiplied by n coefficients c_i. The term *basis function* is used to refer to one of the functions f, while the term *mother function* refers to the basic shape of the basis functions. n basis functions and n coefficient values constitute a functional observation, i.e., the functional model of an observed trajectory. In a way, a functional observation is a smoothed version of the original data, and indeed smoothness of trajectories is a prerequisite for that computational method. The first step in FDA is thus the transformation of our original observations into *functional observations.*

The second step is related to the alignment of the trajectories. Since the lengths of any two utterances are rarely equal, if we want to compare them we need to know which features of the first utterance correspond to which features of the second. This mapping is called *registration.*

Once the second step has been completed, we have a set of functional observations that can be compared to determine the amount of variation in different portions of the trajectories, or that can be submitted to more sophisticated analyses. In this chapter we will use functional principal component analysis, an extension of classical PCA. PCA is commonly used to characterize the extent of variation in multi-dimensional data. As it will be shown in section 2.2.3, with the functional extension of this technique, we can distinguish temporal patterns which maximally change over the curves. In the example that follows we will use this strategy to observe that when the speech rate increases, the jaw movement changes from a repeated pattern consisting of two jaw cycles per utterance toward a pattern with only one jaw cycle.

2.2 Method

2.2.1 First step: Basis expansion

This operation is performed in two steps: 1) the definition of the building-block or basis function and 2) the computation of the coefficients to fit the basis function to the observed sequences.

In cyclic speech, where vertical displacement of the articulators has mostly a sinusoidal shape, it is appropriate to model the observed trajectories with combinations of sine and cosine functions at different oscillation frequencies, adopting a Fourier basis set. With that choice, the parameters needed to define the set of basis functions are their number (i.e. the number of sine components plus the number of cosine components plus 1 for a constant component) and the period of the slowest sinusoid in the set (by default equal to the duration of the signal). We used a Fourier basis of the 11th order with one constant coefficient and 10 sinusoidal coefficients:

$$F(t) = C_1 + C_2 \sin(\omega t) + C_3 \cos(\omega t) + C_4 \sin(2\omega t) + \\ C_5 \cos(2\omega t) + \ldots + C_{10} \sin(10\omega t) + C_{11} \cos(10\omega t) \quad (3)$$

where ω is the lowest period of oscillation, equal to the duration of the utterance. When the signal is not periodic, a basis of B-splines is the usual choice. With B-splines, the signal is divided into a finite number of subsequences and each subsequence is approximated by a polynomial. Often cubic B-splines are used; the basis is built combining polynomials of the fourth order. (In the notation conventions adopted by Ramsey and Silverman the order of the polynomials includes the term of degree 0, so that it is equal to the degree of the polynomial plus one.). Thus the basic polynomial has the form:

$$P(t) = C_1 + C_2 t + C_3 t^2 + C_4 t^3 \quad (4)$$

The entire trajectory is built summing several polynomials of the same degree but with different values for the coefficients. In B-splines each polynomial is different from 0 only over a limited and uninterrupted (i.e. compact) portion of time. The trajectory is thus split into segments modeled by different polynomials. With B-splines the parameters that we have to define are the number of basis functions used and the order of the polynomials. The total number of basis functions used is equal to the number of internal segment boundaries or "break-points" plus the order of the spline (cubic splines being polynomials of order 4). Thus if we want to divide our trajectories into 15 sections, we will need 19 basis functions. The number of internal break points determines the sensitivity of the B-splines to local features of the trajectory and the 4th order polynomials assure that the modeled curve is smooth (its second derivative is a continuous function). The coefficients are obtained through an optimization algorithm which, constrained by a roughness penalty, proceeds by minimizing the second derivative of the smoothed curves (Ramsay and Silverman, 1997).

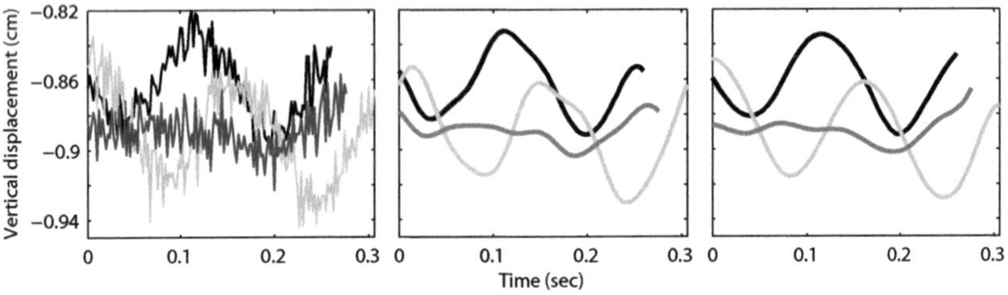

Figure 1: This picture shows the oscillations of the vertical position of the jaw corresponding to three /pata/ utterances (in different shades of gray). On the leftmost panel, the original data are shown; on the middle and rightmost panels we can observe their functional representations obtained with Fourier basis and cubic B-spline basis.

While in the middle panel of Figure 1 we see that a Fourier basis of order 11 constitutes a satisfactory choice for the raw data in the left panel, it is unfortunately easy to obtain results less consistent with the original data. The B-spline basis has its weakness in the fit at the edges of the trajectories, because in these regions a smaller number of data points are available. This problem does not affect the Fourier basis because, since the trajectories are assumed to be periodic, the missing data points at one edge can be extracted from the opposite edge. However the Fourier basis is less flexible than the B-spline approach because it is bounded to cyclic behavior; moreover it is less sensitive to the local transient behavior of the trajectories, which thus tend to disappear in the smoothed curves. It follows that, in order to apply FDA to a set of trajectories, it is necessary to check for the fit of each functional observation to the corresponding original trajectory; this can be quantified by thresholding excessive standard deviation between original and fitted data.

2.2.2 Second step: Registration

Once the functional observations have been created, their time scales can easily be normalized and the trajectories can thus vary over the same interval. In this way, the initial and terminal events correspond. However this necessary preliminary step does not assure that the portions which are equivalent across the trajectories are aligned; they are aligned only if the differences in time scale among the trajectories are uniform. In order to align the events (peaks and valleys) present in all the trajectories, the following procedure (following Lucero et al., 1997) is adopted. The trajectories are computed over the same time interval (that by convention we set from 0 to 1) and a first mean function is obtained by averaging the corresponding data points across the trajectories[1].

Next, for each functional observation, a warping function is defined as a cubic B-spline. A warping function is a transformation of the time scale. Given a functional observation, the warping function defines, for each of its points, the horizontal shift needed to align that point to the corresponding point of the mean trajectory.

The warping function coefficients are then optimized to minimize the distance between the functional observations and the mean trajectory. Applying the warping functions to their corresponding functional observations, the trajectories are aligned. This procedure may be repeated to refine the results (cf. Lucero et al., 1997; Lucero and Koenig, 2000;

1 In order to favor a correct alignment, the original curves can be centered, subtracting the mean from each curve, and scaled through division by the standard deviation (or, more appropriately when comparing time series of different length, through division by their maximum value, cf. Wang and Gasser, 1997; Lucero and Koenig, 2000). Once the aligned curves have been obtained, the initial scale and origin of the axis can be recovered by adding to each curve its initial mean and multiplying by the scale factor used to normalize the curve.

Lucero, 2005, for applications to speech movements). A new mean trajectory is obtained by averaging the aligned values of the functional observations and the warping functions are then recalculated to improve the match to the new mean trajectory.
Once the curves are aligned to the average curve (cf. Figure 2) it is easy to determine the similarity between two curves by applying a Euclidean distance metric. In the same fashion an averaged measure of variability is given by the sum of the standard deviations at different relative times divided by the number of time points, equivalent to the index of spatio-temporal variability (STI) introduced by Smith et al. (1995). However, as a consequence of the nonlinear time-warping, variation in the aligned data is primarily due to amplitude differences between trials, while the individual warping functions show variation in phase. In other words, this method, unlike Smith's linear STI, crucially allows for the separate quantification of amplitude and phase differences.

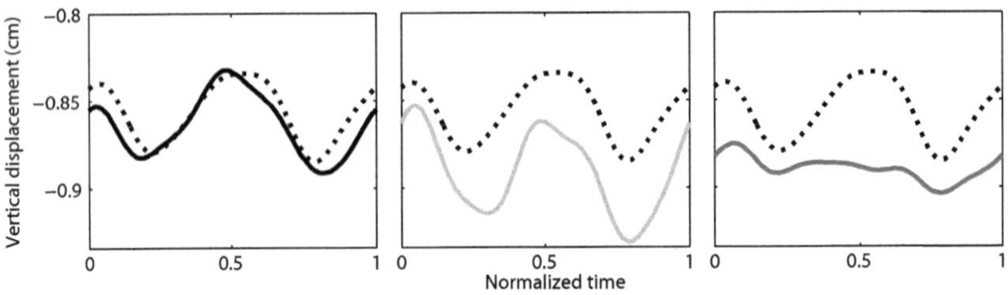

Figure 2: Aligned versions of the three curves plotted in Figure 1. The curves represent the movement of the jaw during the production of the utterance /pata/ (smoothed using a Fourier basis of the 11th order). In each panel, one aligned curve (continuous line) is plotted together with the curve obtained averaging all the 18 aligned curves belonging to the set considered (dotted line).

2.2.3 Third step: Functional principal component analysis

Given a multivariate set of data, classical PCA finds the orientation in that space over which the data vary most. We may think of the functional principal components as those basic curves whose linear combinations give the best approximation of the original set of functional observations. Therefore each curve of the set can be approximated by a linear combination of the principal components. This is a concise way to express that each observed curve can be obtained by summing the principal components, each one multiplied by a different factor. We can thus think of a given principal component as a basic shape which is present with different intensities in the curves analyzed (cf. Gubian et al., 2010; Aston et al., 2010).

The first principal component is that basic trajectory whose variation can explain the highest percentage of the variability observed across the curves. This ranking is extended to the other components which are ordered by the percentage of total variance explained. The effect of a principal component in one particular curve is indicated by the multiplicative factor (or loading) used to approximate that curve. In this section we will focus on the interpretation of principal components but we won't address the issues raised in their extraction and by the computation of their loadings.

Before illustrating an application to real data, it is instructive to understand the meaning of principal components on a set of synthetic curves for which we know the characteristics. As an example we can consider the four curves in the right panel of Figure 3. These come from a set of 100 curves obtained from the curves $S1(t)$ and $S2(t)$ represented respectively by the continuous and the dashed lines in the left panel. These were multiplied by different constant factors (B_i and C_j respectively) and added to a sequence of random values extracted from a uniform distribution between 0 and 0.1.

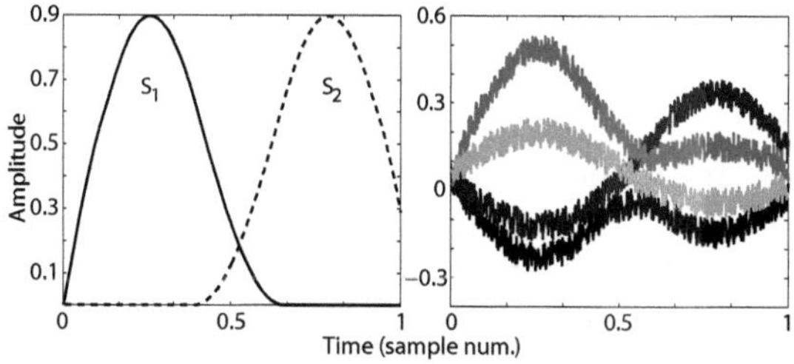

Figure 3: Left panel: basic shapes used to generate the curves in the right panel. Right panel: curves generated by combining the basic shapes in the left panel with uniform noise (see text).

The multiplicative factors B_i and C_j vary from one curve to the other and determine the amplitude of the prototypical shapes in each of the resulting curves. The values for the factors are generated at random, but the factors C_j are multiplied by 0.8. Therefore the average effect of $S2(t)$ on the resulting curves is weaker than the average effect of $S1(t)$. In order to apply FPCA, we need to determine the number of principal components to extract. In our case, we can start with an arbitrarily high number of components, but only two of them account for non negligible proportions of the total variance observed across the curves (as shown in panel a of Figure 4). This is consistent with the fact that all of the 100 curves are obtained by combinations of precisely two basic shapes.

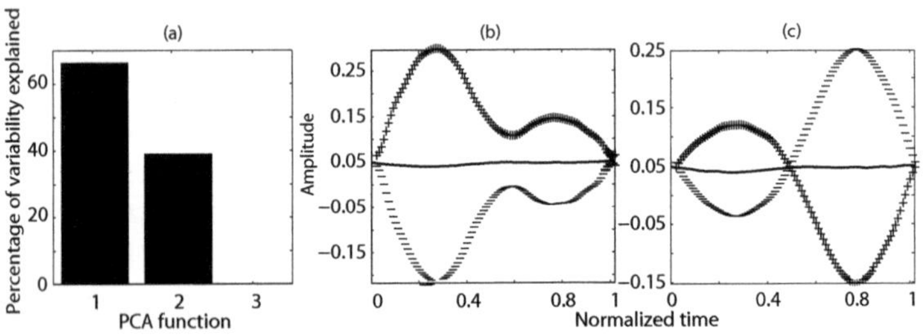

Figure 4: Panel a: Variability accounted by the first two principal components. Panels b and c: effects of the first and second principal components on the mean curve (see text).

Panels b and c from Figure 4 show the effect of the two principal components on the average curve (this is represented in both the panels by a continuous line). The two lines composed by plus signs represent the changes in the mean trajectory which are obtained when the components are multiplied by a positive factor and added to the average trajectory. The lines composed by the minus signs are obtained when the components are multiplied by a negative factor. We can see that each of the two principal components introduces two peaks (or two valleys, if combined with a negative factor); however, when adding to the average curve one of the two shapes in the left panel of Figure 3, only one peak (or one valley) is expected. We can deduce that each component accounts for variability coming from both the basic shapes. This happens because there is an infinite number of pairs of curves, different from the ones in the left panel of Figure 3, whose linear combinations can approximate the observed curves equally well. In other words, given some number of principal components, their uniqueness is not guaranteed. However, no better approximation can be obtained by linear combinations of the same number of curves. Using the Varimax algorithm Kaiser (1958) it is possible to select among the possible sets of principal components for the basic shapes which maximize covariation with the observed curves. In this way the probability of separating the effects of different sources of variability is maximized. The results of this step on the principal components in Figure 4 are presented in Figure 5.

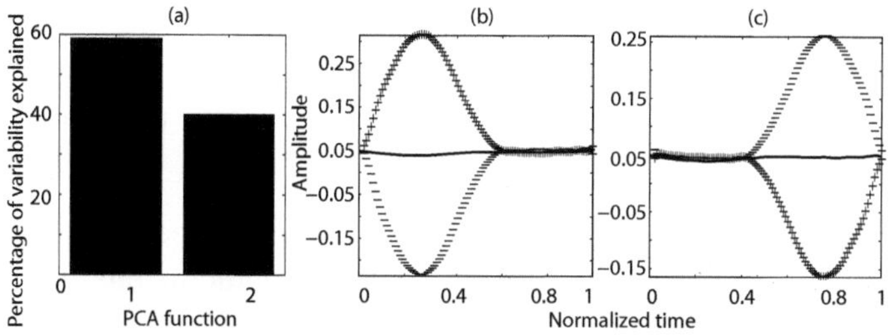

Figure 5: Panel a: Variability accounted by the first two rotated principal components. Panels b and c: effects of the first and of the second rotated principal components on the mean curve (see text).

Here each component introduces only one peak, as expected by adding one of the two curves from the left panel of Figure 3 to the average curve. Let's note that the mean curve is an approximately straight horizontal line centered over the value of 0.05, which is expected because the curves where generated starting from a uniform random distribution between 0 and 0.1.

Turning to real data, we applied functional PCA to the curves aligned in section 2.2.1 and 2.2.2. In order to isolate the components of variability in the shape of the trajectories, we subtracted from each curve its mean and divided the resulting curve for its range. Panel a from Figure 6 shows the amount of variance explained by each of the first three principal components. From panel b of the same figure we can observe that the effect of the first principal component, when multiplied by a positive coefficient and then added to the average curve, is that of reducing the overall amplitude of the jaw movement. However the amplitude of the oscillation which is synchronous with the lower lip movement (the one in the middle of each panel) is reduced only slightly while the amplitude of the oscillation synchronous with the lower lip (the one which is represented at the edges of each panel) is reduced to one third of its amplitude in the average curve. The second principal component (panel c),

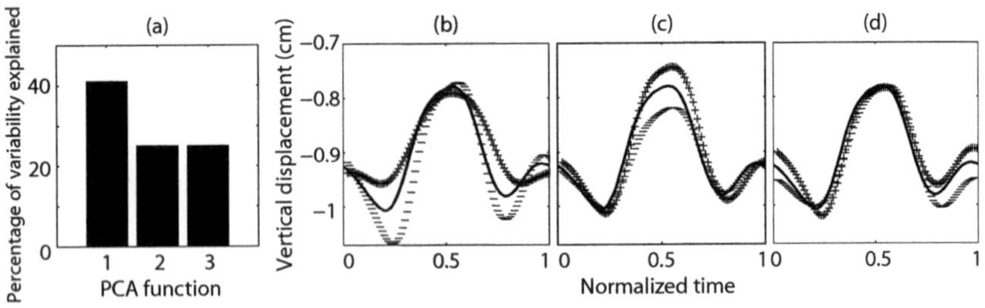

Figure 6: Effect of the Varimax rotated first three components on the mean trajectory of the jaw in the /pata/ utterances from Figure. 2

when multiplied by a positive coefficient, increases the amplitude of the jaw oscillation synchronous with the TTip movement. Finally, the third principal component (panel c), when multiplied by a positive coefficient, has a slightly more complex effect on the oscillation synchronous with the LLip movement. First, the peak height of this oscillation increases; second, the minimum which precedes the oscillation synchronous with the TTip is pushed down; third the minimum following the oscillation synchronous with the TTip is pulled up.

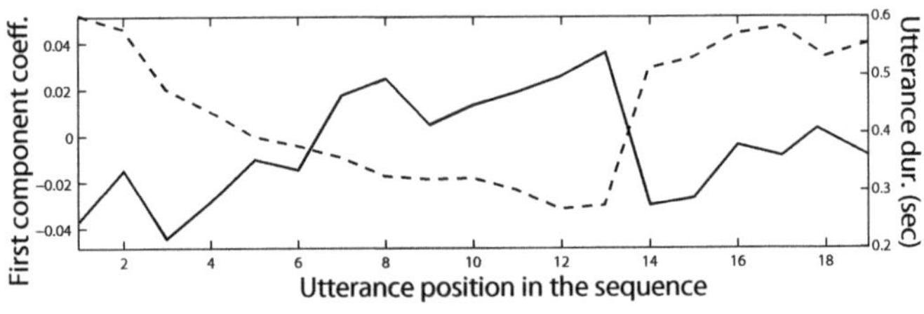

Figure 7: Evolution of the first principal component is plotted against the position of the utterance in a sequence. The continuous line indicates the values of loadings of the first principal component; the dashed line indicates the durations of the utterances measured in time steps. We can observe that as the duration of the utterances gradually decreases (up to the 13th repetition), the loading of the first principal component gradually increases. Between the 13th and the 14th repetitions there is an abrupt return to the initial values for both utterance duration and loading of the first principal component.

In Figure (7), we can see that the coefficient of first principal component, interpreted as tracking the reduction from two to one jaw cycles per sequence, decreases in the middle portion of this sequence of /pata/ utterances (where the speech rate is higher). This is consistent with the reduction from two jaw cycles per utterance to one jaw cycle observed by Rochet-Capellan and Schwartz (2007) at fast speech rates. Moreover, at least in the analyzed sequence, the reduced jaw cycle is the one which is synchronous with the oscillation of the LLip.

3 Part II: Spectral methods

3.1 Introduction

The example outlined in the preceding section concerns the trajectory of the vertical position of the jaw observed in isolation, i.e. without considering its interactions with the other articulators. We are often interested in the relation between two or more variables, as when we study the coordination between the movements of two different articulators. However, if we are interested in their coordination, it is simpler and more appropriate to adopt spectral methods and study their instantaneous relative phase (Torrence and Compo, 1998).

At a given instant, the phase of a signal with cyclic (i.e. periodic) behavior is given by its position in its cycle. The phase is an angular variable and varies from 0, at the beginning of the cycle, to 2π at the end of the cycle. The relative phase between two cyclic signals is the difference between the positions of two oscillators in their relative cycles. If for example, the two oscillators start and end their own cycles at the same time, they are said to be in an in-phase relation (relative phase = 0); if the first oscillator is in the beginning of its cycle at the same time when the second one is in the middle portion of its own cycle the two oscillators are said to be in an antiphase relation (relative phase = π). If the phase angle lies between 0 and π, the first oscillator precedes the second one. When the phase angle lies between π and 2π, the first oscillator lags the second one.

In order to compute the instantaneous phase of a signal or the relative instantaneous phase between two signals, the original time-series must be represented in the time frequency domain. In other words, a spectral representation must be adopted. When we adopt a spectral representation of a signal, we assume that the signal under study can be decomposed into different cyclic trajectories each one characterized by a different frequency of oscillation. The signal is thus approximated by a linear combination of analytic functions which oscillate with different frequencies. Since the characteristic evolution of the analytic functions is known, their instantaneous phase can be extracted. When looking for the temporal relation between two signals, we identify the time scale at which the two signals share more energy (their components at that frequency have higher amplitudes) and then the relative phase of the corresponding components can be computed.

3.2 Wavelet transform

The decomposition of a signal into several oscillators characterized by different frequencies is commonly achieved through the Fourier transform, which decomposes the signal into a linear combination of sine and cosine curves. To obtain the coefficients of the sinusoidal components in the Fourier transform, a section of the signal, whose length is fixed by the choice of an analysis window, is extracted. That section is compared with different combinations of sine and cosine functions which oscillate at different frequencies but have all the same length (i.e. the length of the section). The magnitude of the coefficients depends on the similarity between the sinusoids and the analyzed section of the signal. Once the coefficients of the sinusoidal components have been computed for a given section, the analysis window is shifted by a small amount (the time step of the analysis) and the computation of the coefficients is conducted for the next section. This approach has an important limitation in the fact that a single window is used to resolve all frequencies, implying that the temporal resolution of the analysis is the same in each point of the time-frequency plane. The consequence is that low frequencies produce too few oscillations into one window, affecting the localization of their frequency. At the same time, high frequencies present too many oscillations into a single window affecting the temporal localization of the signal's features.

The wavelet transform approach does not share this limitation because the analytic function (called the mother wavelet, cf. Figure 8) is scaled (stretched or compressed in time) before being compared with the signal (however cf. section 5.2).

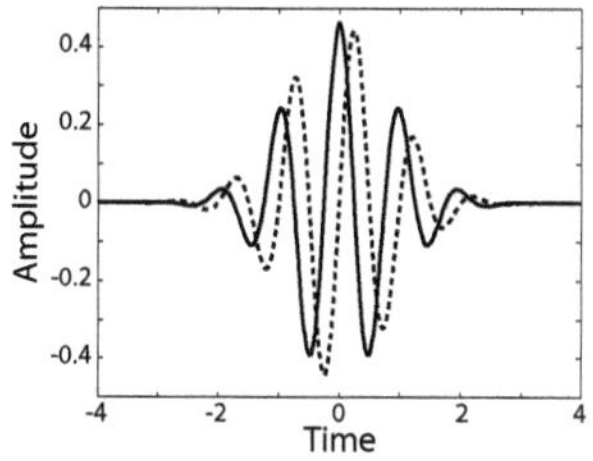

Figure 8: Shape of the complex Morlet wavelet (used as a mother wavelet for the analysis described in this chapter). Note that it is equivalent to a complex sinusoid modulated by a bell shaped curve to have positive energy on a continuous but limited interval of time.

Longer wavelets will be used in conjunction with low frequencies of oscillation, while shorter scales are used in conjunction with high frequencies of oscillation. In this way the wavelet transform can be sensitive to fast local changes in the signal, while maintaining a good separation of the energy at different frequencies.
As for the Fourier power spectrum, a spectral representation is obtained by squaring the absolute values of the coefficients (cf. Figure 9). The instantaneous phase values corresponding to the different frequency components are obtained from the complex argument of the corresponding coefficients. The wavelet equivalent of the Fourier power spectrum is called a scalogram. Time is represented on the x axis, while the y axis represents the scale factor used to stretch or compress the mother wavelet. However it is possible to characterize a compressed wavelet with the frequency of oscillation of the equivalent complex sinusoid (cf. Figure 8). A frequency (or period) scale on the y axis is thus often used to obtain more interpretable results. Figure 9a represents the power spectrum of the oscillation produced by the vertical position of the TTip sensor during a sequence of /pata/ utterances. Dark shades of gray are associated with strong energy. The concentration of the energy on the y axis indicates the oscillatory frequencies of the main compo-

nents. The cone-shaped dashed line delimits the region in the time-scale plane where the wavelet transform gives reliable results (i.e. unbiased by edge effects); this region is called the cone-of-influence (COI; Torrence and Compo, 1998).

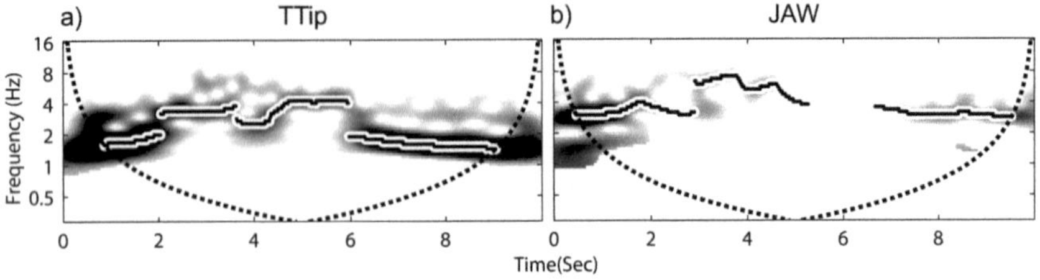

Figure 9: (a) Power spectrum of the oscillations produced by the vertical motion of the TTip during a sequence of repeated /pata/ utterances. (b) Power spectrum of the oscillations produced by the vertical motion of the jaw. The shades of gray represent spectral energy and correspond to the squared coefficients of the scaled Morlet wavelets. Time is represented on the abscissa. The frequencies of the sinusoids corresponding to the different wavelet scales are reported on the ordinate. Time and frequency resolution of the analysis vary over the ordinate. At high frequencies, high temporal resolution and low frequency resolution are observed. The inverse relation between time and frequency resolution holds at low frequencies. Dashed lines show COI; results exterior to this are influenced by edge effects.

Only energy values located within the COI are used in subsequent steps. The bold black line with white outline tracks the evolution over time of the strongest oscillatory component. At the beginning and at the end of the sequence (where the speech rate is low) we can observe a second strong oscillatory component, whose oscillations are twice as fast as the main component's oscillations. This is due to the coupling of the tongue tip with the jaw, whose spectrum is shown in Figure 9b. The duration of a cycle of the secondary component in the TTip spectrum is indeed equal to the duration of a jaw cycle.
The effects of the mutual influence between the jaw and the TTip are observed even in the spectrum for the jaw. Even here, in the regions corresponding to moderate speech rate, two components are distinguishable. Another important aspect of the jaw's spectrum is the weakening of the energy between 5.5 and 6.5 seconds. This event is signaled in the figure by an interruption of the line which tracks the energy of the main component. In the corresponding portion of the sequence, the spectrum

energy is not significantly stronger than the spectral energy obtained by a random process. This is consistent with the "freezing" of the jaw observed by Fuchs et al. (2009) at fast speech rates.

3.3 Cross wavelet transform

The product of the power spectrum of a signal with the complex conjugate of the power spectrum obtained from a second signal returns their cross spectrum, which represents the amount of energy shared by two signals at different frequencies of oscillation. The cross power spectra of the TTip and the LLip and of the jaw and the TTip are shown in panels a and b of Figure 10. At fast speech rates, only one component is present. At slow speech rates (t<2 sec. and t>6 sec.) two components are present. This is shown by the presence of two distinct horizontal gray bands in the regions of the plot. The stronger component corresponds to the lowest band (at a frequency slightly lower than 2Hz); the weaker component lies at a frequency of around 3Hz.

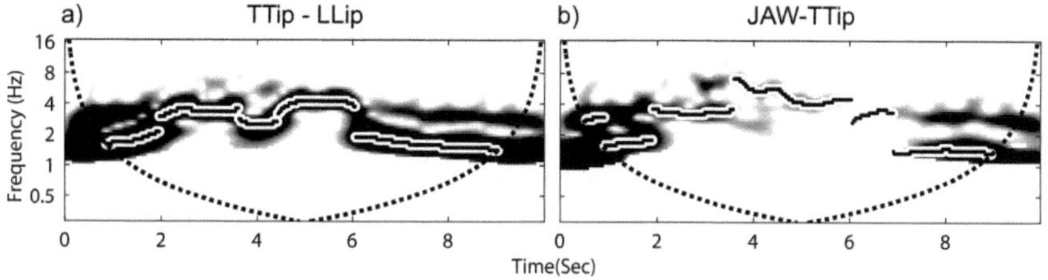

Figure 10: (a) Cross-spectrum of TTip and LLip oscillations; (b) Cross-spectrum of jaw and TTip oscillations

3.4 Obtaining relative phase relations

The relative phase between two signals can also be obtained from the cross spectrum. For each time point, we obtain a whole set of relative phase values characterizing the phase relations at different frequencies. A further step is thus needed to select, at each time point, the frequency of oscillation with the highest-valued coefficients (the band at which the two signals share the most of their energy), and then the corresponding phase value is chosen to characterize the instantaneous relative phase between the two signals at that point in time. The phase plot of the spectrum in panel b of Figure 10 is shown in Figure 11, following Grinsted et al. (2004). The arrows indicate the relative phase at different frequencies (y axis) and different points in time (x axis). The phase angle between the TTip and the jaw is represented by the counter-clockwise angle between the arrows and the horizontal axis. The relevant phase values are those corresponding to the peaks of spectral energy which are indicated by the gray stripe on the background of the figure. It can be observed that the jaw is in phase with the TTip over all the duration of the sequence. This means that when two cycles per utterance are present, the strongest one will be in-phase with the TTip. When only one cycle per utterance is observed this is still in phase with the TTip.

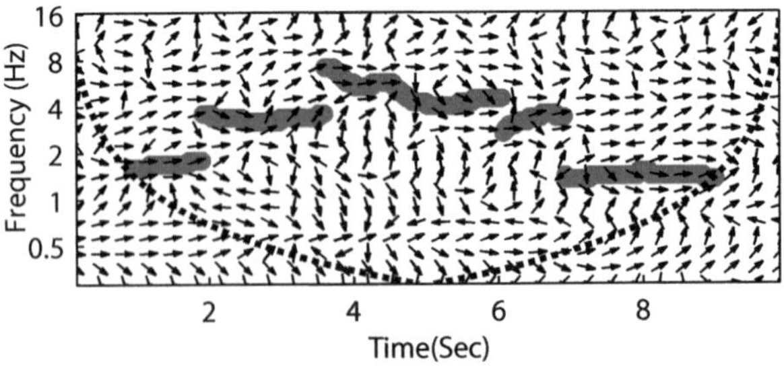

Figure 11: Phase plot from the spectrum in panel b of Figure 10

3.5 Hilbert transform

Discrepancies between the shape of the observed signal and the shape of the mother wavelet may influence the outcome of the wavelet transform. This issue may lead to erroneous results in the presence of noisy signals. An alternative method, based on the Hilbert transform (Rosenblum and Kurths, 1998), should in principle reduce the effect of this kind of artifact and its use will be briefly described here (however cf. Bruns, 2004, for a demonstration of the substantial equivalence of the two approaches). The Hilbert transform, like the Fourier transform and the wavelet transform, is an analytical method; i.e., the signal is represented as an analytic function. The limitation of the Hilbert method is that it cannot handle multifrequency signals. For this reason the two time series are first submitted to a filter bank, obtaining two sets of band passed signals. The Hilbert transform is then applied to pairs of corresponding band passed signals. In this way both the time dependent relative phase and shared energy can be obtained for each frequency band. As with the wavelet transform the relevant values of the relative phase are those occurring at the shared energy peaks.

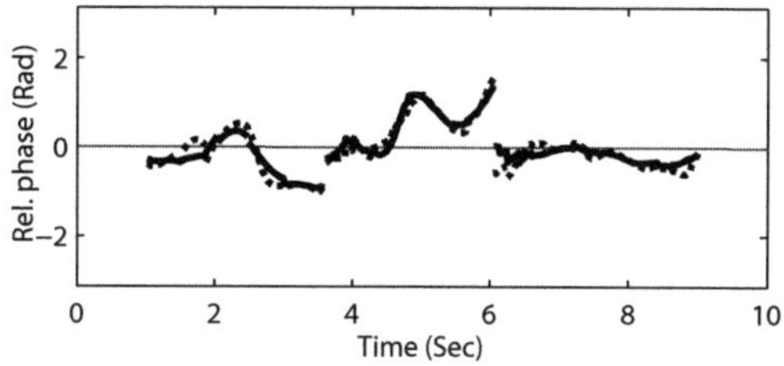

Figure 12: Relative phase between the trajectories of the jaw and the TTip used to produce the spectrum in Figure 10b. The continuous line represents phase values obtained using the cross wavelet transform; the dotted line represents values obtained using the Hilbert transform.

4 Part III: Recurrence and cross recurrence analysis

4.1 Introduction

Up to now we have explored methods to compare low dimensional signals or to study the relations between the components of a multidimensional system. What about comparisons among several high dimensional signals? We may ask for example how similar trajectories of jaw, TTip and LLip might be, across all components of their movement. Or we may want to evaluate the similarity of the evolution over time of the acoustic spectra corresponding to different utterances.

FDA is often used in the comparison of low dimensional time series which contain the same number of events (same number of peaks and valleys). However, the alignment procedure rapidly loses precision when the number of dimensions becomes high ($\gg 2$) and if the number of peaks and valleys varies between the time series. Recurrence analysis methods (Maizel and Lenk, 1981; Eckmann et al., 1987; Webber and Zbilut, 1994; Marwan et al., 2007) offer an alternative approach that can deal effectively with high dimensional non-stationary signals. Such techniques have been developed within the framework of dynamical systems theory to study the stability of a potentially multidimensional signal which repeats its trajectory over time, but they have also been extended to the study of the behavior shared by different systems. In the former case, when the object of study is a signal which repeats its trajectory over time in a more or less regular fashion, recurrence analysis considers the distribution over time of the portions of the signal which are coherently repeated. In the comparisons of two signals, cross recurrence analysis focuses on the distribution over time of the subsections in which the signals show the same behavior (Zbilut et al., 1998; Marwan et al., 2002; Marwan and Kurths, 2002).

4.2 Method

We represent a multivariate time series as a time-varying sequence of state vectors, with each state vector containing the values observed on all the different dimensions of the time series. A recurrence plot (RP) is a two dimensional representation of those points in time when a state is repeated. Both axes of the plot represent the time scale of the signal and a black dot contained at position (i, j) means that the same state is observed at i and j positions in time (cf. Figure 13). The ith column of the plot contains the outcomes of the comparisons among the ith coordinate vector and all the other vectors of the time series. It follows that the plot is symmetric with respect to the main diagonal. This means that a dot at position (i, j) implies the presence of a dot at position (j, i).
On the main diagonal line we will always find black dots in a recurrence plot. This is due to the fact that on the main diagonal each state vector is compared to itself and the distance is thus 0. This line is therefore called the line of identity (LOI).
An isolated black dot at position (i, j) indicates that the state observed at position i is observed again at position j. However a diagonal line going from (i, j) to $(i+n, j+n)$ indicates that the state found at i is observed again at j, that the state found at $i+1$ is observed again at $j+1$, and so on, up to the state $i+n$. In other words, a continuous diagonal line, i.e. a

straight line of slope 1, indicates that a section of trajectory, whose length is equal to the length of the diagonal line divided by $\sqrt{2}$, is repeated in the signal. The bivariate signal represented in the figure is periodic and the same trajectory is perfectly repeated three times. In the RP, on each side of the LOI, we can thus observe two diagonal lines. [2]

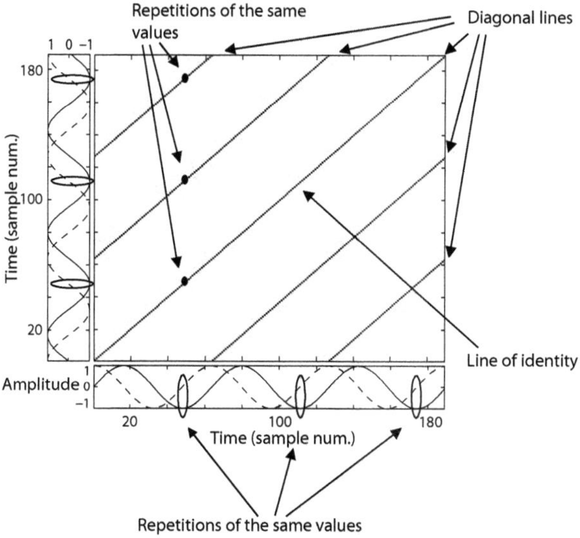

Figure 13: Top: recurrence plot of the bivariate time series plotted near the axes (see text).

2 Readers familiar with recurrence analysis may have noticed the absence of any reference to an embedding procedure. Such processing step is meant to increase the number of dimensions of the observed time series and it is motivated by the assumption that when observing a process we usually do not measure all its relevant features. Let's make the case that we are observing a process which is defined in three dimensions (for example, these may be the heights of the TTip, the LLip and the jaw in the production of our CVCV utterances) and that we can measure only the movement of one of the articulators involved (as if we were measuring the lip movement by means of a camera system such as Optotrack). Adopting an embedding strategy we can in principle reconstruct a three dimensional time series which shares several dynamical properties with the time series obtained by the recording of all the three articulators. The first dimension of the surrogate time series is represented by the recorded LLip height. The other two dimensions are copies of the first one but delayed in time. Although embed-

4.3 Cross recurrence plots

If the state vectors of a signal X are compared to the state vectors of a signal Y, we obtain what is called a cross recurrence plot (CRP; Marwan and Kurths, 2002). Each axis of the cross recurrence plot represents the time scale of one of the signals and the plot will show the points in time where the two signals exhibit the same state vector. A black dot at position (i, j) means that the same state is observed at position i in one signal and at position j in the other signal.

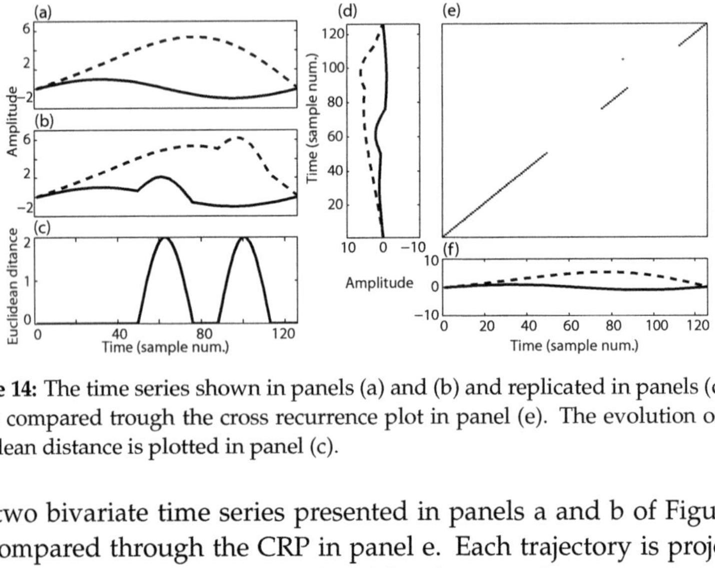

Figure 14: The time series shown in panels (a) and (b) and replicated in panels (d) and (f) are compared trough the cross recurrence plot in panel (e). The evolution of their Euclidean distance is plotted in panel (c).

The two bivariate time series presented in panels a and b of Figure 14 are compared through the CRP in panel e. Each trajectory is projected onto its axis in the CRP (panels d and f). The second trajectory has been obtained from the first one by slightly modifying its amplitude. The effect of the amplitude modification over the duration of the trajectory is

ding is essential for the analysis of mono-dimensional time series, it can be skipped when analyzing multi-dimensional time series. The lack of embedding potentially introduces artifacts in the recurrence plots (mainly the presence of lines with negative slope), however these artifacts are removed by the application of the algorithm presented in section 4.5. However to perform the embedding, two critical parameters have to be established: the number of dimensions to reconstruct and the delay. The computation of these parameters is not a trivial issue; moreover the whole procedure is sensitive to non-stationarity in the time series. Indeed for non-stationary signals an appropriate value for the delay parameter cannot be defined (Marwan, 2010). All this considered, we chose not to use embedding when comparing multivariate time series.

shown in panel c. Here the absolute difference between the time series is averaged over the two dimensions and it is plotted point by point. The two time series are maximally different between frames 50 and 75 and between frames 90 and 110.
A black dot at position (i, j) in the CRP means that a state vector at position i in the horizontal trajectory is replicated at position j in the vertical trajectory. The straight diagonal starting from the lower left corner of the plot indicates that the first 15 points of the horizontal time series match the first fifteen points of the vertical time series. Then a gap is encountered indicating the first mismatch between the time series. Notice that the other diagonal lines present in the CRP correspond to the region where the distance between the time series is smaller, and the gap is consequently located in the regions of maximal mismatch. If a black dot is isolated, i.e. surrounded by white regions, it indicates a random match between the two signals. In a cross recurrence plot, the main diagonal is not necessarily filled with black dots, because points at the same position in the two signals do not necessarily correspond.
Apart from isolated black dots and straight diagonal lines of slope 1, several other structures composed by connected dark dots can be found. Importantly the slope of the continuous lines varies as a function of the relation between the time scales of the two signals. Indeed these slopes correspond to the ratio between the two rates of change of the matching parts of trajectories. A slope which is smaller than one indicates that the signal whose time scale is on the vertical axis is faster, a slope which is greater than one indicates that the signal whose time scale is represented on the horizontal axis is faster. Bowed continuous lines indicate that the relation between the two time scales changes over time. If a bowed quasi-continuous line is found around the main diagonal, this is called the line of synchrony (LOS). Indeed to synchronize the two signals, it suffices to shift the position in time of the points of one signal by an amount which is equal to the vertical distance between the corresponding points on the LOS and the main diagonal of the plot (i.e. the line connecting the opposite corners).

4.4 How a cross recurrence plot is built

Each of the two signals X and Y is represented by N state vectors and each state vector represents the M coordinates of the system at a given point in time. A distance matrix is computed by comparing each state vector of the signal X to each state vector of the signal Y. The vertical side of that matrix has the same length as the signal Y, while the horizontal side is as long as the signal X. Each cell of the matrix contains a measure of the difference between the state vector of the first signal and the state vector of the second signal. If the Euclidean distance is adopted, this will be equal to the square root of the summed squares of the distances computed on the different dimensions:

$$\|X_i - Y_j\| = \sqrt{\sum_{k=1}^{m} \left(X_{i,k} - Y_{j,k}\right)^2} \tag{5}$$

where m is the number of dimensions of the two signals X and Y. In the construction of a CRP a maximum distance is often used as it is generally faster to compute; i.e. the distance between two state vectors corresponding to the maximum among the absolute values of the distances computed on the different dimensions.

$$\|X_i - Y_j\|_\infty = argmax\left(\sqrt{(X_{i,1} - Y_{j,1})^2}, \cdots, \sqrt{\left(X_{i,m} - Y_{j,m}\right)^2}\right) \tag{6}$$

The differences are stored in the matrix in the following way: the first column holds the differences between the first state vector of the signal X and all the state vectors of the signal Y, going from the bottom to the topmost row, where the first state vector of X is compared to the last state vector of Y. The distances from the other points of the signal X are stored in a similar fashion in the columns which follow the first one. The final plot is then derived by the distance matrix, deciding, for each distance measure, if it is sufficiently small such that the compared state vectors can be considered equal. With a fixed threshold criterion, each point of the plot corresponding to a distance smaller than a predetermined threshold will be represented by a dark dot. All the other points will be represented by white dots. The selection of an appropriate threshold is aimed at finding an equilibrium between having a threshold which is as small as possible, while being capable to detect a sufficient number of recurrences. Thiel et al. (2002) show that the threshold should be 5 times larger than the standard deviation of the observational noise present in the time series. However, how to obtain the appropriate threshold in the general case where no estimate of the observational noise is available, remains an open issue (cf. Marwan, 2010, for a review of the relevant approaches).

In computing a cross recurrence plot different approaches involving an adaptive threshold can be adopted. For example, with the **fixed recurrence rate** criterion, the number of recurrence points to be found in the plot is fixed at a given percentage of the number of locations in the plot (corresponding to the maximum possible number of recurrence points given the lengths of the time series compared). The threshold is then adapted in order to obtain the desired number of recurrences. With a **fixed amount of neighbors** criterion, the threshold changes from one column of the plot to the other in such a way that the same number of recurrences is found in each column. In this way, each point of the time series represented on the horizontal axis of the plot has the same number of recurrences in the other time series.

4.5 Recurrence quantification analysis (RQA)

Quantitative indices of the relations between two signals are often derived by counts of the points belonging to diagonal lines of slope 1 (Marwan and Kurths, 2002). For example the percentage of determinism (%DET) is equal to the number of points belonging to diagonal lines divided by the total number of dark points present in the plot. This means that it is equal to the ratio between the number of points belonging to repeated trajectories and the number of the random matches. The mean length of the diagonals and their maximum length are used as well.

There are at least two reasons not to use these measures for signals derived from speech when comparing different realizations of the same motion pattern. One is related to the differences in their time scales. Indeed bowed lines are not captured by the measures described above. For this reason, the above measures are not able to separate variability in the amplitude of the time series from variability in their rate of change. This is particularly problematic if we want to compare different produc-

tions of the same utterance to measure variability (cf. Lucero, 2005). The second reason is related to the smoothness of the signals. If X and Y present a match at position (i, j), and X is particularly smooth, there are good probabilities that the two signals will also match at position $(i + 1, j)$ because of the small difference between $X(i)$ and $X(i + 1)$. A random match can easily be transformed in a continuous horizontal line, if the signal whose timescale is represented on the X axis is particularly smooth. For the same reason a continuous diagonal or bowed line can become thicker and thicker as the smoothness of the signal Y increases. While differences in the time scales of the two signals can obscure the similarity between sections of the two signals, smoothness introduces false matches. To reduce the bias introduced by these two features, in our recent work (Lancia, Fuchs and Tiede, in preparation) we introduce an algorithm based on image processing techniques combined with a skeletonizing strategy proposed by Marwan et al. (2002).
The main processing steps are the following:
1) Each group of connected dark dots is distinguished through a standard algorithm for connected components labeling (Ballard and Brown, 1982, pp. 13-62).
2) Each group is then reduced to a thick line which follows its shape. The tracking is constrained to proceed towards the top-right direction. This is achieved by first identifying the dark dot nearest to the bottom left corner of the smallest rectangle including the group. Then the tracking algorithm described by Marwan and his colleagues is used. In summary this algorithm starts looking for recurrence points by placing a square window with its bottom left corner on the starting point. The size of the window is increased until it includes at least another black dot. When this happens, the center of mass of the area under the window is computed and it is considered as the second point of the tracked line. A new window is placed with the bottom left corner onto the found point and its size is increased until a new dark point is found. The procedure is repeated until the tracked line reaches the right or the top side of the plot. The percentage of determinism is then computed by dividing the number of dark dots belonging to the thick continuous lines by the total number of possible dark dots.

4.6 Application to speech

We consider here 21 sequences of /pata/,/fata/ and /pasa/ utterances produced by three speakers[3]. In each sequence, we compare pairs of successive utterances using recurrence analysis and consider the %DET as a measure of similarity between the utterances of each pair. This choice was motivated by the assumption that two utterances produced one after the other are more likely to be similar than two utterances far away in the sequence. Comparisons among successive utterances are thus expected to better differentiate among levels of variability observed in different conditions.

Since we study the joint motion of the jaw, the TTip and the LLip, a six dimensional coordinate vector is needed to store the vertical and horizontal positions of the three articulators at different moments in time. Before performing the comparison each trajectory is down-sampled to a standard length. This step is performed in order to compare measures derived from different pairs of utterances[4].

The recurrence plot shown in Figure 15b is obtained by comparing two consecutive utterances. The actual multi-variate trajectories are plotted along their respective axes (panels a and d). To avoid crowding of trajectories, only the vertical positions of the articulators are displayed. In panel c we can observe the output of our algorithm when that recurrence plot is processed.

Note the presence of continuous lines going downward in the unprocessed RP. This means that a portion of the signal in Figure 15b is pulled in the opposite direction by the signal in 15a. This is reasonable, considering that the motion of the articulators has an oscillatory nature and that a movement in one direction is always followed by a movement in the opposite direction. However the points belonging to these lines do

3 In order to match the results from recurrence analysis with the results from functional PCA, we selected the three speakers in the following way: we extracted the first principal component separately for each speaker and utterance; we then chose speakers for whom the first principal component reduces the amplitude of the jaw cycle synchronous with the labial constriction. The loadings obtained in this way were used to compute the correlation shown in Figure 16.

4 Using the fixed recurrence rate criterion, the probability that the outcome of a comparison between two coordinate vectors produces a recurrence point depends on the number of coordinate vectors compared, i.e. on the lengths of the two time series.

not represent deterministic matches, in the sense defined in the preceding section, and thus they are correctly discarded by our algorithm.

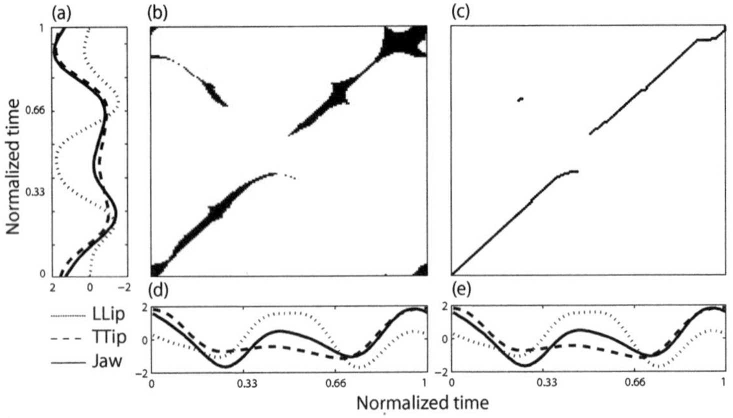

Figure 15: Cross recurrence plots of the 6 trajectories produced by the jaw, the TTip and the LLip in the horizontal and vertical dimensions during two successive utterances. Trajectories in the horizontal dimension are omitted for clarity. The first trajectory is plotted on the horizontal axis of each plot, the second trajectory is plotted on the vertical axis common to the two plots. The plot in panel b is the classic CRP, the plot in panel c is obtained by submitting the plot in panel b to the algorithm described in the text.

Once the comparisons have been performed and the %DET has been computed for all pairs of successive utterances, we obtain a sequence of values for each sequence of utterances. We will compare the values of the %DET index with the values of the coefficient relative to the first principal component of the jaw motion described in the first section. This comparison is motivated by the following reasoning:
We adopted the hypothesis that in this particular task, the labial coronal ordering is favored by the weakening of the jaw cycle which is synchronous to the movement of the LLip. Using functional PCA we observed that jaw behavior evolves from two jaw cycles per utterance to one cycle per utterance. This change is captured by the variation of the first principal component of the jaw's motion which, when averaged over the nine sequences, explains just under 90% of the total spatio-temporal variation. We could then observe that, at the beginning of the sequences, each utterance presents two jaw cycles of comparable amplitude and, after a transient portion during which speech rate increases,

the second behavior is observed, with a reduction of one of the two jaw cycles. If the behavior of the whole system changes because the initial behavior becomes unstable at high speech rates, we expect to observe that, for short utterance durations, %DET increases as the coefficient of the first principal component decreases. In fact, this is supported by the weak but highly significant negative correlation (r^2=-0.37, $p<10^{-5}$) shown in Figure 16 where the two indices are plotted against one another.

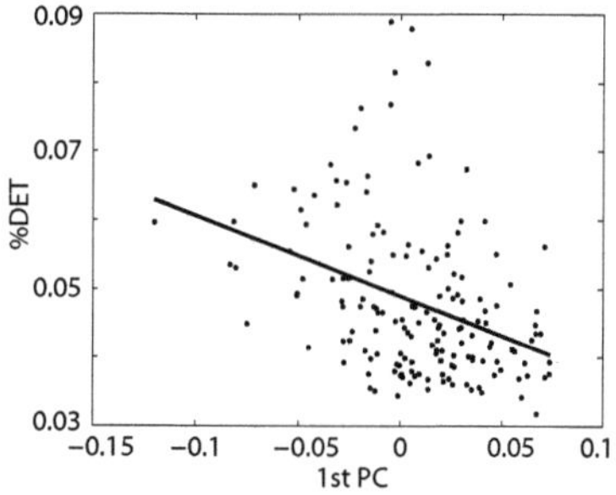

Figure 16: %DET regressed with the value of the coefficient of the first principal component obtained by applying functional PCA to 24 CVCV sequences obtained from three speakers r^2=-0.37, $p<10^{-5}$).

5 Part IV: General discussion and conclusions

5.1 Parameterization of the analysis

Functional data analysis: Given a set of curves and a shape for the basis function, a certain number of parameters are responsible for the quality of the fit of the smoothed curves to the original trajectories. The first parameter to be set is *the number of the basis functions* used to model the original observations. For the Fourier basis, this corresponds to the number of sine and cosine components plus one; for the B-spline basis, this corresponds to the number of segments in which the original curves are decomposed, plus the order of the polynomials used to model the different segments. In both cases, a higher number of basis functions determines an increase in the sensitivity to local features of the trajectories. An automatic method has been proposed to determine the optimal number of basis functions needed to model a trajectory (Friedman and Silverman, 1989). However this approach does not always give useful results and often visual inspection remains the only way to evaluate the fit to the original data.

When using a B-spline basis, *the order of the polynomials* may be changed too. This affects the smoothness of the modeled curve and of its successive derivatives. The basis functions are constrained to match at the break points, and their successive derivatives up to the order minus two. Increasing the order of the polynomials increases the number of successive derivatives which are constrained to match the break points, and as a consequence the modeled curves appear smoother. When working with tangential velocity, the original observations should be modeled by means of splines of the fourth order or higher to obtain appropriately smooth derivatives.

The last parameter for the basis expansion represents *the emphasis given to the roughness penalty constraint* in the optimization algorithm which determines the weights of the basis functions. The higher the values for this parameter (λ; Ramsay and Silverman, 1997), the smoother the modeled curves will be. The optimal value for this smoothing parameter can be obtained by using a generalized cross validation criterion (Craven and Wahba, 1978). However, even for this parameter, it is necessary to inspect the results obtained with different values (Ramsay and Silverman, 1997).

When the functional observations need to be aligned, the same set of parameters must be controlled in the basis expansion of the warping functions. These curves are generally built starting from a B-spline basis of the fourth order. The general advice is to start with a very small number of bases (i.e. a small number of break points) and then to increase this number if the results of the registration are not satisfactory.

Cross wavelet transform: The wavelet transform is subject to the usual tradeoff between time and frequency resolution. In the implementation of the cross wavelet transform discussed in this chapter, the equation of the Morlet mother wavelet is defined by only one parameter which represents a dimensionless frequency. A good balance between localization in time and frequency is obtained using a value of 6 for this parameter (Torrence and Compo, 1998).

Recurrence analysis: In this chapter we used recurrence analysis with a fixed recurrence rate criterion to determine if two state vectors of two different multivariate signals can be considered similar. With this choice, the parameter that controls the behavior of the analysis is *the ratio of dark dots to the number of possible dots* in the plot. If this value is too small, recurrence points can be missed; however if this value is too high, false recurrences may be detected. The choice of this parameter for a nonstationary signal is an unresolved question. Schinkel et al. (2008) propose to use the value which best separates the classes of trajectories to be studied. For example, in the case discussed in this chapter, we could have maximized the difference in the %DET index between curves which show high values for the first principal component and curves which show low values for this component. This maximization can be conducted computing the ROC curve from the obtained %DET index values. The algorithm outlined in this chapter for post-processing the recurrence plots reduces the impact of this parameter on the final results in that false recurrences are detected and discarded. When using such a method, is thus advisable to choose a value smaller than the 10% of the total number of possible dots in the plot.

5.2 Limits of this survey

The analyses described in this chapter cover only a small portion of the possibilities offered by the methods proposed. This is especially true for FDA and RQA.
Indeed several methods related to multivariate statistics and linear regression have been adapted to the analysis of functional data. Moreover FDA has been shown to be successful in the assessment of the dynamical laws underlying the evolution of time series (cf. Ramsay and Silverman, 2002, for a review of several variants and applications of FDA).
Concerning the spectral methods in section 3, it must be noted that, although the different approaches are formulated in different terms, all correspond to a convolution of a known function with the analyzed signal and can be implemented to give the same results (Bruns, 2004; Le Van Quyen et al., 2001; Quiroga et al., 2002; Kiebel et al., 2005). Even the Fourier transform can reach the same flexibility of the other methods when the window size is varied along the signal according to its local

frequency. We chose to focus on the wavelet approach due to its ease of application: no filter bank has to be implemented and no tracking of the frequency of the main component has to be conducted before applying the transform. The only preprocessing needed is a normalization of the signals compared.
Cross recurrence analysis has been used to detect different kinds of synchronization between time series (Marwan et al., 2007). Recurrence analysis has been used to recover the dynamical invariants of the processes underlying the time series and to detect the presence of chaotic behavior (Romano et al., 2005). However, these uses of recurrence analysis are controversial if the evolution over time of the system is not drawn in its reconstructed phase space, i.e. the space defined by the actual degrees of freedom of the system underlying the observed time series (Thiel et al., 2004).

5.3 General conclusions

In contrast with these advanced uses, the examples illustrated in this chapter are meant to represent situations in which the application of the techniques is quite straightforward and requires the smallest possible number of choices. FDA is a good alternative when the trajectories observed are low dimensional, smooth, and characterized by moderate variability (i.e. all the trajectories present the same number of peaks). Spectral methods as the cross-wavelet transform are useful for characterizing the coordination among different signals. Finally, recurrence analysis becomes particularly useful when comparing multivariate trajectories having high levels of variability.

6 Acknowledgements

This paper was made possible by the public availability of the software reported in Appendix B, made freely available through the efforts of several generous researchers. We wish to thank Pascal Perrier for much useful discussion, and Susanne Fuchs both for promoting the production of this chapter and for her contributions in the development and application of the method summarized in section 4.6. Finally, we would like to thank two anonymous reviewers for useful and important suggestions. This work was supported by a grant from the German-French University to the PILIOS project.

References

Aston, J. A. D., Chiou, J. M., and Evans, J. P. (2010). Linguistic pitch analysis using functional principal component mixed effect models. *Journal of the Royal Statistical Society: Series C (Applied Statistics)*, 59(2):297–317.

Ballard, D. H. and Brown, C. M. (1982). *Computer Vision*. Prentice-Hall, New York.

Bruns, A. (2004). Fourier-, hilbert-and wavelet-based signal analysis: Are they really different approaches? *Journal of Neuroscience Methods*, 137(2):321–332.

Craven, P. and Wahba, G. (1978). Smoothing noisy data with spline functions. *Numerische Mathematik*, 31(4):377–403.

Eckmann, J. P., Kamphorst, S. O., and Ruelle, D. (1987). Recurrence plots of dynamical systems. *EPL (Europhysics Letters)*, 4:973–977.

Friedman, J. H. and Silverman, B. W. (1989). Flexible parsimonious smoothing and additive modeling. *Technometrics*, 31(1):3–21.

Fuchs, S., Hartinger, M., Ziervogel, M., and Weirich, M. (2009). On coordinative patterns and transformation effects in reiterant speech. In *Proceedings of the Conference Progress in Motor Control, Marseille*.

Goldstein, L., Pouplier, M., Chen, L., Saltzman, E., and Byrd, D. (2007). Dynamic action units slip in speech production errors. *Cognition*, 103(3):386–412.

Grinsted, A., Moore, J. C., and Jevrejeva, S. (2004). Application of the cross wavelet transform and wavelet coherence to geophysical time series. *Nonlinear Processes in Geophysics*, 11(5-6):561–566.

Gubian, M., Cangemi, F., and Boves, L. (2010). Automatic and data driven pitch contour manipulation with functional data analysis. In *Proceedings of Fifth International Conference on Speech Prosody, Chicago, USA*.

Hertrich, I. and Ackermann, H. (2000). Lip-jaw and tongue-jaw coordination during rate-controlled syllable repetitions. *The Journal of the Acoustical Society of America*, 107:2236–2247.

Kaiser, H. F. (1958). The varimax criterion for analytic rotation in factor analysis. *Psychometrika*, 23(3):187–200.

Keating, P. A., Lindblom, B., Lubker, J., and Kreiman, J. (1994). Variability in jaw height for segments in english and swedish vcvs. *Journal of Phonetics*, 22:407–422.

Kiebel, S. J., Tallon-Baudry, C., and Friston, K. J. (2005). Parametric analysis of oscillatory activity as measured with eeg/meg. *Human Brain Mapping*, 26(3):170–177.

Koenig, L. L., Lucero, J., and Löfqvist, A. (2003). Studying articulatory variability using functional data analysis. In *Proceedings of the 15 th International Congress of Phonetic Sciences*, pages 269–272.

Lancia, L. and Fuchs, S. (2011). The labial coronal effect revisited. In *Proceedings of the ninth International Seminar on Speech Production, Montreal.*

Le Van Quyen, M., Foucher, J., Lachaux, J. P., Rodriguez, E., Lutz, A., Martinerie, J., and Varela, F. (2001). Comparison of hilbert transform and wavelet methods for the analysis of neuronal synchrony. *Journal of Neuroscience Methods*, 111(2):83–98.

Lindblom, B. (1983). Economy of speech gestures. In MacNeilage, P., editor, *The Production of Speech*, pages 217–245. Springer, New York.

Lucero, J. C. (2005). Comparison of measures of variability of speech movement trajectories using synthetic records. *Journal of Speech, Language, and Hearing Research*, 48(2):336—-344.

Lucero, J. C. and Koenig, L. L. (2000). Time normalization of voice signals using functional data analysis. *The Journal of the Acoustical Society of America*, 108:1408–1420.

Lucero, J. C., Munhall, K. G., Gracco, V. L., and Ramsay, J. O. (1997). On the registration of time and the patterning of speech movements. *Journal of Speech, Language, and Hearing Research*, 40(5):1111–1117.

Maizel, J. V. and Lenk, R. P. (1981). Enhanced graphic matrix analysis of nucleic acid and protein sequences. *Proceedings of the National Academy of Sciences*, 78(12):7665.

Marwan, N. (2003). *Encounters with Neighbours - Current Developments of Concepts Based on Recurrence Plots and their Applications.* University of Potsdam.

Marwan, N. (2010). How to avoid potential pitfalls in recurrence plot based data analysis. *International Journal of Bifurcation and Chaos*, 21(4):1003–1017.

Marwan, N., Carmen Romano, M., Thiel, M., and Kurths, J. (2007). Recurrence plots for the analysis of complex systems. *Physics Reports*, 438(5-6):237–329.

Marwan, N. and Kurths, J. (2002). Nonlinear analysis of bivariate data with cross recurrence plots. *Physics Letters A*, 302(5-6):299–307.

Marwan, N., Thiel, M., and Nowaczyk, N. R. (2002). Cross recurrence plot based synchronization of time series. *Nonlinear Processes in Geophysics*, 9(3-4):325–331.

Mooshammer, C., Hoole, P., and Geumann, A. (2007). Jaw and order. *Language and Speech*, 50(2):145–176.

Pouplier, M. (2007). Tongue kinematics during utterances elicited with the slip technique. *Language and Speech*, 50(3):311–341.

Quiroga, R., Kraskov, A., Kreuz, T., and Grassberger, P. (2002). Performance of different synchronization measures in real data: a case study on electroencephalographic signals. *Physical Review E*, 65(4):041903.

Ramsay, J. O., Hooker, G., and Graves, S. (2009). *Functional Data Analysis with R and MATLAB*. Springer, New York.

Ramsay, J. O. and Silverman, B. W. (1997). Functional Data Analysis.

Ramsay, J. O. and Silverman, B. W. (2002). *Applied Functional Data Analysis: Methods and Case Studies*. Springer, New York.

Rochet-Capellan, A. and Schwartz, J. L. (2007). An articulatory basis for the labial-to-coronal effect: /pata/ seems a more stable articulatory pattern than /tapa. *The Journal of the Acoustical Society of America*, 121:3740–3754.

Romano, M., Thiel, M., Kurths, J., Kiss, I., and Hudson, J. (2005). Detection of synchronization for non-phase-coherent and non-stationary data. *EPL (Europhysics Letters)*, 71(3):466–472.

Rosenblum, M. and Kurths, J. (1998). Analysing synchronization phenomena from bivariate data by means of the hilbert transform. In Kantz, H., Kurths, J., and Mayer-Kress, G., editors, *Nonlinear Analysis of Physiological Data*, pages 91–99. Springer, Berlin.

Schinkel, S., Dimigen, O., and Marwan, N. (2008). Selection of recurrence threshold for signal detection. *The European Physical Journal-Special Topics*, 164(1):45–53.

Shockley, K. (2005). Cross recurrence quantification of interpersonal postural activity. In Riley, M. A. and Van Orden, G. C., editors, *Tutorials in Contemporary Nonlinear Methods for the Behavioral Sciences, Web Book*, pages 142–177. National Science Foundation, Arlington, Virginia.

Smith, A., Goffman, L., Zelaznik, H. N., Ying, G., and McGillem, C. (1995). Spatiotemporal stability and patterning of speech movement sequences. *Experimental Brain Research*, 104(3):493–501.

Thiel, M., Romano, M. C., Kurths, J., Meucci, R., Allaria, E., and Arecchi, F. T. (2002). Influence of observational noise on the recurrence quantification analysis. *Physica D: Nonlinear Phenomena*, 171(3):138–152.

Thiel, M., Romano, M. C., Read, P. L., and Kurths, J. (2004). Estimation of dynamical invariants without embedding by recurrence plots. *Chaos: An Interdisciplinary Journal of Nonlinear Science*, 14(2):234—243.

Torrence, C. and Compo, G. P. (1998). A practical guide to wavelet analysis. *Bulletin of the American Meteorological Society*, 79(1):61–78.

Van Lieshout, P. and Namasivayam, A. K. (2010). Speech motor variability in people who stutter. In Maassen, B. and van Lieshout, P., editors, *Speech Motor Control: New Developments in Basic and Applied Research*, pages 190–214. Oxford University Press.

Wang, K. and Gasser, T. (1997). Alignment of curves by dynamic time warping. *The Annals of Statistics*, 25(3):1251–1276.

Webber, C. L. and Zbilut, J. P. (1994). Dynamical assessment of physiological systems and states using recurrence plot strategies. *Journal of Applied Physiology*, 76(2):965–973.

Webber Jr., C. L. and Zbilut, J. P. (2005). Recurrence quantification analysis of nonlinear dynamical systems. In A., R. M. and C., V. O. G., editors, *Tutorials in Contemporary Nonlinear Methods for the Behavioral Sciences, Web Book*, pages 26–94. National Science Foundation, Arlington, Virginia.

Zbilut, J. P., Giuliani, A., and Webber, C. L. (1998). Detecting deterministic signals in exceptionally noisy environments using cross-recurrence quantification. *Physics Letters A*, 246(1-2):122–128.

7 Appendices

A Further readings and tutorials

Ramsay and Silverman (2002) offer a collection of case studies analyzed through FDA with a reduced emphasis on mathematical formulations. The commented Matlab and R implementations of the analysis described in this book (and the relative datasets) are available at this address `http://www.stats.ox.ac.uk/~silverma/fdacasebook/`.
Ramsay et al. (2009) wrote an introduction to FDA and its variants with examples in both R and Matlab languages. Ramsay and Silverman (1997) is the principal reference on FDA with a detailed discussion of the mathematical and computational aspects. An introductory tutorial with emphasis on the concept of spline smoothing is available at this address: `http://www.psych.mcgill.ca/misc/fda/examples.html`.
Lucero's first applications of FDA to study the variability of speech signals are published in Lucero et al. (1997). A tutorial-like presentation can be found in Lucero (2005). Gubian maintains a web page on functional data analysis for speech research

(http://lands.let.ru.nl/FDA/). The available tutorials cover FDA registration, functional PCA and functional linear models.
A general tutorial on the use of cross wavelet transform has been written by Torrence and Compo (1998). Grinsted et al. (2004) build on the work by Torrence and Compo in their very accessible tutorial on the use of cross wavelet transform for the analysis of geophysical data.
Marwan (2003) provides a comprehensive introduction to recurrence and cross recurrence analysis, while Marwan et al. (2007) can be considered the most complete reference on recurrence analysis and its variants. Van Lieshout and Namasivayam (2010) report results obtained by using recurrence analysis with speech articulators[5]. However in that application no method to compensate for non-stationarity was adopted. Non-stationarity implies that the rate of change of the signals analyzed varies, introducing bowed lines in the plot and, as a consequence of that, the results obtained in that paper are hard to interpret. Webber Jr. and Zbilut (2005) and Shockley (2005) wrote accessible tutorials on the use of recurrence and cross recurrence analysis. A web based tutorial can be found at the following address: http://www.recurrence-plot.tk/glance.php, in which an animated introduction presents in an intuitive way the concept of phase space reconstruction. This topic has not been covered in the present chapter but constitutes the basis for more advanced uses of this technique.

B Software

With the exception of our algorithm designed for post-processing cross recurrence plots, all the analyses described in this chapter can be performed through available Matlab and R commands. The FDA software page is maintained by Ramsay at this address: http://www.psych.mcgill.ca/misc/fda/downloads/FDAfuns/. Here Matlab, R, and Splus versions of the software can be found.
Torrence and Compo's cross wavelet transform software is available at: http://paos.colorado.edu/research/wavelets/software.html.
Grinsted et al. (2004) wrote a Matlab package that integrates Torrence and Compo's toolbox with several useful routines. One of these routines has been used to produce the phase plots presented in this chapter. The package can be found at this address: http://www.pol.ac.uk/home/research/waveletcoherence/.
Marwan's Matlab toolbox for recurrence and cross recurrence analysis can be found at the following address: http://tocsy.agnld.uni-potsdam.de/crp.php. Webber produced a series of programs to perform recurrence analysis in DOS/Windows environment. This can be found at the following address: http://homepages.luc.edu/~cwebber/.

5 To be more precise, recurrence analysis (RA) was not conducted directly on the movements of the articulators. First the relative phase was computed from pairs of kinematic signal, then the RA was applied to the time series of the relative phase values.

Speech Production and Perception

Edited by Susanne Fuchs and Pascal Perrier

Vol. 1 Susanne Fuchs / Melanie Weirich / Daniel Pape / Pascal Perrier (eds.): Speech Planning and Dynamics. 2012.

www.peterlang.de